NAVAJO AND HOPI ART IN ARIZONA

NAVAJO AND HOPI ART IN ARIZONA

CONTINUING TRADITIONS

RORY O'NEILL SCHMITT, PHD

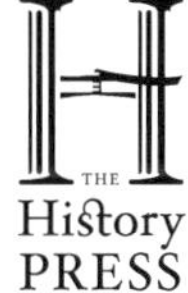

Published by The History Press
Charleston, SC
www.historypress.net

Front cover, top left: "Spider Woman" by Edward Charlie. *Photo by Rory O'Neill Schmitt (2015), all rights reserved*; *top center*: "Winter Apparition" by Marlowe Katoney. *Courtesy of Marlowe Katoney, all rights reserved*; *top right*: *Blue Yazzie Sits at the Ganado Post Office* by Melanie Yazzie. *Courtesy of Glenn Green Galleries, all rights reserved*; *bottom*: Artistic materials for Manuel Chavarria's katsina doll carvings. *Photo by Rory O'Neill Schmitt (2015), all rights reserved. Back cover, top*: Piki Wadsworth prepares turquoise stones. *Photo by Rory O'Neill Schmitt (2015), all rights reserved*; *middle*: Turquoise necklaces by Piki Wadsworth. *Photo by Rory O'Neill Schmitt (2015), all rights reserved*; *bottom*: "The Dawn of the Day" by William Carpenter (1915). *Courtesy of the Library of Congress, all rights reserved.*

First published 2016

Manufactured in the United States

ISBN 978.1.46711.789.0

Library of Congress Control Number: 2015955718

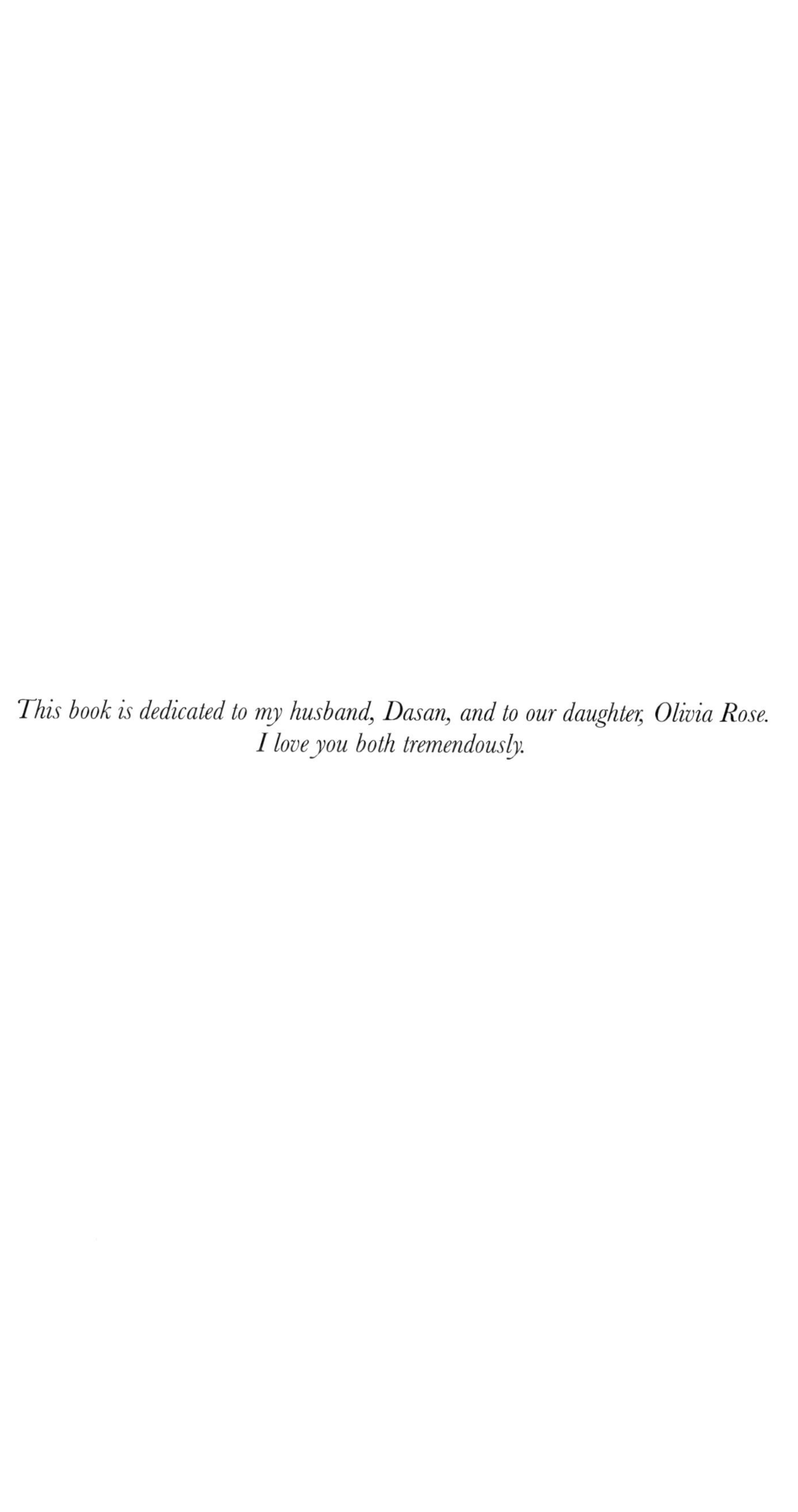

This book is dedicated to my husband, Dasan, and to our daughter, Olivia Rose.
I love you both tremendously.

CONTENTS

CONTENTS

FOREWORD

N*avajo and Hopi Art in Arizona* is an engaging collection, indeed, a complex weaving of artistic journeys presented by author Dr. Rory O'Neill Schmitt. Rory invites the reader to best appreciate these journeys by providing a brief foundation of pertinent history, gained from literature and primary sources, related to the arts of the Navajo and Hopi tribal communities. Drawing on her unique education and practical experiences as author, art therapist, educator and professional photographer, Rory next vividly introduces us to several contemporary artists who share their lives and artist journeys. Parallel to these artists' life stories, Rory reveals her own journey of awakening to a far better understanding of native arts, an awakening that evolved into a commitment to lifelong learning regarding the fascinating and ever-changing topics of native arts. Whether you are already well grounded in native arts or a novice on the topic, this book will further provide an invitation to all readers to begin or refresh a similar personal journey.

The substantive weaving of content and journeys in *Navajo and Hopi Art in Arizona* is crafted to engage and challenge all readers. Fortunately, the collective wisdom shared by the artists whom Rory has selected provides guidance to maximize our reading and resulting life experiences. There are some frequent themes to keep in mind as the informational levels unfold.

Read and listen carefully to the stories and voices of the artists. I found myself returning and reading again such passages. Ramson Lomatewama (one of the Hopi artists selected) urges our attention to native voices in his poem "Words of Wisdom." Listen!

Absorb my words into your heart
As our mother the earth
Absorbs the summer rain.

Appreciate the many relationships and shared values among the chosen art media, styles and forms. As Melanie Yazzie sought advice regarding her choice of art over weaving traditions of her family, her grandmother said, "You are weaving…in a different way…weaving your ideas and stories in this new way." Ric Charlie observed, "Art was art…anything I could do with my hands and be creative about it falls into the category as art."

Recognize the strong influence of landscape/environment in all native art. The sky, horizon, earth, wind, rain and sun consistently emerge throughout the native art forms. Melanie Yazzie assists our understanding again as she expresses this key influence in a few words: "I need to see the sky. I need to see the mountains."

Celebrate the power of family reflected in both traditional and contemporary native arts. Artists repeatedly refer to the strong role of family, especially as artists experience life in two worlds. Navajo weaver Barbara Teller Ornelas is a proud part of seven generations of weavers. In speaking about her choice of transition between a business career and art she stated: "I was already an artist. My art is learned from generation to generation… My art is passed down in my family."

Contemplate the sometimes less-than-visible but nevertheless vital roles of the mind and spirituality. Weavers are especially open about the spiritual aspects of the weaving process. Barbara Teller Ornelas notes, when speaking about Navajo woven art, "They have no blankets or rugs without spirits in them. I had to learn to be calm…because sometimes your weaving will take on how you feel or your attitude." Several artists, including Melanie Yazzie and Jesse Monongya, refer to the role of dreams in determining life direction and in their creative processes. In Ramson Lomatewama's poem "The Dawn," he reflects on the confluence of sky and dreams: "The Stars were made to be dreams—Mysterious and eternal."

Like Fred Katbotie and Charles Loloma, several of the artists featured in *Navajo and Hopi Art in Arizona* in time bring their artistic journey to a point of reflection, influence and teaching. Although young, Navajo weaver Marlowe Katoney wants to support change by transforming expectations regarding contemporary art forms. Likewise, Hopi glass artist and poet Ramson Lomatewama is an educator who believes that, through art, people gain a greater appreciation of the world around them, better responding to their environment and reflecting on their spirituality: "To me the artwork and what it does for a person's growth on the inside is more important than anything else." As we assess our own personal artistic journeys, such lofty stages might seem a challenge, but we can take comfort from a native blessing:

> *You have everything you need.*
> *Look North: the spirit runs through your body.*
> *Look East and feel the power of the Sun, our family, our people.*
> *Look West and hold on to a healing guide.*
> *Look South and make harmony with your life.*

—Lee Peterson
Immediate Past Chair of the Board of Trustees
Heard Museum
Phoenix, Arizona

PREFACE

EMBRACING NATIVE ARTS

Have you ever had a profound experience that changed your life? When I moved to Phoenix, Arizona, in the summer of 2010, I first visited the Heard Museum, an institution that promotes greater understanding of the arts, heritage and ways of life of native peoples of the Americas. Directly at the entry of the "Home: Native People in the Southwest" exhibit (curated by Dr. Ann Marshall), viewers interact with a contemporary ceramic and glass sculpture. *Indigenous Evolution*, by Tony Jojola and Rosemary Lonewolf, introduces visitors to a main theme: American Indians are a people not only of the past but of the present, as well. Contemporary native artists work in a variety of nontraditional and traditional mediums; these are the tools that they use to express their individual and shared histories.

Determined to gain knowledge on American Indian art and culture, I joined the guild of the Heard Museum (Las Guias) and began volunteering at events, such as the Heard Museum Guild Indian Fair and Market. During a yearlong docent-training program at the museum (2010–11), I was part of a class that met each week and was guided by a museum educator and anthropologist, Gina Laczko. She taught us about histories of native peoples of the Southwest. We also visited nearby sites in Arizona, such as Montezuma's Castle, ancient cave dwellings that are still intact. Each time that I was introduced to an incredible fact about American Indian innovation or adaptation, I thought to myself, "This is fantastic! Everyone should know this. How can I share this knowledge with others?"

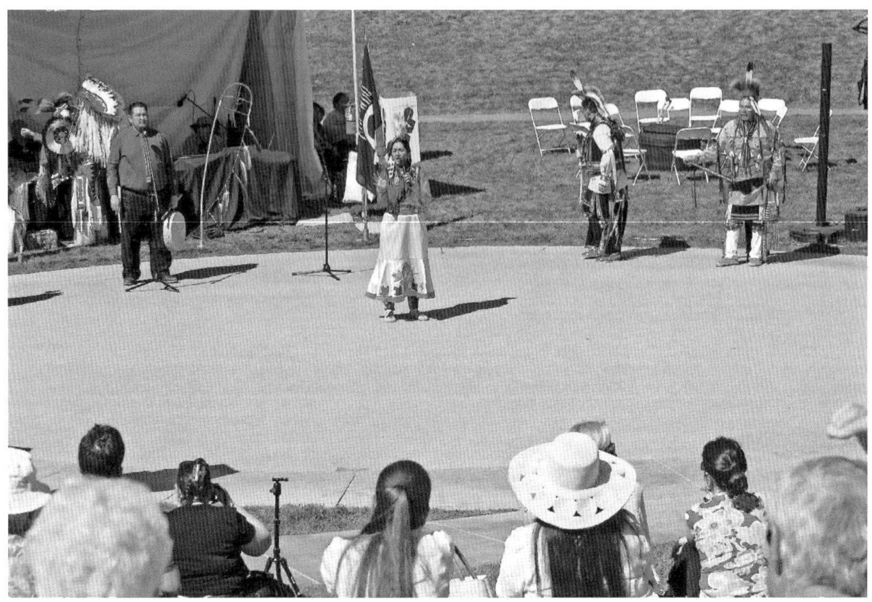

Performances at the 2015 Heard Museum Guild Indian Fair and Market include storytelling, dance and music. *Photograph by Rory O'Neill Schmitt, all rights reserved.*

Why Is Learning about Contemporary Native Artists Important Today?

Since the 1970s, critics, such as Linda Nochlin, have noted that the western art canon has often focused on European male artists. Furthermore, art educator Graeme Chalmers explains that colonialists often ignored or denigrated indigenous art, referring to it as primitive or child-like. Chalmers stresses the importance of learning from disempowered groups and urges contemporary culture to use a plurality of perspectives. Focusing on artists who traditionally have held less power than dominant groups is a progressive means of teaching art.

Any approach to studying the art forms and the history of the Southwest must include the ancient peoples who lived there for thousands of years. Today, native artists in Arizona continue to create exceptional artworks that have extraordinary value. Learning about the makers of art and their backgrounds is integral to understanding, appreciating and celebrating their artworks.

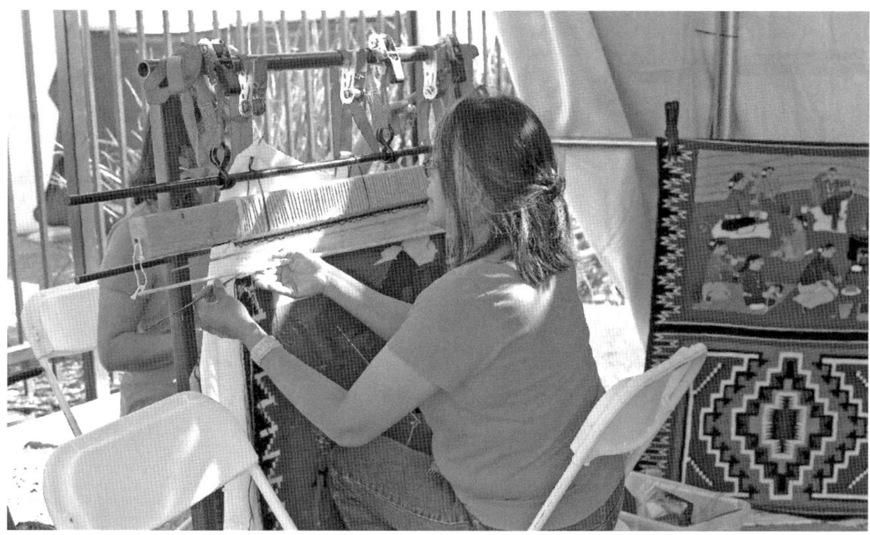

Exceptional living artists exhibit and interact with visitors annually at the Heard Museum Guild Indian Fair and Market. Pictured here are esteemed Navajo artists from the family of Louise Nez (a leading pictorial weaver): Florence Nez Riggs (left) and Laverne Nez Greyeyes (right). In 2013, Florence Riggs was the signature artist at the Heard Museum Guild Indian Fair and Market. Displayed in the background of this photograph are pictorial and geometric weavings. *Photograph by Rory O'Neill Schmitt, all rights reserved.*

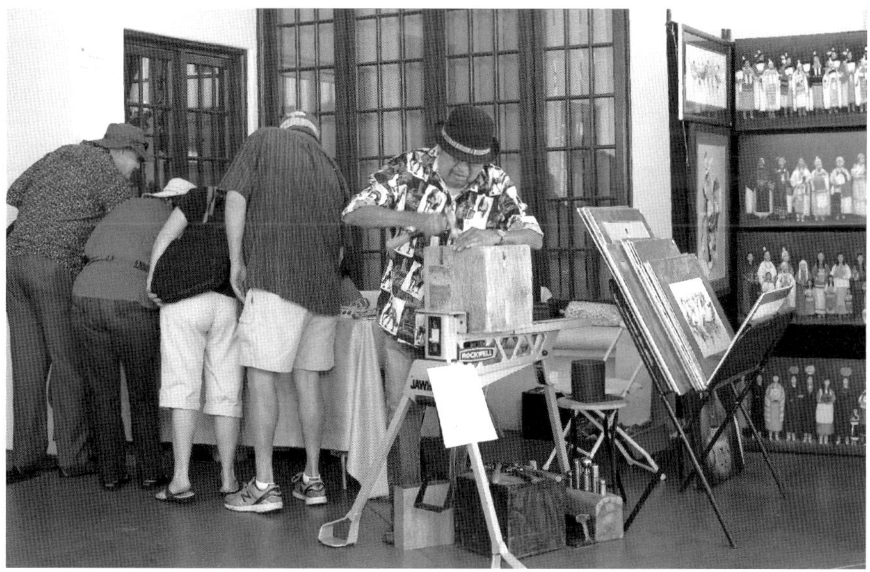

A craftsman demonstrates his process as he hammers his wood piece outside at the 2015 Heard Museum Guild Indian Fair and Market. Visitors interact with original artworks. *Photograph by Rory O'Neill Schmitt, all rights reserved.*

Book Organization

Who

In this book, featured native artists depict the range and diversity of art forms currently emerging from Arizona. It is my goal to share a bit of biography about the artists, identify how they find inspiration, describe their artworks and explain the meanings that they hold for their powerful creations. My criteria for selecting artists included:

- Artists have a recognizable body of work;
- Artists have been exhibited in art museums and fine art galleries;
- Artists have received acknowledgement in print publications and/or online sources;
- Artists are from Arizona (or have resided here for substantial portion of their lives);
- Artists have membership in the Navajo or Hopi tribe;
- Artists have biographical information that is both available and accessible;
- Artists may use any of a variety of media and may work in traditional and/or contemporary methods;
- Artists create visual artworks that do not serve as solely utilitarian or ceremonial objects;
- Artists are living and are currently creating new works;
- Artists are willing to participate in interviews;
- Artists demonstrate creative vision.

What

This book is by no means an exhaustive, encyclopedic account of contemporary native artists in Arizona. It is a glimpse into the amazing world of leading and emerging artists who are contributing to the development of twenty-first-century American art. Though there are twenty-two federally recognized tribes in Arizona, this book features a plethora of artists from two specific tribes: the Navajo Nation and the Hopi tribe, which are two of the largest tribes in the state.

Arizona's Indian Reservations

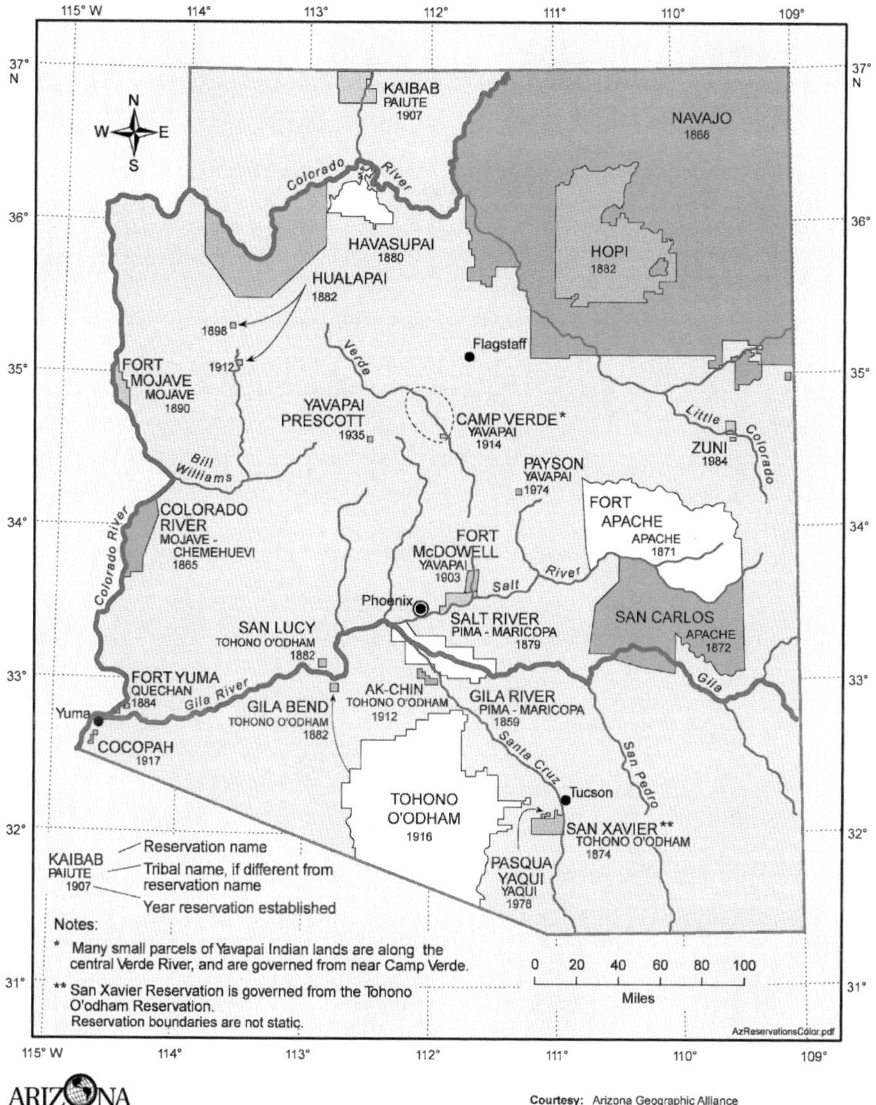

ARIZONA GEOGRAPHIC ALLIANCE

http://geoalliance.asu.edu

Courtesy: Arizona Geographic Alliance
School of Geographical Sciences and Urban Planning
Arizona State University
Cartographers Douglas Minnis and Becky L. Eden

American Indian tribes and communities in Arizona include those of the Hopis, Yavapai-Prescott Indians, Kaibab-Paiutes, Zuni Pueblos, Cocopah Indians, Colorado River Indians, Hualapais, Havasupais, San Juan Southern Paiutes, Yavapai-Apaches, Fort McDowell Yavapais, Fort Yuma–Quechans, Gila River Indians, Pascua Yaquis, Salt River Pima–Maricopa Indians, Tohono O'odhams, Tonto Apaches, White Mountain Apaches, Ak-Chin Indians, Fort Mojave Indians, Navajos and the San Carlos Apaches. *Courtesy of Arizona Geographic Alliance, Arizona State University and cartographers Douglas Minnis and Becky L. Eden, all rights reserved.*

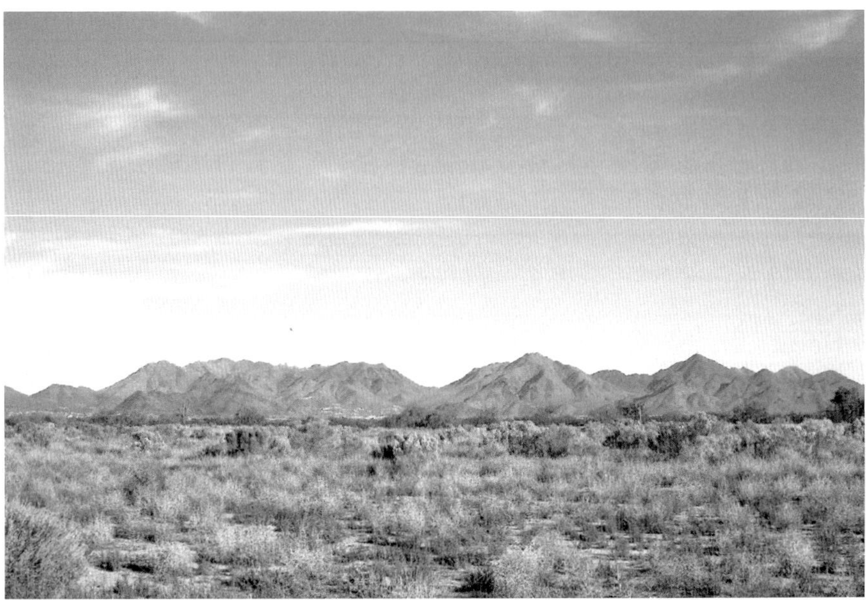

Though it is a popular residential area located just north of Phoenix, Scottsdale also contains expanses of desert lands and mountains. *Photograph by Rory O'Neill Schmitt, all rights reserved.*

When and Where

Research, interviews and photography were completed from 2014 through 2015 throughout several regions of Arizona, including Polacca, Hotevilla, Winslow, Verde Valley, Goodyear, Glendale, Phoenix and Scottsdale. Some artists in this book, such as Melanie Yazzie, may no longer live in Arizona. This diaspora reflects a current trend, according to the book *Reservation X*, of native artists leaving homelands and moving to urban centers for economic survival. Some participating artists in this book, such as Kevin Chavarria, reflected their desire to one day return to life on the reservation.

How

Research about native art and artists in Arizona was completed through reviewing literature, as well as interviewing art specialists and community members. Like Olivia Gude, a Chicago artist and educator, I believe that an artwork cannot be understood as pure form. Rather, as an artwork was made by a maker, it represents the maker's lived experiences. Therefore, I completed interviews with all of the participating artists. Visits to artist studios, art museums, galleries and reservations enabled me to create photographic documentation of artists and their original artworks. It is my hope that my previous experience as a board-certified art therapist (2005–10) enabled me to approach visual artwork and their creators in respectful and authentic ways. Through meeting artists in their studios and homes, I developed a deeper understanding of the unique personalities and artistic processes of these creative visionaries. My hope is that the photography created during these sessions enables readers to glimpse into these vivid Arizona art worlds.

I have written this book for an audience who may be new to the study of American Indian culture in Arizona and who, like me, are yearning to learn more. This text documents information about the unique ways of making art, responding to one's culture and forging new traditions. It serves as a contemporary witness to native artists who, despite challenges, continue to create art and share their art forms with the world community. It is my hope that this book contributes to multicultural art education and deepens an awareness of the art and culture of native peoples in the United States of America.

ACKNOWLEDGEMENTS

I would like to acknowledge my editor, Megan Laddusaw, for her continued support. It has been an incredible opportunity working together on my first publication with The History Press.

I would like to thank my family, who have been supportive every step of my life and who continue to bring me happiness: my father, Richard Patrick O'Neill; sisters, Dale Ellen and Rachelle; and brother, Barret. I would like to acknowledge my mother's support and belief in me. Rosary O'Neill Harzinski introduced me to The History Press after her book, *New Orleans Carnival Krewes: The History, Spirit and Secrets of Mardi Gras*, was published (2014). Thank you, Mom, for teaching me to "write, write, write. And, when you're tired, write some more!" You instilled in me the belief that what I had to say mattered. I am also extremely grateful to my Arizona family, who have embraced me into their lives and keep me motivated, joyful and inspired: Dasan, Olivia, Vicki, Brett, Jasmine and Maya.

I wish to voice special thanks to the Heard Museum. I am grateful to the museum's past chair of the board of trustees Lee Peterson, who continues to support my research in native art. I wish to express gratitude to Jaclyn Roessel, public programs and education director, and Dr. Ann Marshall, director of curation and education. Special thanks go to the Heard Museum Guild, as well as the communications manager, Mark Scarp, and the museum's librarians, Betty Murphy and Mario Nick Klimiades.

I would like to thank my inspiring teachers, friends and colleagues: Gina Beyer, Mary Erickson, Bernard Young, Mary Stokrocki, Richard Toon,

Peter Held, Kerry Green, Eric Margolis, Mark Klett, Herman Leonard, Jenny Bagert, Mike Willmon, Joe Lawton, Zeke Berman, David Storey, Debi Farber and Ashley Dorr.

I am enormously grateful to each of the artists who participated in interviews for this book. In particular, I would like to thank Melanie Yazzie, who has an incredible sense of kindness and compassion. I would like to acknowledge her trust in me and her willingness to be the first person to say, "Yes!" to an interview. I could see her authentic support when she connected me to other native artists through the gallery who represents her work, Glenn Green Gallery. I am grateful to Jesse Monongya for the new lessons that I gained from him. He is an incredible storyteller and has a warm heart and soul. In addition, I am thankful to Barbara Teller Ornelas and Linda Teller Pete, who are very giving people and have a deep commitment to preserving, educating and sharing Navajo weaving with the world. Lastly, I wish to thank Verma Nequatewa. Her humility is incredible; it matches her extraordinary talent.

Thank you to all of the artists. I appreciate your trust and your willingness to share with me your life, your culture and your art.

Part I

Native Peoples of Arizona

1
AN INTRODUCTION

American Indians in Arizona

Between twelve and fifteen thousand years ago, the first known inhabitants of the Southwest, known as the Paleo-Indians, crossed the Bering Straight from Asia. Different groups spread to diverse areas and adopted customs to support life in their new environments. Native peoples of Arizona adapted to the natural environments, which had an incredible range of life and native plant zones. For example:

- In the northern region, native peoples adapted their lifestyles to the lofty plateaus and huge canyons.
- In the central region, they lived among high mountain ranges.
- In the southern section, they thrived in the river plains and deserts and along the Gila River.

The first inhabitants were hunters and gatherers. Later, they settled into areas and built homes and farmed. Around 6000 BC, groups of people from California desert regions and northern Mexico moved into Arizona. Prehistoric cultures developed, including the Hohokam, Anasazi and Mogollon peoples. (See Figure 1.)

The Hohokam people, or "Ancient Ones," migrated to the Salt and Gila River areas of southern and central Arizona from Mexico in 300

BC. Hohokams were brilliant farmers who developed an incredible canal irrigation system. They lived in permanent buildings, created pottery and traded with people in Mexico.

In about 200 BC, the Anasazi people came to the Four Corners area, located in northern Arizona, where the state meets with Utah, Colorado and New Mexico. They had evolved from a nomadic lifestyle to a more sedentary lifestyle by 500 AD. Anasazis were known as "basket makers," as they wove delicate storage baskets out of yucca fiber. They migrated from caves to pit houses, from pit houses to apartment-style dwellings (which the Spanish referred to as *pueblos*) and from those to extraordinary cliff dwellings on the tops of mesas.

Lastly, the third group, the Mogollons, left archaeological evidence that dates their culture to AD 300. Mogollons lived in one-room pit houses overlooking fields in eastern Arizona, southwest New Mexico and northern Mexico.

Figure 1: A Timeline of American Indians in Arizona

10,000 BC (approx.)	First known inhabitants of Southwest arrive.
300 BC–AD 300	300 BC: Hohokam people, or "Ancient Ones," migrate to the Salt and Gila River areas of Arizona. 200 BC: The Anasazi people come to the Four Corners area. AD 300: Mogollons live in one-room pit houses overlooking fields in eastern Arizona.
AD 500–1492	Pre-contact cultural life remains steady. American Indians battle invaders after Columbus arrives in America in 1492.
1540s	Spanish settlers intrude the Southwest.

1800s	1848: U.S. war with Mexico leads to Arizona territory. U.S. government establishes reservations. Transcontinental railroad connects the Southwest.
1900s	U.S. government establishes Indian boarding schools. Reforms lead to the "Indian New Deal."
2000s	Arizona has one of the largest American Indian populations in the United States.

A PERIOD OF GREAT CHANGE

Pre-contact native life remained steady for hundreds of years, but great changes occurred due to the influence of European outsiders in the fifteenth century. American Indians began to fiercely battle invaders after Columbus arrived in America in 1492. The Spanish intruded in the Southwest in the 1540s, and for three centuries, Spanish settlers fought to gain control of land and also indoctrinate American Indians in Christianity. Franciscans, Jesuits, Protestants and Mormons established missions and churches throughout Arizona.

The 1800s were a period of great change for American Indians in Arizona. During this century, the Spanish withdrew and Anglo-American settlers forcibly flooded the Southwest. In 1848, the United States won the war with Mexico, leading the country to acquire the New Mexico and Arizona Territories. American soldiers built forts in traditional American Indian homelands, such as within Navajo lands. Due to fights between native peoples and the new settlers in their homelands, the U.S. government relocated American Indians, redistributed lands and established reservations. American Indian groups were allotted smaller portions of their original homelands or were forced to relocate to entirely new areas. Reservation policies resulted in devastation and poverty.

During the twentieth century, U.S. federal Indian policies included assimilating tribes into the dominant culture, as well as protecting tribes as cultural entities. The government established compulsory Indian boarding schools, wherein children were removed from their families and homelands. In an effort to support western acculturation, the children's traditional clothes were destroyed, and their long hair was cut. In school, where they were often permitted to speak only in English, they learned vocations and participated in western sports.

Today, Arizona has one of the largest American Indian populations in the United States. The capital, Phoenix, is considered the third-largest city in the United States with the most American Indians, accounting for approximately 5 percent of the state's total population. According to the most recent U.S. census report, of the twenty-five reservations with the largest American Indian and Alaskan native populations, seven are located in Arizona, including the Navajo Nation and the Hopi tribe. In addition, nearly 25 percent of the land in Arizona is covered by reservations, and approximately 63 percent of American Indians in this state live on these reservations. The remote locations of many reservations enable these communities to thrive, supporting American Indians in retaining many of their cultural traditions.

NATIVE ART FORMS IN ARIZONA

Traditional native art forms in Arizona include basketry, jewelry, sculpture and pottery. Weavings, such as Navajo rugs, and sculptures, such as Hopi katsina dolls, are also well known. Originally, ancient nomadic tribes in the Southwest created art forms that were easily transportable, such as baskets, rather than objects that were fragile, such as pots.

With the establishment of trading posts on reservations in the nineteenth century, native artists began selling and trading their artworks. They traded weavings, sheep hides and other local products for goods like flour, canned foods and tools. The oldest Navajo trading post currently in operation—since 1876—is the Hubbell Trading Post in Ganado, Arizona.

With the establishment of the transcontinental railroad in the late 1800s, the Southwest was connected with the rest of the United States, enabling tourism in Arizona to skyrocket. Tourists contributed to native economies by purchasing crafts and goods, watching craft demonstrations and performances and taking tours of reservations and villages. The types of artworks purchased by tourists influenced what native artists were making.

During the twentieth century, federal policy reforms led to the period of the "Indian New Deal," wherein art was promoted for economic development. The federal government's support of American Indian art affected whether art education was in schools. Many schools began having systems for selling student art. In 1935, there was a federal law that established a criminal penalty for misrepresentation of Indian goods or products for the purposes of sale.

In 2015, contemporary native artists have a range of diverse art forms, including sculpture, jewelry, fashion, photography, ceramics, weavings, paintings and mixed media. Artists are responding to both their lived experiences, as well as local and global events. Many contemporary American Indian artists mix traditional forms with new forms of media. For example, in 2014, the Arizona State Museum featured "Neoglyphix: All-Indigenous Aerosol Art Exhibition" by native graffiti artists from Arizona.

American Indians are not a people of the past. They are living, breathing peoples contributing to a dynamic world. This book presents individuals from an array of Navajo and Hopi artists from Arizona who use different tools, materials and processes to express themselves in visionary ways. The next section is an overview of the Navajo Nation, which provides a foundation for understanding how culture and traditions influence the artists featured in this book.

Part II

Contemporary Navajo Artists

2
THE NAVAJO NATION

The Diné

Many Navajos refer to themselves as Diné, meaning "the People," as the term, *navajo*, meaning "enemy," was given to them by the Zuni Pueblos. In their homeland, about 80 percent of Navajos speak their own language. Today, Navajo school curriculum includes their culture and language, called Athabaskan.

Families play a vital role in Navajo society. The clan system unites the people. Each person belongs to a clan, and clan membership dictates responsibilities. This kinship system, *K'é*, follows the lineage of the women; children belong to their mother's clan. Each person belongs to four unrelated clans in the following order: the mother's first clan, the father's first clan, the maternal grandfather's first clan, and the paternal grandfather's first clan. Navajo men are not permitted to marry someone from their own clan, even if the person is not related by blood.

For many Navajos, religion is a part of daily life; it is not separate. Navajos seek to create beauty in their own worlds, and this continues to be a guiding influence of Navajo artists today. Love and respect are paramount, and Navajos value the welfare of others in their community. The Navajo Way focuses on staying in harmony with nature and finding balance between mind, body and soul.

Many Navajos do not worship one supreme God; they believe that multiple gods intervene in human affairs. They worship their gods by

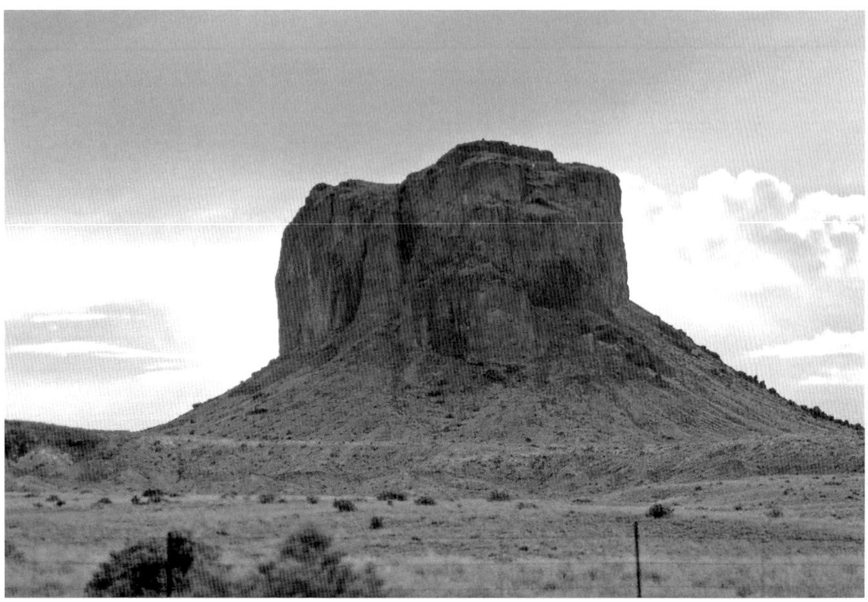

The Navajo reservation features incredible rock formations, such as the one in this photograph. *Photograph by Rory O'Neill Schmitt, all rights reserved.*

making offerings and participating in ceremonies. For example, when a person is ill, many believe that he or she is out of sync with the universe. To find healing, the person may participate in healing ceremonies led by a medicine man, called a singer. Ceremonies may include herbs, prayers, chants, songs and dances. Rituals can last several days and involve many community members. Navajo singers might request the assistance of the Holy People, called *yeibichais*, to create a sand painting. The ill person sits on the sand painting, which serves as portal for the spirits and healing energy to enter. As a part of custom, sand paintings are destroyed after the ceremony, as they have absorbed toxic energy.

Ceremonies often take place in traditional round-shaped dwellings, which resemble the roundness of the body of Mother Earth. Called hogans, these wooden structures have a single entrance that faces east, in order to catch the rising sun's blessing. Many Navajos build a hogan near the main house where they live and spend time in the hogan to reconnect to teachings. When someone dies inside the hogan, owners might abandon this building from fear of the ghosts. They break a hole on the hogan's northern side to remove the corpse.

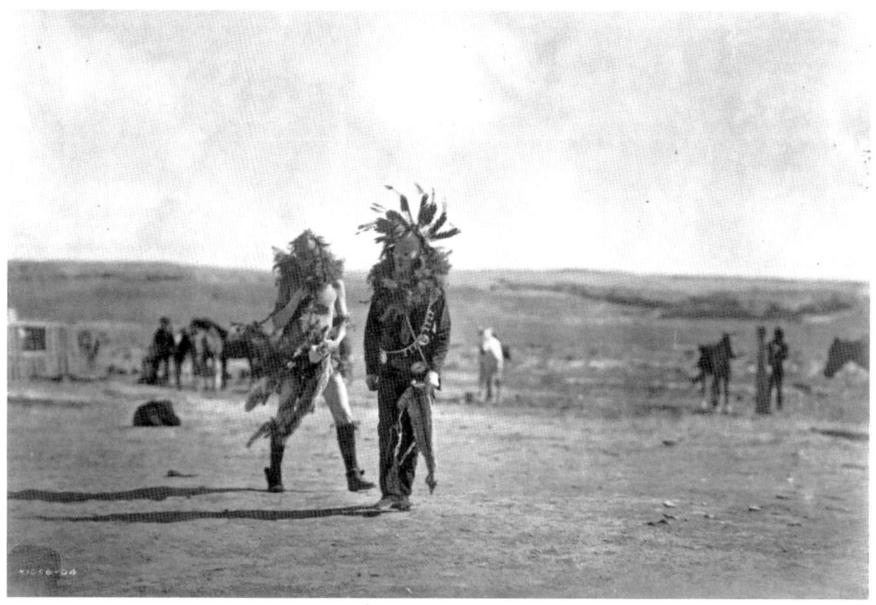

In this 1905 picture by Edward Curtis, called "Toneneli and Haschelti," Navajo men are shown participating in a Yebichai ceremony. *Courtesy of the Library of Congress, all rights reserved.*

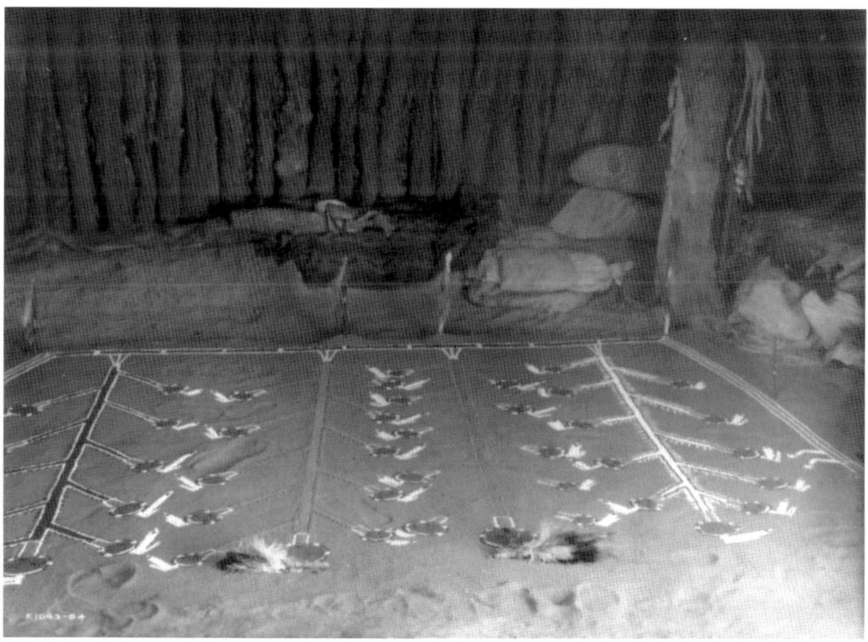

This 1906 photograph, "Sand Painting, Wind Doctor's Ceremony—Navaho," by Edward Curtis shows a Navajo sand painting; sand paintings are often created during ceremonies and then destroyed. *Courtesy of the Library of Congress, all rights reserved.*

Figure 2: Navajo Timeline

AD 1000	Navajos migrate south from Canada.
1400	Navajos arrive in the Four Corners region. They learn agriculture and weaving from their Pueblo neighbors.
1500s & 1600s	Spanish introduce horses, sheep and cattle, as well as silversmithing.
1700s	Navajos struggle to maintain their homeland.
1800s	Navajos surrender to U.S. military, face the Long Walk and are imprisoned. Later, Navajos receive only a fraction of their homeland back.
1900s	More land was progressively returned to Navajos following several treaties.
2000s	The Navajo Nation is the largest federally recognized reservation and the most populated tribe in the United States.

Navajo Homeland (AD 1000–2015)

The Navajo people trace their lineage back to AD 1000, when their ancestors began to migrate from their northern homelands in Canada. A severe drought had challenged their ultimate survival, and they needed to move to areas with rivers and a dependable water supply. The Navajos arrived in the Southwest about four hundred years later. Navajos refer to their ancestral homeland as *Dinétah* or *Diné Bikéyah*, and it is located in northwestern New Mexico. When the Navajos arrived, they were originally a nomadic band of hunter-gatherers. They later learned agriculture and weaving from their Pueblo neighbors. (Refer to Figure 2, Navajo Timeline.)

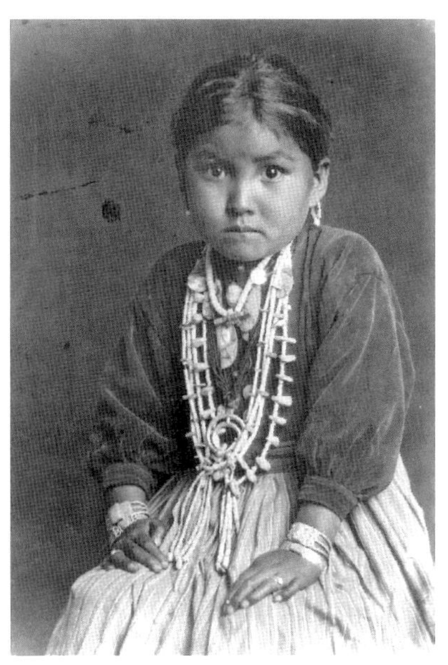

This historic photograph, "The Silversmith's Daughter—Navajo Indian," was created between 1920 and 1930 near Gallup, New Mexico, by an unknown photographer. *Courtesy of the Library of Congress, all rights reserved.*

With the arrival of the Spanish in the late 1500s and early 1600s, Navajos were introduced to horses, sheep and cattle. Throughout their history, Navajos learned from their neighbors and adapted customs to improve their quality of life and ensure their survival. Neighboring influences drove the basis of the Navajo economy to include agriculture, woven textiles and herding.

During the 1700s and into the 1800s, Navajos struggled to maintain their homeland from others' approaches, including those of neighboring tribes, Mexicans, New Mexicans and the U.S. military. In the 1860s, Navajos were in direct conflict with the U.S. military, which was encroaching on their homeland. To disempower the Navajo people, the army destroyed their homes, crops and livestock. In 1863, Colonel Kit Carson led the removal of eight thousand Navajos from their lands and forced them to walk three hundred miles to prison camp in Bosque Redondo, New Mexico. During the Long Walk, hundreds of Navajos died. Those who made it to the camp had to survive despicable living conditions for four years. In 1868, a treaty was signed establishing the Navajo Nation, wherein Navajos gained tribal sovereignty and received a fraction of their homeland (about one-tenth the size) in the Four Corners region of the United States, where present-day northern Arizona meets with Utah, Colorado and New Mexico.

Additional homeland was returned to the Navajo tribe during the 1900s, following several treaties. It is noted that friction between the Navajos and Hopis occurred, as the tribes experienced land disputes. The Hopi

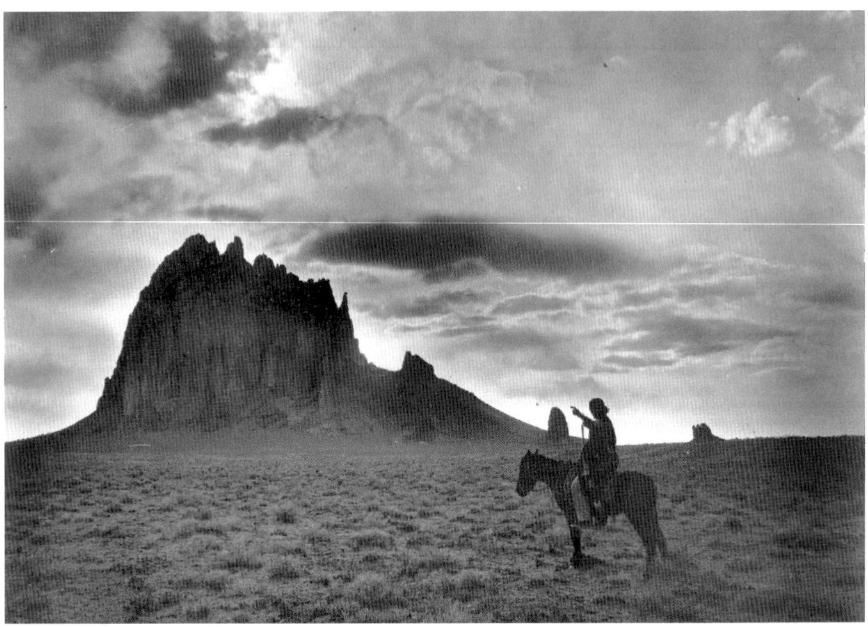

In "The Dawn of the Day," a Navajo man sits on horseback and points toward a butte in the background. In 1915, William Carpenter created this photograph. *Courtesy of the Library of Congress, all rights reserved.*

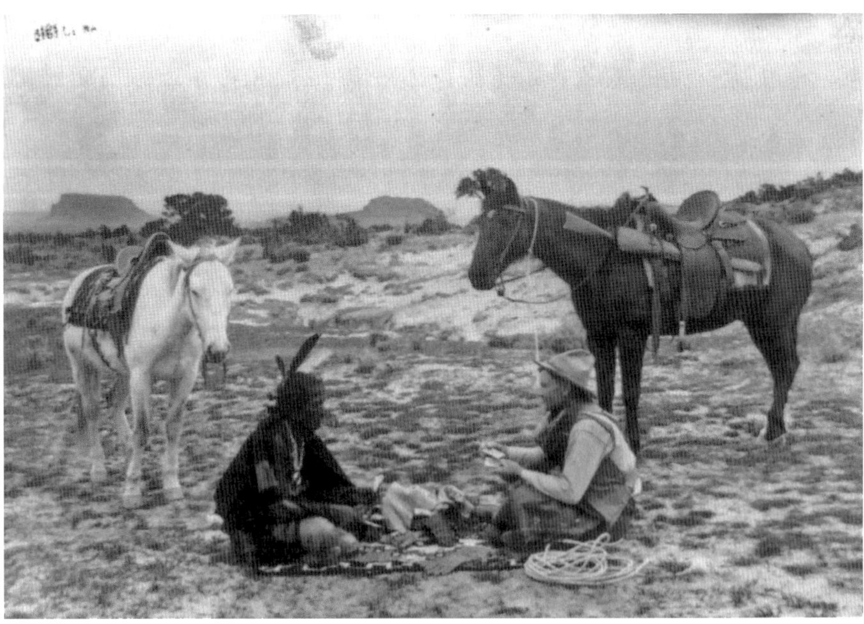

In this 1915 photograph by William Carpenter, entitled "Life on the Plains," a Navajo man and a cowboy play cards. *Courtesy of Library of Congress, all rights reserved.*

reservation today is indeed much smaller than the Navajos' reservation; their three mesas are completely surrounded by the Navajo reservation. Following the 1974 Settlement Act, Hopis were granted some contested lands and over ten thousand Navajos were relocated. In 2011, Malcolm Benally described stories of Navajo women who experienced this relocation in *Bitter Water: Diné Oral Histories of the Navajo-Hopi Land Dispute.*

The Navajo Nation is the largest federally recognized reservation in the United States, approximately the size of West Virginia. In fact, the total area of the reservation is larger than Vermont, Massachusetts and New Hampshire combined. Comprising approximately sixteen million acres (twenty-seven thousand square miles), the Navajo Nation expands throughout Arizona, Utah and New Mexico. The geography includes arid deserts, as well as alpine forests, deeply incised canyons, mountains and mesas. Natural boundaries mark the Navajos' homeland in the Southwest. To the north is Mount Hesperus (near Durango, Colorado), to the east is Sierra Blanca Peak (near Alamosa, Colorado), to the south is Mount Taylor (near Grants, New Mexico) and to the west is San Francisco Peaks (near Flagstaff, Arizona). Navajo people believe that their Creator placed them in the area between these four sacred mountains.

The Navajo Nation is the most populous reservation in the United States, according to the most recent U.S. census. In 2015, the Navajo Nation government declared that over 300,000 members of the Navajo Nation currently exist. Within the state of Arizona, there are 140,000 Navajos. Today, many Navajos make their livings through farming and raising sheep, as well as creating artwork, such as Navajo weavings and jewelry.

Navajo Art

Throughout their history, Navajo peoples have created artwork. Their artwork has continued to evolve based on influences of historical events, as well as artists' dedication to preserving cultural traditions and meanings. Art forms include basketry, pottery, painting, jewelry and weaving. As this book features many contemporary jewelers and weavers of Arizona, the next two sections focuses on an examination of those two mediums.

Jewelry

Throughout their history, Navajos have celebrated beauty, creating special objects for ceremonies and crafting items to adorn their bodies. Archaeologists have recovered Southwest native artifacts with turquoise dating from 200 BC. Turquoise carries spiritual and ceremonial significance. It was used as a medium for exchange, as well as an indicator of status. In addition to turquoise, many Navajos favored in their jewelry coral, which was brought to the Southwest in the 1700s. Navajo jewelers also incorporated sacred stones, such as abalone and jet, as well as white shell.

In the mid-nineteenth century, Mexican and Spanish peoples introduced silversmithing to the Navajos. (The Navajos then taught silversmithing to the Zunis in the 1870s, who in turn taught the craft to the Hopis in the 1890s.) Silverwork traditionally involved using such tools as crucibles, bellows, hammers and anvils. Several methods for working silver exist:

- Wrought work: To create wrought work, silversmiths cut the silver and then hammered, filed and stamped it.
- Repoussé method: Using the repoussé method involves hammering one side of the flat metal piece, which creates a raised design on the opposite side.
- Wirework: When creating wirework, Navajos twist strands of wire. They also shape and flatten the wire with a hammer.
- Tufa-casting method: In the tufa-casting method, artists carve a design into a mold from soft volcanic stone (tufa), back the stone with another stone and then pour liquid metal into the mold. Finishing details are then completed by hand. Artists may cut and solder semiprecious and precious stones and incorporate them into the jewelry.

Southwestern American Indian jewelry had two main phases. The first phase (1864–1900) included simple designs made for personal use. Early Navajo jewelry can be noted by the use of silver and large stones. The second phase (1900–1930s) involved lighter-weight jewelry made for the tourist trade. Due to the high tourist demand, it is noted that, during this time, many inauthentic Navajo jewelry pieces were created out of nickel silver with nonnative symbols and sometimes imported from Japanese sweatshops.

In the 1900s, popular Navajo accessories included the concho belt and the squash blossom necklace. Circular or oval silver ornaments, called *conchos*, were hammered, stamped or cut by hand and then uniformly attached to

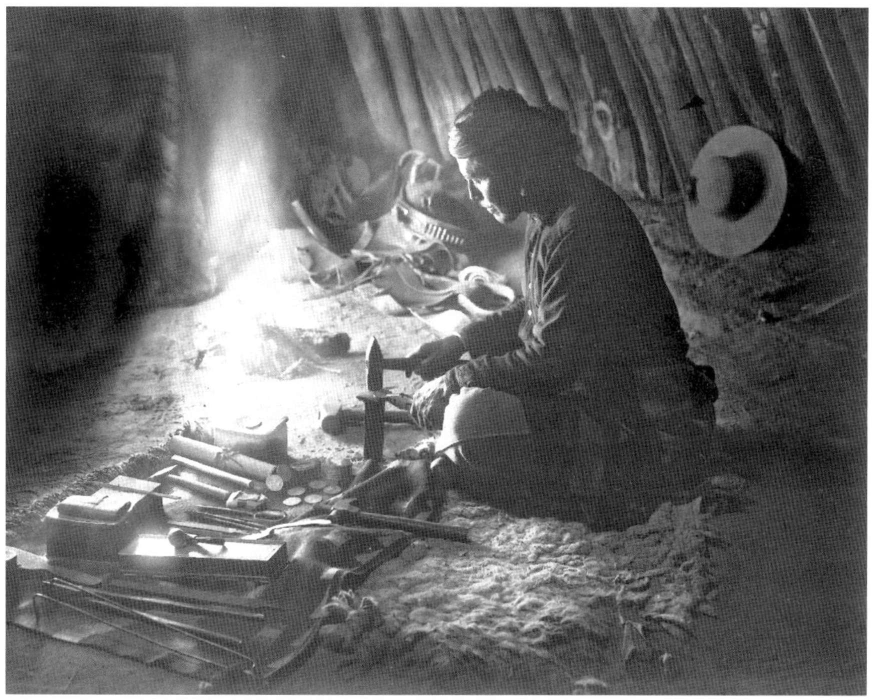

William Carpenter created this photograph, called "Navajo Silversmith," in 1915. *Courtesy of the Library of Congress, all rights reserved.*

a leather belt. Squash blossom necklaces included plain beads and a silver squash blossom design. Later, the inlaying of turquoise stones on silver beads of squash blossoms occurred. Hanging at the center of the squash blossom necklace was a silver crescent shape, called a *naja*. It is believed that Navajos first viewed the *naja* symbols on the bridles of Spanish horses; it was an amulet that was believed to ward off the evil eye.

A legendary Navajo jeweler of the twentieth century is Kenneth Begay. Kenneth Begay brought about major changes to the art form, transforming the massive silver jewelry with large turquoise stones into pieces with elegant and simple designs and paving the way for jewelers in the twenty-first century.

Today, contemporary Navajo jewelers still use elements that refer to their cultural symbols and traditions. They are responding to contemporary life around them, as well. Jewelers might use a variety of precious gems, determined by collectors' preferences. They might also follow art galleries' advice regarding the most sellable styles. According to Lois Jacka's book *Navajo Jewelry: A Legacy of Silver and Stone*, galleries act like trading posts today.

Weaving

Many Navajos believe that Spider Woman first taught mortals the art of weaving. Others note that Navajos learned weaving from their Pueblo neighbors around AD 1350. Master weavers, the Pueblos had woven for centuries prior to the Navajos' arrival in the Southwest. The Navajos modeled their weaving techniques, upright looms and styles after the Pueblos. Though Pueblo men traditionally created weavings, the women traditionally are the weavers in Navajo culture. This craft is passed down from generation to generation. Girls learned weaving from their female relatives: mothers, grandmothers and aunts.

Navajos use a vertical loom that have a wood-pole frame. When creating weavings, they often set up their looms inside their homes. First, weavers create a foundation of equally spaced vertical yarns on their loom; this is called the warp. Then, they weave yarn into the warp to create a pattern; this is called the weft. Weaving involves patience, as one sits for long periods of time, as well as dedication, as one must be careful to ensure precision so that the designs have symmetry.

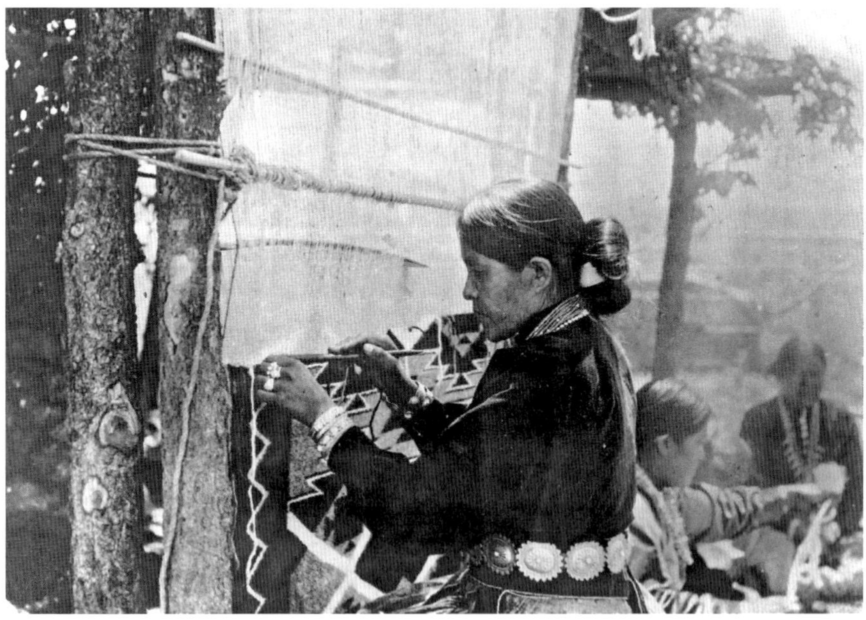

In this historic photograph, "Navajo Indian" (1909), a Navajo woman weaves while two women sit in the background. Notice the type of traditional Navajo dress: long billowing skirts, long-sleeved shirts, large silver necklaces and concho belts. Photographer unknown. *Courtesy of the Library of Congress, all rights reserved.*

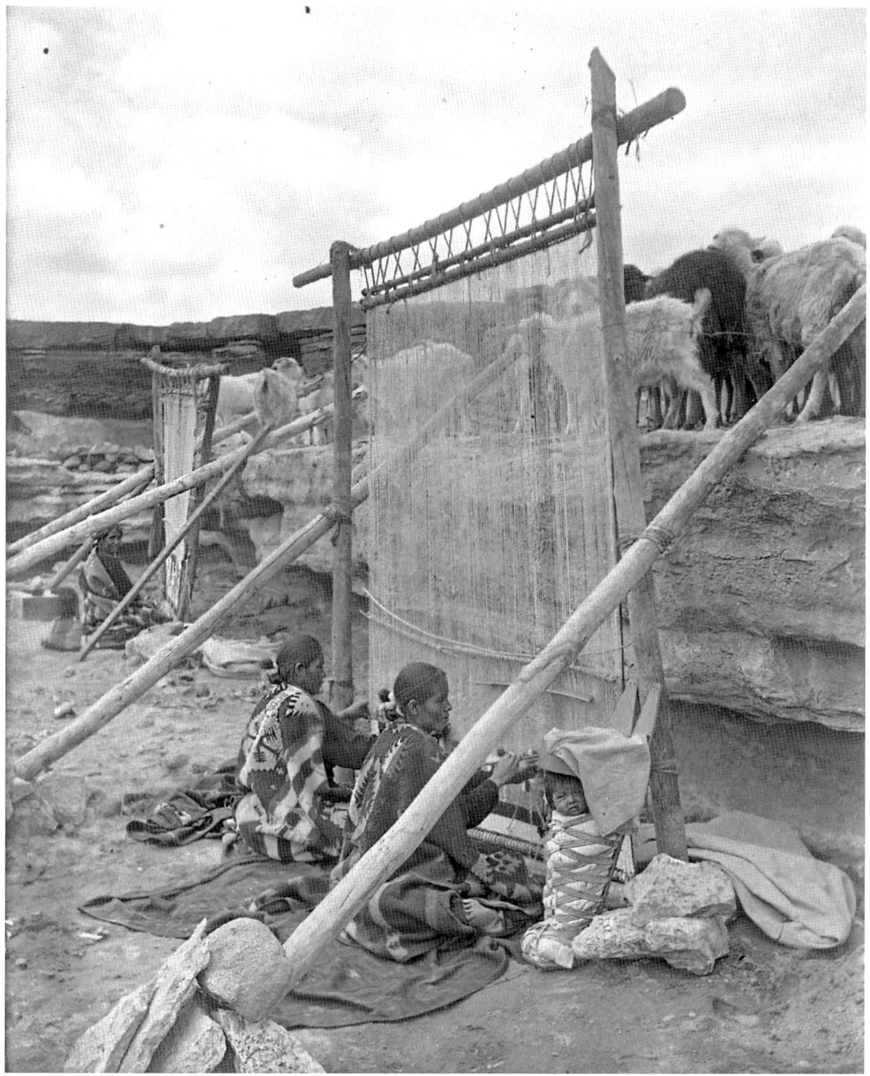

Navajo female weavers work on a large-scale weavings outdoors while a baby rests nearby in a hooded cradleboard. William Pennington & Wesley Rowland created this photograph, "Navajo Weavers," in 1914. *Courtesy of Library of Congress, all rights reserved.*

Navajos' first weavings were utilitarian; many were primarily blankets or clothing, such as mantas (for women) and blankets (for men). Originally, weavings were made of cotton. When the Spanish introduced churro sheep around 1598, Navajo weavers began using wool. Sheep were sheared, and their wool was carded, spun and dyed. During this time, Navajo blankets

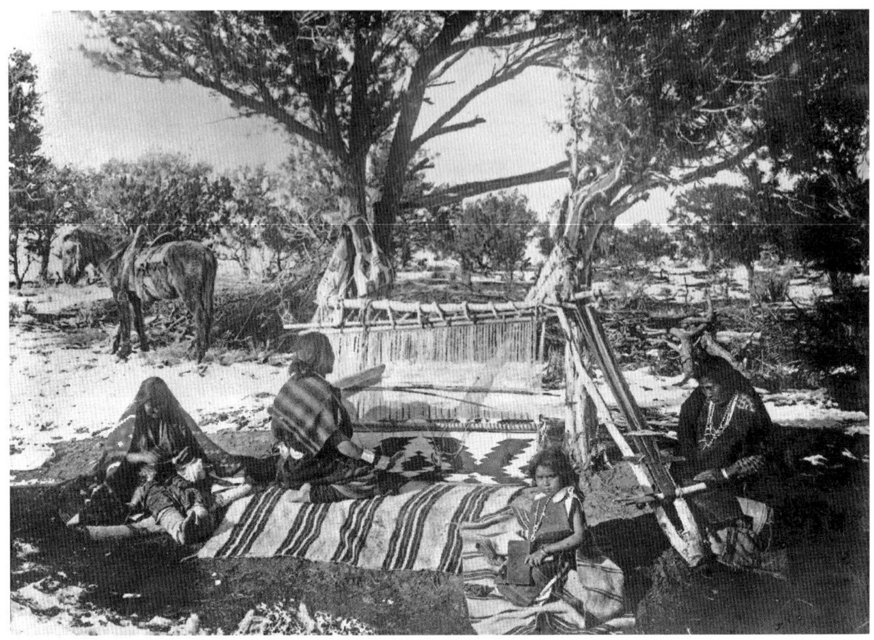

James Mooney created this photograph, "Navajo Indians, Blanket and Belt Weavers" (1892–93), in Keams Canyon, Arizona. The photograph depicts several components involved in Navajo weaving: carding wool, spinning wool and weaving at the loom. *Courtesy of the Library of Congress, all rights reserved.*

included subtly hued yarn, which had been dyed with vegetable colors. By 1650, Navajos had earned a reputation as fine weavers.

In the 1800s, many Navajo weavings were composed of handspun wool of churro sheep or merino sheep. Navajo blankets had simple designs of edge-to-edge bands, as well as geometric motifs. Navajo chiefs' blankets contained bands of white, black, blue and red colors in various widths. Beginning around the 1880s, weavers also created pictorials, which were often combined with geometric designs. Pictorials featured images weavers encountered in daily life—such as sheep, cows, houses, trains and later trucks—as well as images that reflected their cultures: dances, spirit beings and trees of life. Some Navajo weavers began to use brightly colored commercial woolen yarns, for example, wool from Mexico and Germantown, Pennsylvania.

Toward the end of the nineteenth century and into the twentieth century, ready-made clothing and commercial cloth became available, and Navajo weavers stopped making garments. Trading posts encouraged weavers to create sellable, thicker weavings that were like rugs to be sold to Anglo tourists. When trading post operators put Navajo weavings in catalogues, their popularity grew. Navajo rugs became known for the beauty in their designs.

Traders became interested in different parts of the Navajo reservation, and regional rug types developed. By the 1930s, distinct styles of weaving developed and were named after their respective areas, such as the following:

- Two Grey Hills style is composed of earth-tone colors, central geometric patterns radiating outward and a dark border.
- Ganado style often features the color red, strong geometric patterns and a black border.
- Crystal style has borders and horizontal bands and radiating geometrics at the center.
- TeecNosPos style is composed of bright colors and intricate geometrics.

By the late twentieth and early twenty-first centuries, weavers were selecting weaving styles that they preferred and not necessarily weaving style of the region where they lived. Weavings frequently reflect the weaver's individuality and experiences, and traditions continue to evolve. For example, Navajo male weavers are creating weavings today.

CLOSING

This chapter presented an introduction to the history and culture of the Navajos. The following chapters showcase the biographies and artworks of contemporary Navajo artists in Arizona. Included are multimedia artist Melanie Yazzie; jewelers Jesse Monongya, Ric Charlie and Edward Charlie; weavers Barbara Teller Ornelas, Lynda Teller Pete and Marlowe Katoney; and quilter Margaret Wood. The large grouping of participating Navajo artists can be attributed to the fact that the Navajo Nation is currently believed to be the most populated tribe in the United States.

3
MELANIE YAZZIE

I think what I do is I hold true to everything that's traditional inside of me and in my heart and soul and mind. With the work that I'm making, I'm connecting with stories...I transform those relationships into symbols and images that come into the work. It isn't like a traditional type of Navajo art-making, but it is very much Navajo-centered in that I'm thinking about it in a good way, and making this history or story known throughout my work.
—Melanie Yazzie

Growing Up Navajo in Arizona

Melanie Yazzie was born in 1966 in Ganado, a chapter of the Navajo Nation that is located in the northeastern corner of Arizona. In Spanish, *ganado* means "livestock" or "cattle," and many ranches and farms can be found in this region. Belonging to the Salt and Bitter Water clans, Melanie Yazzie was raised on the Navajo reservation by her Navajo parents, Bessie B. Yazzie and Albert A. Yazzie, and by her grandparents. Her family instilled in her a strong work ethic. A typical family workday included waking at 4:30 a.m. and having breakfast. Her grandfather would begin herding sheep, and her grandmother would begin with housework and weaving rugs. Like her relatives, Melanie begins each day in the early morning hours. She explained, "I'm very Navajo in that way in that we wake up really early. You're not to be idle, and you're supposed to be useful and working all the time. I live and breathe my art-making and my teaching."

Melanie's mother and grandmothers were traditional Navajo weavers. Her maternal grandmother, Thelma Baldwin, wove rugs in the Wide Row style. And her paternal grandmother, Nesbah Yazzie, wove rugs in the style of the Crystal, New Mexico region. Melanie said, "We had art teachers throughout the time I was growing up on the reservation, and they all inspired me. But it really was my grandparents and my mom…who *always* inspired me." In addition to introducing her to the art of weaving, Melanie's family stressed Navajo cultural values. For example, when Thelma saw a sand painting on a placemat at a local diner, she explained to Melanie, "They are very special and sacred and should not be used as decoration." In Navajo culture, a sand painting is traditionally created by a medicine man in a hogan during sacred healing rituals.

Formative Education

Melanie received her early formative education on the Navajo reservation, as well as at a Quaker school in Pennsylvania, called Westtown School. She decided to attend Westtown after receiving encouragement from her father, who had also attended on a scholarship. When her father was growing up on the Navajo reservation near Window Rock, a Quaker couple had asked his teacher if she had any students interested in studying U.S. history. The teacher selected Albert. Melanie later learned that at the time, her father spoke very little English, as Navajo was his first language. Melanie explained, "This was back when you had to go travel on the train for a week to get to the East Coast. It was a very different time."

During Melanie's senior year at Westtown, an exceptional art educator, Caroline Loose, introduced her to printmaking. This teacher inspired her, believed in her and treated her equally to the other students. To this day, twenty-five years later, Melanie and Caroline remain in communication.

Melanie explained that venturing to Pennsylvania led her to appreciate home. She said:

> *When I went away to the Quaker school, to Westtown, being away from home, being very, very homesick…it heightened my awareness of what a beautiful place I grew up in. It made me see Arizona and home in a totally new light because I'm in the East where there are trees…everywhere. I ached for brown, for the colors of home, for the big open space, to see the*

sky, to see the stars. I needed that, and I realized…I need to be in the West, I need to see the sky. I need to see mountains. I love the West. It's something about the colors and landscape and the openness that draw me home. The smell of the earth after a rain makes me want to eat the dirt.

Nearing high school graduation in 1984, Melanie was pulled in two different directions: to attend art school at the Kansas City Art Institute or to move back to Arizona. At that time in her life, her parents were not supportive of her attending an art school, as they felt that she should go to a liberal arts school. Melanie realized she was very passionate about making art, and she also longed to be close to her grandparents. She was accepted to Arizona State University. However, a week before school started, she secretly planned to go to Mexico and live for a year.

Living in Irapuato, Mexico, allowed Melanie to gain a broader understanding of diverse peoples. She witnessed that many native people in Mexico were treated harshly and were not encouraged to take pride of their heritage. Living abroad also gave her the opportunity to gain a deeper appreciation for her home and for the opportunity of education. She said, "I saw how indigenous people were treated and how in Mexico during that time, a lot of people didn't want to relate to any of their indigenous heritage. I just realized how fortunate we were in the U.S. as natives, but just as Americans, also."

Higher Education

Melanie returned to Arizona and enrolled at Arizona State University. Initially, she took coursework required for becoming an English and Spanish teacher because she wanted to respect her parents' concern for her ability to make a living. Later, following the urging of her younger sister, Melanie decided to pursue studio art. When the deadline of selecting a major was approaching, her sister asked, "What do you really want to do? Mom and Dad always told us to choose what we love, our passion." Melanie told her, "Well, my passion is art." Her sister said, "Why don't you just do that? It's going to alter everything, and you don't even have to think about it."

Melanie went on to complete coursework in a wide array of studio art disciplines, including ceramics, printmaking, and 3-D design. Her influential professors in the art department included Jeanne Otis, Randy

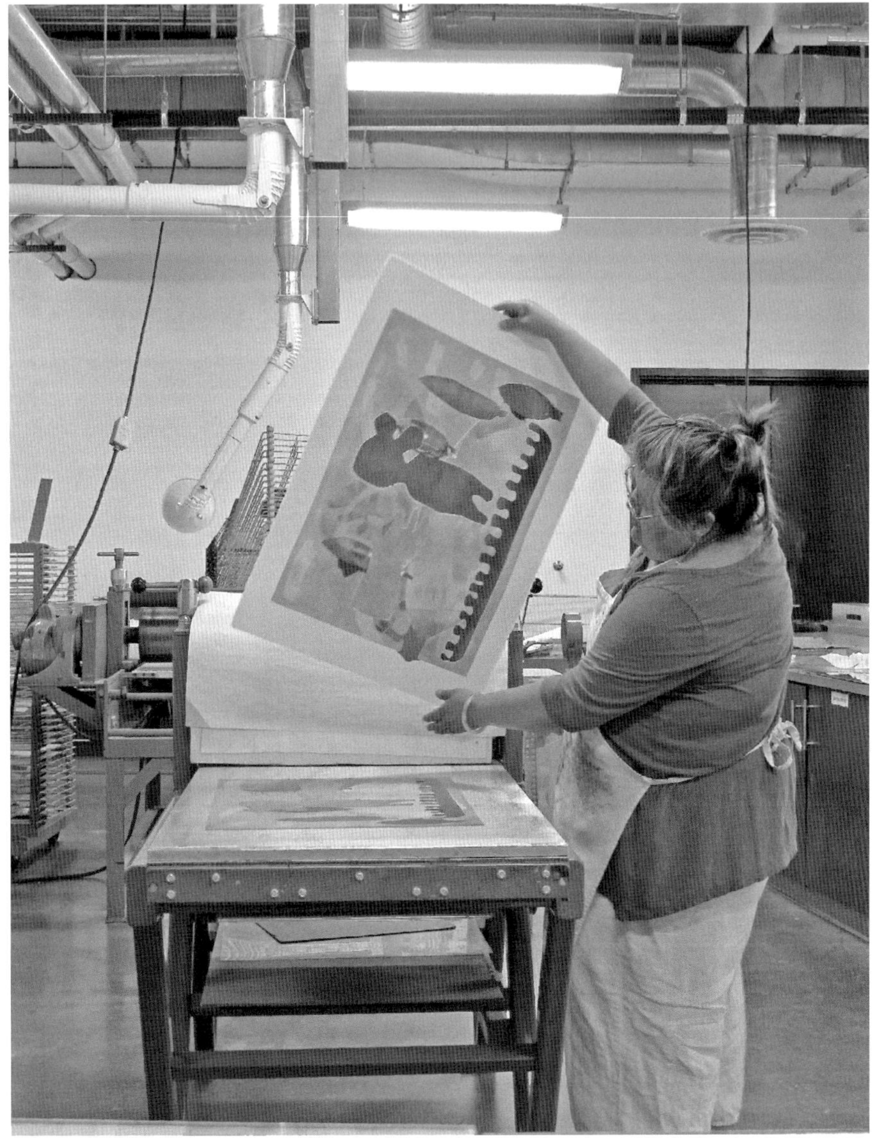

In the studio, Melanie Yazzie inspects one of her prints. *Courtesy of Glenn Green Galleries, all rights reserved.*

Schmidt, Kurt Weiser, Katherine Maxwell, John Risseeuw, Jules Heller, Joe Segura, Dan Britton, Denis Gillingwater, Daniel Mayer, Betsy Fahlman and Jan L. Stanley-Muchow. Introductions to various media and processes enabled her to adapt multiple methods in her professional

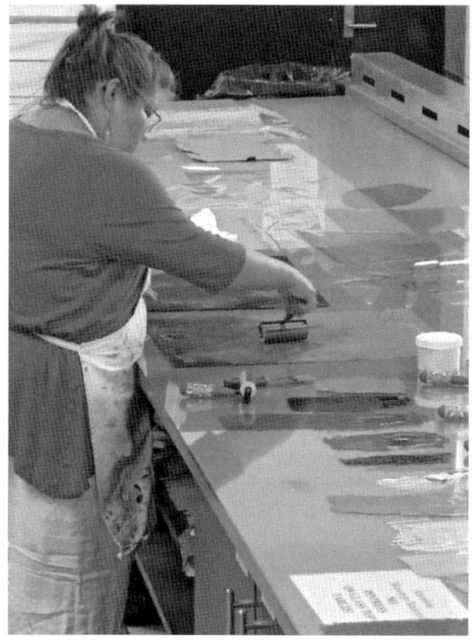

Master printmaker Melanie Yazzie carefully applies paint in her studio. *Courtesy of Glenn Green Galleries, all rights reserved.*

career. She attributes her current use of stencils to the influence of esteemed artist and professor Jules Heller, who wrote *Printmaking Today* (1973) and *Papermaking* (1978).

In preparation for graduation, Melanie was determined to be able to continue making art. Like other recent college graduates, she knew that she would not have access to many expensive lithography tools, such as a slab of limestone and a lithographic press. For her senior honors thesis paper and exhibition, "Images Inspired by the Navajo Creation Myth," she selected the screen-printing process. This medium involved accessible and easily portable tools, such as paper or plastic film, a fine mesh screen and a squeegee. She decided that she wanted to teach this art form to youth on the Navajo reservation in order to help bolster their self-esteem.

Following earning bachelor's degree in fine arts/studio printmaking in 1990, Melanie pursued a master of fine arts degree in printmaking at the University of Colorado at Boulder. During graduate school, Melanie experienced a dilemma in her artistic development. She questioned her artistic forms and considered if she should become a traditional weaver like her relatives. She asked her grandmother Thelma, "Should I stop making this work? Should I start making some weavings, and work like you?" In Navajo, her grandmother responded, "You are weaving. You're weaving in a different way. You're weaving your ideas and stories in this new way. I don't know how you do it, but it's amazing. You're a different type of weaver. We are both weavers." This experience helped her feel validated in her path as a contemporary native artist and empowered her to pursue creating mixed-media artworks.

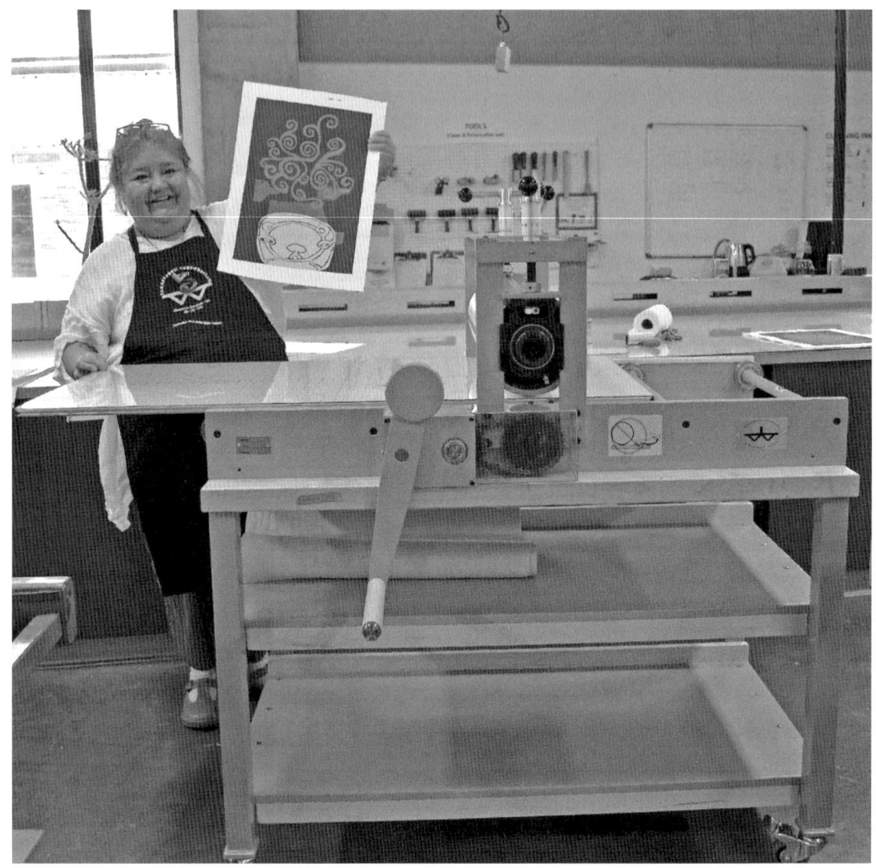

Melanie Yazzie stands by a Luna printmaking press in her studio in 2014. *Courtesy of Melanie Yazzie, all rights reserved.*

Artistic Processes, Inspiration and Imagery

Melanie uses controlled, formal methods when creating screen prints, etchings, collagraphs, reliefs, monotypes and lithographs. She often combines several processes together to make unique works of art. She often transfers photographic images over to a screen or photo litho-plate and prints them in different layers of a print. The theme of the more controlled pieces frequently relates to colonization. She includes photographs of family members in some of these politically charged prints. She pointed out, "Those aren't out there as much because I think, at one point, I felt the pieces were very in your face and difficult to handle. I've realized within the past year or two that some of our own native people probably need to see some of the images."

At other times, she participates in informal processes that allow room for more movement. For Melanie, the central concept directs the choice of medium and artistic process. For example, her monotypes, which are created on rag paper, can be likened to one-of-a-kind paintings. She noted, "They exist uniquely to themselves, and there may be a series, but none of the pieces are exactly the same." The process is long and very labor intensive before she even arrives to the printing press. There are weeks before a session in which she is planning and cutting her stencils for a series of work.

A prolific artist, Melanie creates paintings, gouache drawings, mixed-media installations, bronze-and-steel sculptures, porcelain hand-built ceramics, linocuts, monotypes, woodblocks, etchings, lithographs and paper-pulp prints with photo-lithographic elements. An element of her concern is for the world environment; therefore, she remains dedicated to using safer printmaking materials and methods whenever possible.

Melanie discovers imagery for her artworks in her dreams, a process that her grandmother and mother also used. Once, Melanie asked her grandmother how she came up with a weaving design. Thelma responded, "I just woke up this morning, and I saw it in my mind. Now, I know how to make it, and I'm going to make it." Melanie is also constantly drawing as a process to support ideas and development for her artworks. She explained, "A lot of my work is based off drawings and different dreams or stories that I've put together from my own…my own creative place in my mind, in my heart and in my soul."

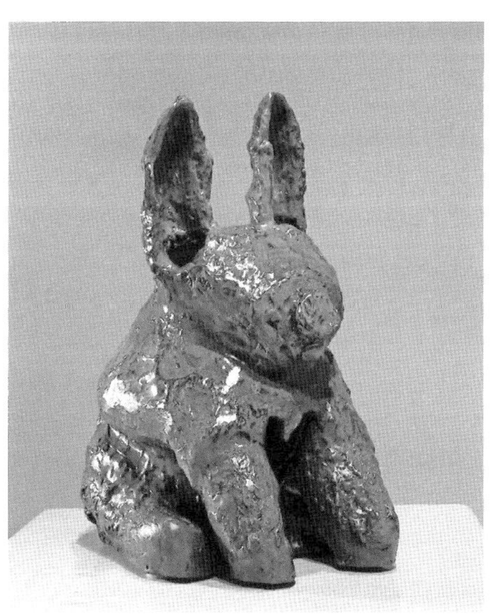

In this sculpture, *Blue Yazzie Sits at the Ganado Post Office*, Melanie Yazzie reflects her affinity for animals, as well as her connection to her hometown. *Courtesy of Glenn Green Galleries, all rights reserved.*

Melanie explained the artful ways of Navajo peoples. She said, "I broadened the scope of what an artist means to how somebody would prepare a meal, how somebody teaches. I know this is about art, but the way in which we think of art-making is the way you live your life as a Navajo person. You do things in a beautiful way. You think things in a beautiful way, and in that way, we're all artists."

The colors of Arizona, such as those found in the Canyon De Chelly and the Painted Desert, inspire her artwork. In addition, Melanie often includes in her work animal imagery, such as animals found on the reservation (dogs, cats, sheep and horses), her pets and imaginary hybrid animals. Melanie grew up with many animals, including a St. Bernard, Doberman, rat, hamster and fish. Currently, she has one dog named Gus Gus.

Melanie pieces together diverse symbols in her artwork, such as transformation, travel and womanhood. In recent exhibitions, her painting and sculpture subject matter included native ceremonies, rituals, prayers and sacred foods and addressed themes of indigenous women and post-colonial challenges.

Raggedy Ann

Melanie's family greatly influenced her path to using mixed materials as an artist. Her grandfather "built a lot of things from found materials. He would use Coke and Pepsi-Cola signs for doors of a shed, old milk crates to build fences, just found objects were things that he would use that I think would save on materials. I think a lot of that played a role in how I became an artist."

An example of Melanie's exploration with mixed media can be found in *Raggedy Ann* (1996). In this artwork, the artist re-contextualizes objects in innovative and powerful ways to create a new story. This artwork was an installation exhibited at the Heard Museum in which she juxtaposed a Navajo weaving from the Heard Museum's permanent collection; an old, weathered trunk, which was open to reveal tattered dollar bills and postcards of European sculpture and American Indian pottery; and collages of the character Raggedy Ann.

As Navajo weavings are traditionally associated with Navajo women's art forms, Melanie may be reflecting on her own grandmothers' weavings, as well as her own challenges with pursuing new media as a contemporary Navajo artist. The trunk may be referencing remnants of Melanie's voyages (from boarding school at Westtown to more recent international travels to New Zealand) and serves as a witness to her life journey. A recurrent message in her work is sharing the knowledge that she has gained through traveling and meeting diverse peoples. Lastly, Melanie's selection of the cartoon Raggedy Ann seems to show her connection to the character's adventures and physical resemblance. Male classmates at Ganado Public School would call Melanie "Red Ant" because her unique hair looked reddish in the sun, and when she ran around the schoolyard, her face would turn bright red.

Combatting Stereotypes and Advocating for Native Communities

At times humorous, at other times political, themes of Melanie Yazzie's artwork explore issues that many native peoples encounter, including racism. In *Indian Look Alikes* (1993), she addresses American Indian stereotypes. Text from a vintage coloring book reads, "Circle the Indians in each row that look the same, color the pictures." Next to the cartoonish American Indian figures, Melanie placed her own school photographs. Through her artwork, Melanie challenges assumptions that people in the past held about American Indians. She brings current viewers to also consider whether they also continue to hold stereotypes.

Melanie Yazzie uses her artwork as a catalyst for a respectful discourse about tolerance and diversity. To this day, many people assume that Navajo artists exclusively work as weavers or silversmiths. Melanie said, "I've always been approached by people who don't know a lot about art and native arts, and they'll always say, 'Wow. You're an artist? Can you make me a silver bracelet or can you make me a weaving? How come you don't weave?' [There will be] accusations of not being native—Navajo—enough, if I'm not a weaver because both of my grandmothers were weavers."

Melanie advocates for educating others about the contemporary lives and challenges of native communities in the United States and across the globe. She has worked with communities in New Zealand, the Arctic, France, Russia, Siberia, Australia, Canada, Japan and Mexico. She finds connections with indigenous peoples through their stories and their similar histories of being colonized. Through sharing their wisdom, individuals strengthen their communities. Melanie validates others' tremendous strength, which enables them to survive amid adversity. She said, "Everybody has a beautiful story to tell and share. That is valuable. In that way, we're connected, not just as Navajos or nonnative people but just as human beings."

Melanie collaborates with other artists of different cultures, thus demonstrating her belief that creating artwork is a process that diverse people can do. In 2007, she took part in a group exhibition at the C.N. Gorman Museum, called "Understandably Connected," in which forty artists connected through their indigenous identities and the challenges of cultural survival. Later, in 2010, she participated in the exhibition with Sue Pearson, who is of Norfolk Island ancestry, at Tawero Studio Gallery in New Zealand.

PROFESSIONAL CAREER

Melanie Yazzie is an esteemed educator and lecturer. Her teaching experience includes institutions such as the University of Arizona (Tucson), the Institute of the American Indian Arts (Santa Fe, New Mexico), Boise State University (Boise, Idaho) and the Pont Aven School of Contemporary Art (Pont Aven, France). She has led workshops in printmaking throughout the United States and abroad for over twenty years. Melanie has also served as an artist-in-residence at the Denver Art Museum (2012), Missoula Art Museum (2014) and the Crow Shadow Institute of the Arts (2012). Currently, she is a professor and the head of the Printmaking Department at the University of Colorado at Boulder.

Melanie has exhibited her artwork in over 150 solo and group exhibitions, including at the following locations: the Gallery of Visual Arts at the University of Montana (2015), University of New Mexico Art Museum (2014), Missoula Art Museum (2014), Denver Botanic Garden (2011), Museum of Natural History, University of Colorado at Boulder (2010) and Khalil Sakikini Center (2006), Shemer Art Center and Museum (2005), Institute of American Indian Arts Museum (1994) and CU Art Galleries (1993). In 2014, she was featured in a solo exhibition, "Melanie Yazzie: Geographies of Memory," at the University of New Mexico Art Museum. Layered imagery referenced her Navajo heritage, as well as aspects of geography and her autobiography.

Several esteemed institutions have collected her artwork, including the Heard Museum, the Corcoran Museum, Missoula Art Museum, Sante Fe Museum of Fine Arts, Anchorage Museum of History and Art, the Museum of Art of Rhode Island School of Design, Arizona State University Art Museum, Rhodes University, Te Waka Toi Maori Contemporary Arts and the Australian National Gallery.

Additional Publications and Resources

You can find additional information about Melanie in the following books: *Melanie Yazzie: Geographies of Memory* by Lisa Tamaris Becker and Lucy Lippard (2014), *About Face* by Zena Pearlstone (2008), *The Lure of the Local* by Lucy Lippard (1998), *Native American Art in the Twentieth Century* by Jackson Rushing (1999) and *Printmaking in the Sun* by Dan Welden and Pauline Muire (2001). Additional publications exploring her work include *Focus Magazine, Los Angeles Times* and *New Zealand Herald.*

Since 1994, Glenn Green Galleries in Santa Fe, New Mexico, has exclusively represented and sold her artworks. Melanie explained that the Green and Yazzie families have been lifelong friends. Gallerist Kerry Green acknowledged the complexity of Melanie Yazzie's artistic layering process. Kerry said, "When I look at her work and get to spend time with it, I see more and more layers. It's like conversations we have about life and art that reveal subtext and depth. The artwork is beautiful, and it has a lot happening that is seen and not seen. She dedicates herself to some complicated art-making processes, which are so refined in her hands that it looks effortless."

She also shared: "Melanie is naturally creative. It is always fascinating to watch her in the print studio or sculpting when she is in 'the zone.' It is even more amazing to watch her try a process that is new and foreign to her. You can see the wheels turning in her mind and when it clicks for her. She is totally engaged and immersed in what she is making. Creativity flows from her."

Indeed, Melanie Yazzie is a visionary artist.

4

JESSE MONONGYA

Navajo Roots

Jesse Monongya was born on August 13, 1952, to Navajo mother Ida Mae Costello (Water-Flows-in-a-Circle clan) and Hopi father Preston Monongya. While his father was deployed in the military, Jesse's mother disappeared, abandoning their four children. Jesse was only three years old. It was never revealed to Jesse what happened to his mother: Did she die? Did she move away and leave her family? About fifteen years ago, human remains were found in a shallow grave at the Grand Canyon (where she previously worked), and Jesse believes these could have belonged to his mother.

Jesse's grandfather David Monongya, a respected Hopi elder, tried to adopt Jesse. However, Jesse explained, "With your mother's side is your census. Your number is on that side. You go back to that side, if you're ever adopted." Therefore, distant Navajo relatives, Lucille and Allen Mailman, whom he called Grandmother Yellow and Grandfather, raised Jesse and his siblings on the western part of the Navajo Reservation in New Mexico. As tribal elders, they instilled in Jesse the traditions of Navajo Way, which were led by discipline and beauty. He learned agriculture and ranching ways of life, as well. Grandmother Yellow was a "very strong spiritual leader." Jesse shared, "She gave me all of her tools and pushed me to be a very true believer in our traditional ways and spiritual ways." To this day, Jesse finds inspiration through his family's teachings. He explained:

> *The inspiration comes from the traditional teaching, from my grandmother... Everything was instilled when I was young...I was raised with the old people. I had to reach back to Grandmother and all of her teachings. I bring her up before me and I see all the traditional ways of dances, all the traditional colors, all the sand paintings, all the weavings, the Two Grey Hills rug weavings. These became fascinating to me.*

The technical perfection and a sense of balance of Two Grey Hills weavings, which he often saw as a child, later inspired Jesse's work as a jeweler.

Like many other American Indians at the time, Jesse attended boarding school. Jesse reported that at Wingate High School, some Navajo students would get into trouble with abusing alcohol. He explained, "A lot of them died. They were getting run over by a train or getting run over by traffic or in jail or getting killed. The city the school was in, Gallup, was the drinking capital of the world for the Indians." Jesse's school often asked him to accompany students home to the reservation. He began to ask himself what living environment issues were leading to students turning to alcohol and not succeeding academically. He explained, "When something is not too right, I go investigate. That's what I did in high school."

Jesse found that the children were raised in "pretty much poverty and welfare." Parents had been removed from the home, leading the children to act out rebelliously. Grandparents were raising the children and teaching them traditional Navajo ways of life and often Christian values. However, Jesse noticed, "The word *love* wasn't really expressed among Navajos at the time that I remember. The kids themselves didn't know what love was really about." Jesse presented his report to the school administration and the entire student body, for which he received a standing ovation. He showed tremendous leadership skills at an early age and also exhibited his deep commitment to healing the wounds of his community. Jesse's commitment to his native community continued throughout adulthood, when he advocated for drug and alcohol treatment centers on the Navajo reservation. He recognizes that alcoholism is still plaguing native communities:

> *Most of my cousins' relatives have died from alcoholism. The saddest thing that I do now today is go back home and bury my cousins, relatives. Every year, I go home and bury another one. It's always they died from alcoholism or something like that...*
>
> *It's* [the reservation's] *so rampant with alcohol...There's a gene in our body—this small radar that sits in our body that* [is] *longing for*

> *alcohol. You put alcohol in one kid's body* [and] *that's what they always want, to have that feeling—that first drink. Then, a lot of them will become alcoholics—sniffing glue, gasoline, paint. They're doing all kinds of stuff now.*
>
> *It's sad. Our traditional ways, our spiritual ways are pretty much really dim. It's really sad. How alcohol can take over a whole family and kill a whole family.*

BECOMING A JEWELER

In his twenties, Jesse served as a marine in the Vietnam War, and when he returned home, he was reunited with his father, Preston Monongya, a well-known jeweler. Initially, Jesse was not interested in pursuing his father's profession. He said, "When I came back from Vietnam, when I found my dad…I had no interest in what he was doing. I was more interested in going to college and playing basketball, baseball, softball. Sports was my main thing…One day, I stopped. And I said, 'Hey, I'm getting behind here. I'm going to school, and I'm learning nothing.'"

Preston Monongya had mastered a variety of artistic processes, including sculpture, katsina doll carving, pottery and jewelry. Jesse recognized that Preston was influential in the art world. He stated, "He was famous when I found him—Preston Monongya, who opened a market to the world of Indian jewelry, who changed the world with his art." Jesse continued:

> *The Indian jewelry at that time was only identified with the tribe, the tribe, if you made an overlay piece, you know that's from the Hopi Reservation. If you made turquoise and squash blossom, you know it came from the Navajos, and so forth and so on.*
>
> *That came to be that way until my Dad comes along and calls it art. The whole thing changed. It went to the individual: Preston Monongya became an artist, not so much Hopi jewelry.*
>
> *You see what I'm saying? Because he changed the style completely with the tufa stone. When he changed that, everybody said, "Oh my gosh, these guys call themselves artists." The artisan was born into the overall, the tribe in the Southwest.*

When Jesse found his dad, everything changed in Jesse's world. Jesse remembers accompanying Preston with his wealthy collectors to the Hopi reservation. Many were Hollywood movie stars, like Dick Van Dyke, who were filming at the studios in Carefree, Arizona. Jesse said:

> *We used to take them all up to the Hopi Reservation, because the Hopi people were very interesting to the movie world…You could be in the city two hours ago, and then you go back to the Hopi reservation* [and] *it's like you're in a foreign country…*
>
> *The setting, where they lived, they* [Hopis] *lived in the cliffs, up in the cliffs and their homes are out there. Their dances have been the same way they said* [for] *over one thousand years. They kept their dances. They kept all of their traditional ways. All their dances, and all the activity, and all the ceremonies they would have for their people stayed the same all these years, never changed. The living never changed. I think maybe ten years ago, they started getting electricity up there.*

Jesse learned basic metalworking skills and traditional tufa stone processes from his father. He attributes his talent to Preston and said, "That's where the talent all comes from—from my dad's side." Jesse admitted that it wasn't always easy working together. Jesse would come to his father's aid when he had troubles, such as "bailing him out of prison" for tax evasion. Jesse shared, "We had such huge egos, my Dad and I. If we were to stay together as a father and son, probably him and I would been one of the richest Indians or probably [would have] died of early alcoholism."

Jesse dedicated himself to developing his jeweler skills, and his skills progressed exponentially. In the mid-1970s, Jesse realized he had surpassed his father when he discovered Preston had entered one of Jesse's pieces in a Hopi art show in Flagstaff with his name on it. Jesse stated:

> *My dad, Preston—I finish a piece, he enters it in July the Fourth. He takes the Best in Show, with my piece, with his name on it, right? I knew I was already better than my dad. My dad is number-one jeweler in the world by this time….*
>
> *There was my piece in the middle of all these ribbons hanging off of it…I picked up my piece, and…I turned it over, and on the back, it says the price on this piece was $2,800…I keep trying to get that in my mind of what $2,800 would look like, I'd never seen $2,800 in my life.*

Jesse realized the monetary value of the jewelry he could gain if he set off on his own. In Phoenix, he visited a gem store. The salesperson offered limited options for Jesse's fifty-dollar budget. All he could afford was a bucket of inexpensive coral pieces. Jesse remembered:

> *He said, "Jesse, this stuff is really small stuff, you shouldn't even worry about this."*
>
> *I took it out and looked at it, and I said, "This is exactly the stuff I'm looking for."*
>
> *I took the whole bucket and put it in my car. It smelled like fish; it smelled like you were in an ocean or something. I said, "Oh my gosh, this is horrible." I brought it all home and I started cutting because I had beaten my dad* [at the art market competition].

Dreaming of His Mother

Jesse was also driven to pursue jewelry-making after being inspired by a dream of his mother. He continues to recognize that strong spiritual experiences and beliefs direct the course of his life. Jesse was on his way to heavy equipment operator training in Chicago when he had a life-changing dream.

It was June, and he was sleeping outside his father's home. He dreamt that he heard a crying bear. He said, "This little bear is making these cries. And, we were raised on the reservation, when you hear a little bear cry you don't want to be around, you know?" He awoke at 4:00 a.m. and looked around for the bear, but he saw nothing. He returned to sleep, and his dream continued:

> *This guy was bringing a little coffin in the back of a small wagon, and there's a little mule in front of it…He says, "Anybody want to see their parents or family member?" I said, "I do, I do. I'm looking for my mom."*
>
> *He said, "I had a hard time finding your mother. Because she had changed her name, we couldn't find her. We have her over here now, we can talk to her." He opened the coffin and my mom's sitting in there. And she says, "Oh, hi, son." Her and I were talking, and she's telling me all about what's going to happen to your dad, what's going to happen to your brother. And I said, "I don't want to hear that."*
>
> *She reached down to her side and picks* [up] *this bundle of tools wrapped up in cloth. She says, "Take this, and you're going to be the most famous man in the world."*

> *I'm holding this stuff, and I said, "What do I do with this?" She said, "You'll figure it out...I've got to leave, son, but you need to think about not going to Chicago and just take these tools."*

When he awoke, he was energized and inspired to create art. He said:

> *I jump up and wow! I don't know. I got this dream, and I was so excited...I went in my dad's studio, and...I'm standing in there. I'm thinking that this little bear is still coming down this alley.*
>
> *I said, "Oh my gosh." Just then I saw it...I saw one of my dad's bears sitting underneath the lamp. The light was shining on it. I walk up to it, I'm looking at it and it was instant, just like that. I mean it was like, I knew all the colors, what colors it should have...I'm going to cut me one out and make my own...Inlaid, it was already all cut out to be inlaid. I went home and bezzeled mine, bezzeled the bear, and I worked at my studio, my little kitchenette.*

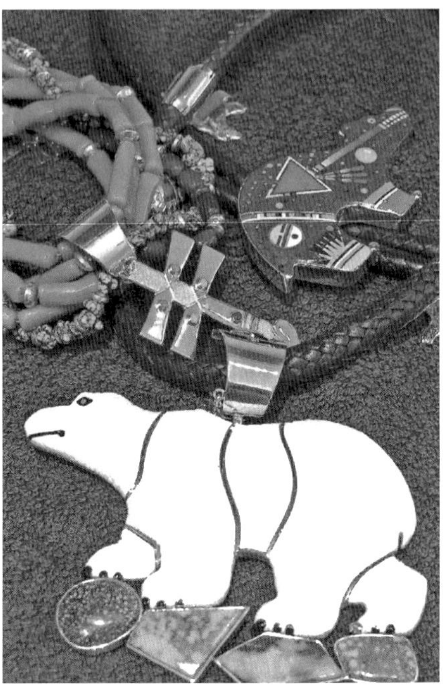

Bear imagery is a common theme found in Jesse Monongya's artwork. Some of Jesse's opal bears are called *shánídíín* bears. In the Navajo language, *shánídíín* means "healing ray of light," and for Jesse, they reflect a new beginning. *Photograph by Rory O'Neill Schmitt, all rights reserved.*

Jesse realized that he needed to set off on his own. He heeded his mother's advice and indeed found success. Jesse has been in business as a jeweler for forty years.

Paving the Way for New Art Forms

Jesse is committed to making jewelry that defies expectations of native jewelry. He has refined skills in lapidary, the art of cutting, polishing and engraving precious stones. Jesse creates gorgeous jewelry featuring scenes of galaxies, mountains and nighttime skies, as well as bears, turtles and the Sun Face. Deep blue skies are formed from lazuli, moons are made of opals and constellations are created of inlays of jade, malachite and diamonds. Intricate details, such as those found on the caps of mountains in a design, can include up to one hundred stones to express utter beauty and render striking three-dimensionality.

Jesse appreciates the traditional jewelry-making processes. He stated, "With the modern society, with the modern technology that we have: with the diamond machine, diamond drills...and the dentist equipment, it makes it possible to do the things that you thought you couldn't do. At the same time, the elders did it without it...That gives you the inspiration."

Jesse's spirituality is also his driving force. He said, "You have to have a spiritual nature, growth, inside to understand what you're doing and why you're doing [it]." Jesse recognizes the connection between the precious stones he uses in his jewelry and the Creator. He said, "The amazing thing is God created the universe, our Creator created this universe. And he did not put the stones in [one place]...They're all over the world. Any kind of colors, shape, size, and they always prove to you that he is the Great Creator.

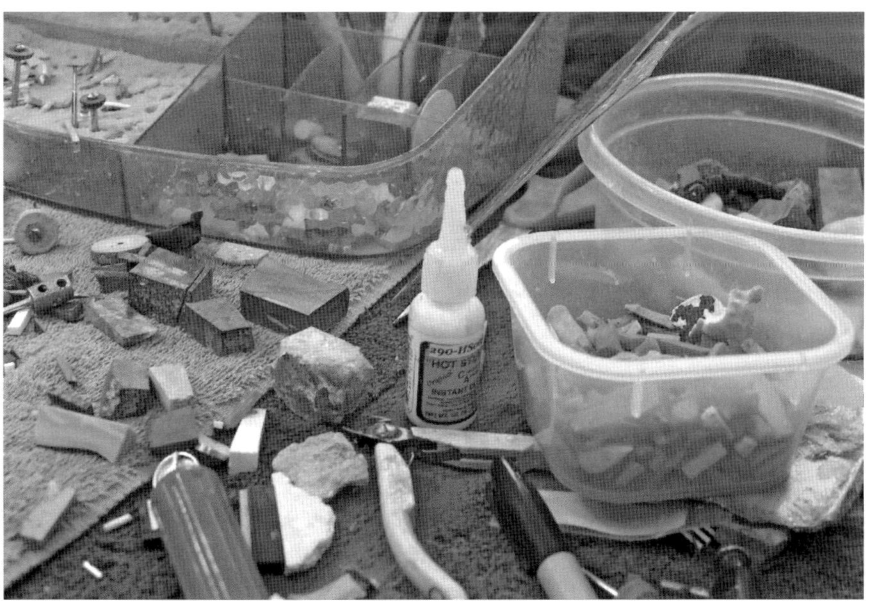

Jesse Monongya's secret ingredient in constructing his jewelry is super glue. *Photograph by Rory O'Neill Schmitt, all rights reserved.*

People don't really understand that. They overlook that. Now today, we just take the beauty back into our work."

For decades, Jesse worked out of his garage. He said, "I don't know if you've seen that commercial, it's a Cadillac commercial…'All great people came out of their garage.' I guess I'm one of them." Years of dedication to pushing his jewelry art form to the highest standard have led him to become a leader in the field. Today, Jesse's state-of-the-art studio in Scottsdale has multiple workstations with several specialized machines, such as tufa stone–casting equipment and laser-welding and diamond-cutting machines. Windows poetically look onto his residence, patios and exquisitely groomed yard. A large, rust-colored Navajo weaving hanging on the far wall and katsina doll carvings and eagle sculptures exhibited on shelves reflect Jesse's rich Navajo and Hopi heritage. Magazines, books and cherished family photographs in the studio document and celebrate Jesse's life.

For several years, Jesse has been working closely with his team: his son, Jesse "Bo" Monongya, and his son's best friend (since junior high school), Brent Goswick. Bo described his training:

> *I started with my dad when I was about thirteen. He started me from the bottom up, sweeping floors, learning how to take care of all of the machines*

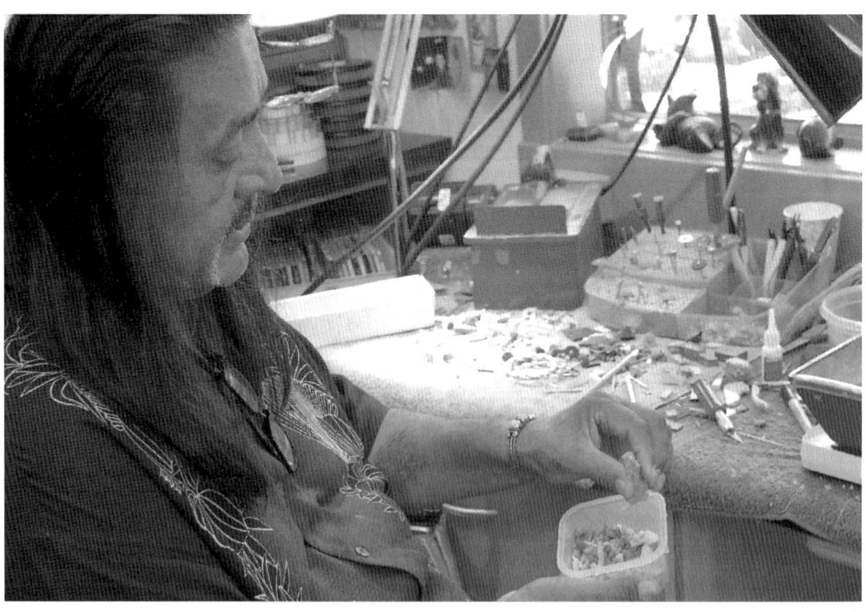

Jesse Monongya examines coral pieces that he will select, cut, shape and polish to use in a future jewelry piece. *Photograph by Rory O'Neill Schmitt, all rights reserved.*

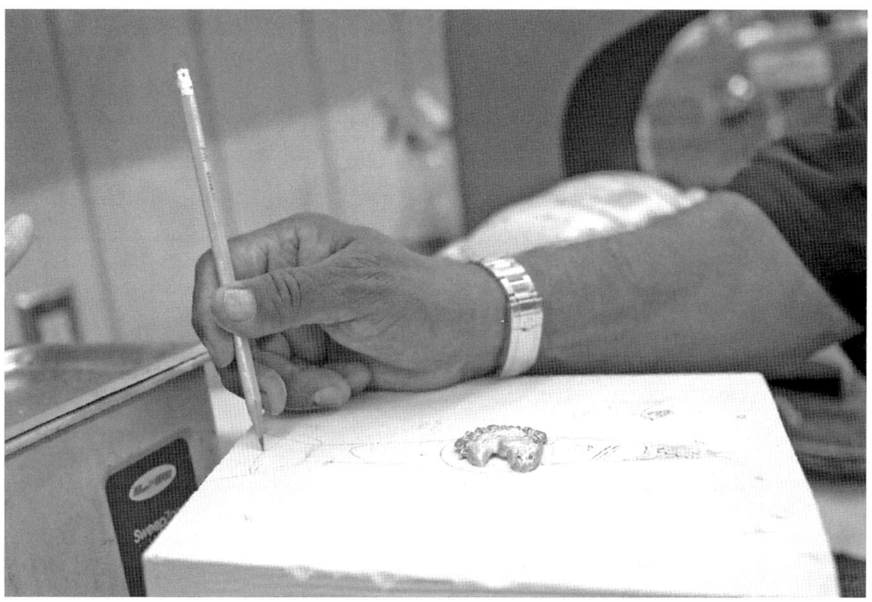

Jesse sketches a design onto tufa stone for a private collector who has commissioned a piece of jewelry with the theme of horses. *Photograph by Rory O'Neill Schmitt, all rights reserved.*

> *and respecting the machines. That equipment is what your livelihood is, so you had to take care of it.*
>
> *He showed me that, and then he pushed me into just cutting out simple patterns for him. Then, it turned into basically the steps of silversmithing. Now I'm in full fabricating all his jewelry, helping him with whatever he needs, just day-to-day stuff.*

As Bo is a third-generation jeweler, his son, Jager, is showing interest in becoming a fourth-generation jeweler. Bo shared, "My son, he's starting to hint around with it. He loves what his grandpa does." Gifted jewelers run in the Monongya family.

Being a leader in the field, Jesse recognizes his responsibilities. He shared, "When you become a leader like I am in what I do, you got to stay ahead of the game." He explained:

> *Teaching the young generation—people of all walks of life, giving it to them and letting them do whatever they want to do with it.* [The reason] *I stay ahead of the generation is because I'm considered probably the top two in the world today. I have to maintain it...*

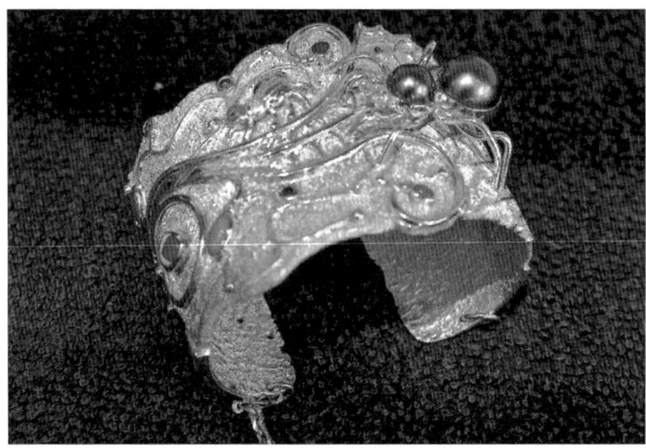

This gold cuff bracelet by Jesse Monongya reflects a modern design and includes insect imagery composed of semiprecious stones. *Photograph by Rory O'Neill Schmitt, all rights reserved.*

> *To do that, I have to get up with the morning stars and the moons and learn to pray, learn to develop good prayer lines. Then, help others. The inspiration will always be there when you give to others."*

To set a standard for the next generation, he started the Jesse Monongya Lapidary School. He is committed to saving native arts. He said, "I have a lot of knowledge. You know that saying, if you have a lot of knowledge that means nothing if you can't give it away."

Family

Jesse teaches traditional values to his children and grandchildren. He notes that families need a strong leader at the core. He said:

> *My kids, were pretty much* [raised] *the way I was raised but in a different way...It stays in your mind when you're young.* [It's important to] *learn how to pray with the children, learn how to be the leader that you are with your family. A lot of this has been taken out of a home. The children are within the circle by themselves without the main core. When you are the main core of the home, they all come back together. They stay together, and they think pretty wisely.*

In addition to Bo, Jesse has two daughters: Sophia and Stephanie. Sophia works as a registered nurse and has a son named Wesley. In 2002, Jesse lost his twenty-year-old daughter, Stephanie, in a car accident in Phoenix. This tragedy shattered his world. He said:

> *Life wasn't all that easy, even though I made a lot of money…I lost my daughter Stephanie.* [She was] *twenty years old and got killed on the* [Highway] *101. It broke my whole world apart. Twenty-year-old child, beautiful girl, daughter…*
>
> *My world just went tumbling straight down to the bottom again. I didn't want to live, just want to be alone, shun everybody away from me…It took me about three years. I almost killed myself* [with] *drinking and drugs."*

Following this event, Jesse had a dream of his daughter that gave his life meaning again. He shared: "My daughter came back in my dreams and said, 'Dad, you're not coming to heaven. You have one purpose, and you taught us all what that purpose was. You need to fulfill your purpose before you come up.'"

Jesse's commitment to a healthy life can be seen in his daily attendance of Alcoholics Anonymous meetings. He said, "I went back to Alcoholics Anonymous. I had twenty-three years by that time in Alcoholics Anonymous then. Now, I have nine years again and rebuilt my whole life. My family and my children all came back, and life is much better now today." Jesse's family brings him tremendous joy.

Awards and Exhibitions

Jesse has won the highest awards at several competitions, including the Northern Arizona Museum (1975), Gallup Intertribal Indian Ceremonial Arts and Crafts Show (1978, 1991, 1992 and 1993), the Heard Museum Guild Indian Fair and Market (1977, 1979 and 1998), Od'Ham Tash (1984), Santa Fe Market (1979 and 1992) and the Gene Autry Museum (2011). He has been featured in solo and group exhibitions, such as those at the Museum of Man (1977), Heard Museum (1986, 1997–98 and 2010–11), Museum of Northern Arizona (1991), Desert Caballeros Museum (1995) and University of Pennsylvania Museum of Anthropology and Archeology (1995).

Jesse's jewelry has been in the collections of the Heard Museum, Northern Arizona Museum, Museum of Man, Cooper-Hewitt Museum and Denver Art Museum, as well as in the private collections of Senator Barry Goldwater, artist Allen Houser, benefactor John Rockefeller and actors Goldie Hawn and Burt Reynolds. You can see his service to the community in his acting as a board member on the Scottsdale American Indian Art Invitations and the Arizona Indian Arts Alliance.

Additional Information

Jesse's jewelry is considered the finest inlay work done today. He strives each day to become better as a jeweler, to make strong, durable jewelry with no mistakes. More information about Jesse can be found in *Jesse Monongya: Opal Bears and Lapis Skies* (2002) by Lois Dubin, *Navajo Jewelry: A Legacy of Silver and Stone* (1996) by Lois Jacka, *Enduring Traditions: Art of the Navajo* (1994) by Lois and Jerry Jacka and *Beyond Tradition: Contemporary Indian Art and Evolution* (1991) by Lois and Jerry Jacka.

Jesse's website is www.jessemonongyastudios.com, and his studio can be contacted through the e-mail address Monongye@cox.net.

5

RIC CHARLIE

Tuba City, Arizona

Ric Charlie grew up north of Flagstaff in Tuba City, Arizona. Ric's grandparents and parents raised him on the reservation using traditional Navajo fundamentals, as well as modern ways of life. He explained that they spoke only English to him and his seven siblings because they were "preparing us for the off-the-reservation type of living." Devoted to supporting the community, Ric's mother worked as a nurse at the Indian Hospital, and his father was a police officer. In addition, his grandmother worked as a cook for the elementary school, and his grandfather was as an engineer at the power plant.

As a child, Ric spent his days drawing birds, horses and dinosaurs. In junior high school, he enjoyed pottery, drawing and woodshop classes. For Ric, creating ceramics and drawings did not seem very different from making jewelry. He said, "It was all the same. I mean: Art was art. Anything I could do with my hands and be creative about it to me all falls into the same category as art."

Ric was inspired to pursue jewelry-making by the famous Hopi jeweler Charles Loloma. Ric shared:

> *Charles Loloma…was a big influence in high school. He'd come with the fancy car, and he's got the gold-rimmed sunglasses, the fun diamond jewelry. He's looking real sharp, and I'd go, "Wow."*

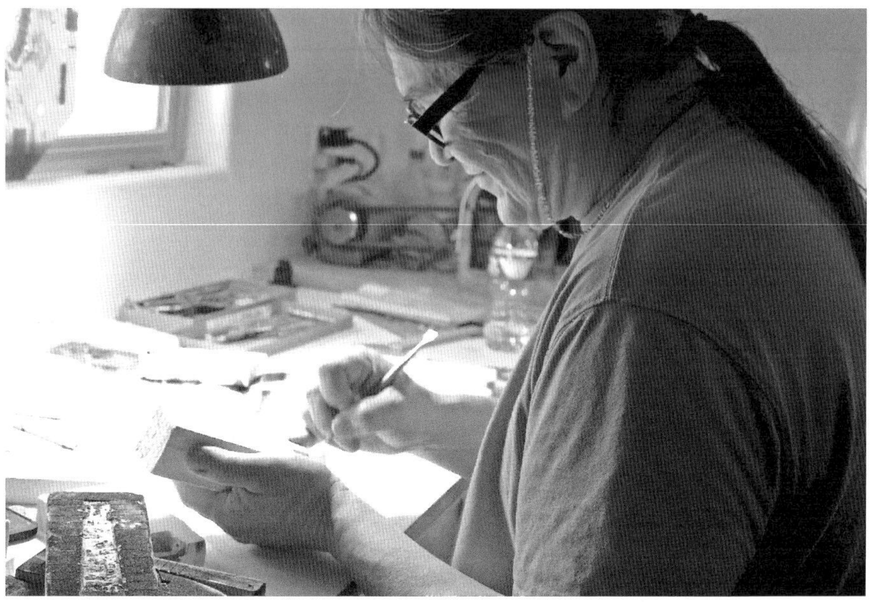

Ric Charlie carefully carves his geometric designs into tufa stone at his studio in Goodyear, Arizona. *Photograph by Rory O'Neill Schmitt, all rights reserved.*

> *At that time, growing up, art was a big business. It still is today. I wanted a piece of that. I thought—I was just out of high school—I had to create something totally unique and different that I could call my own."*

In high school, he studied advanced art and jewelry-making. He learned the basic fundamentals of soldering and cutting stones. Later, he continued his studies in studio art at a community college in Mesa, Arizona.

Resurrecting and Developing Tufa Casting

Ric uses silver, turquoise and other precious stones in his bracelets, rings, earrings, bolo ties and belts. To meet the current demands of the market, he creates gold pieces with diamonds and other precious gems. Ric is known for creating his signature patinas in his silver jewelry. He is able to make rich colors of blue, green and purple through controlling the process of diluting the liver of sulfur solution to capture a rainbow of colors in his gold jewelry. Due to the time expended to achieve extremely detailed, one-of-a-kind jewelry, Ric creates limited pieces each year, usually about fifty.

For over forty years, Ric has been resurrecting and further developing the tufa casting method. He explained:

> *Tufa stone casting was a dying art, and there was only a handful of artists out there that was considered very talented in this method, but there was nobody out there to teach. Everything that I've learned was based on trial and error. I am self-taught in tufa casting...I figured that tufa stone was going to be my niche in the jewelry business because there weren't very many people out there doing casting. Not only that—I had this dream of being the best, and I wanted to be the best. I kept pursuing and improving my technique. Today, they consider me to be one of the finest in the nation."*

For one piece of jewelry, like a bracelet, Ric may carve several tufa molds, as each mold may pertain to a different type of gold (for instance, yellow, green and rose gold) that he intends to use. Working at his home studio, Ric carves abstract designs with intricate geometric detailing into the tufa stone. Carving into the stone is like drawing on canvas. Commanding precision dental tools, he draws out fine lines meticulously and methodically, reining control of the medium. He is fastidious about his work area, cleaning up tufa scraps after he has carved the molds.

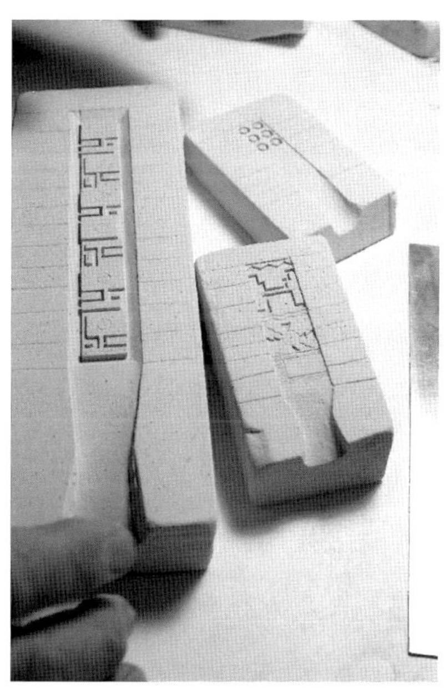

Ric Charlie fastidiously carves designs into different sizes of tufa stone. Each cast he makes will be integrated into the final jewelry piece: a bracelet composed of three types of gold and set with diamonds. *Photograph by Rory O'Neill Schmitt, all rights reserved.*

Usually, he casts his tufa stone in his garage, but sometimes, he casts at a station in his backyard. With long dark hair down his back in a low ponytail, Ric works in red camouflage shorts and a T-shirt. Confident in his ability after decades of doing this craft, Ric just puts

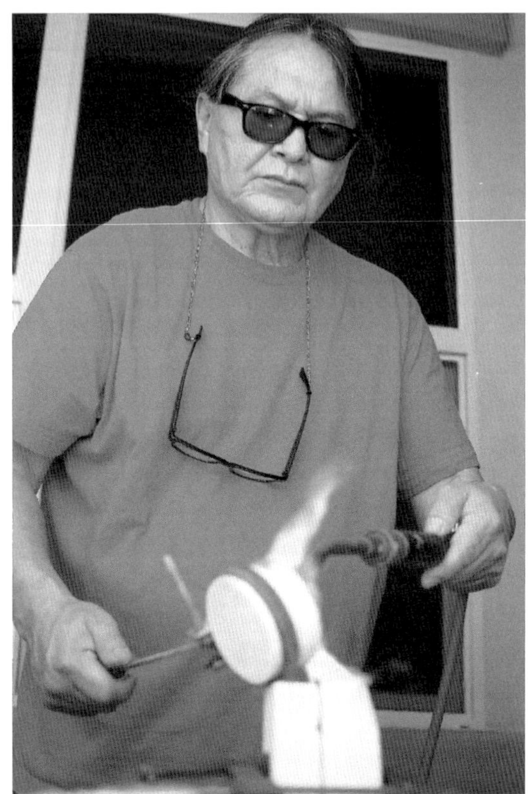

Right: Using a torch, Ric Charlie melts gold and pours it into the tufa cast. *Photograph by Rory O'Neill Schmitt, all rights reserved.*

Below: Soon after dipping the metal into the pickling solution, the piece is cool enough for Ric Charlie to touch. *Photograph by Rory O'Neill Schmitt, all rights reserved.*

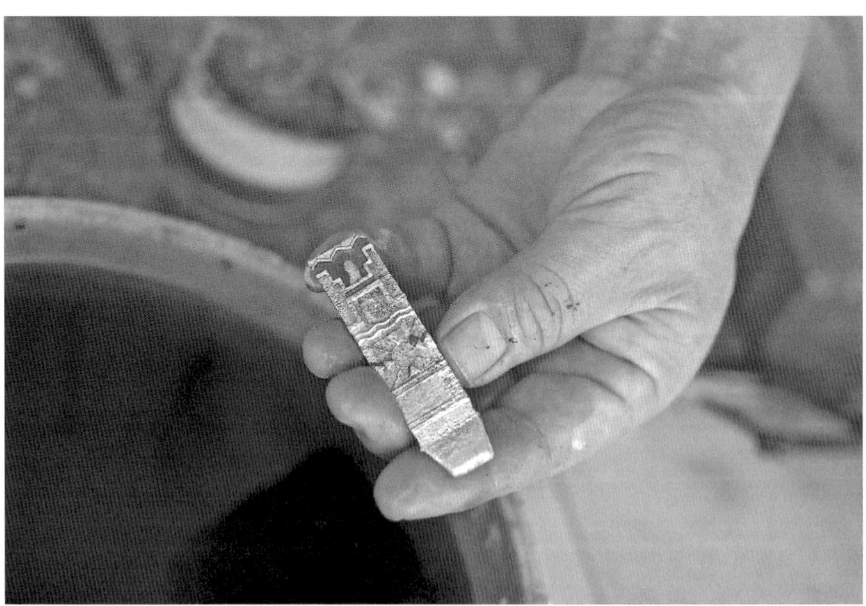

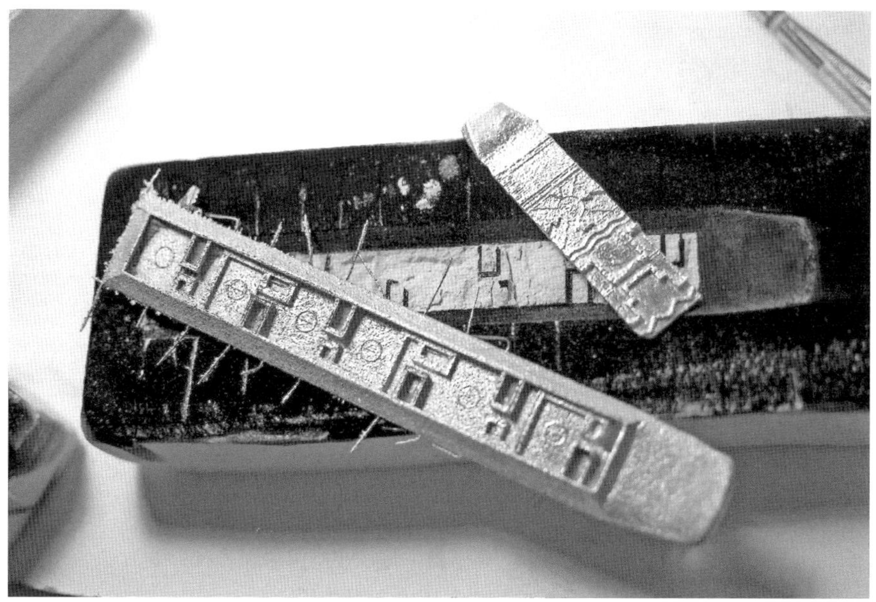

Result from a recent pour of gold into two tufa casts. Ric Charlie will later cut out shapes from the piece (on the right) to place into the base of the bracelet (on the left). *Photograph by Rory O'Neill Schmitt, all rights reserved.*

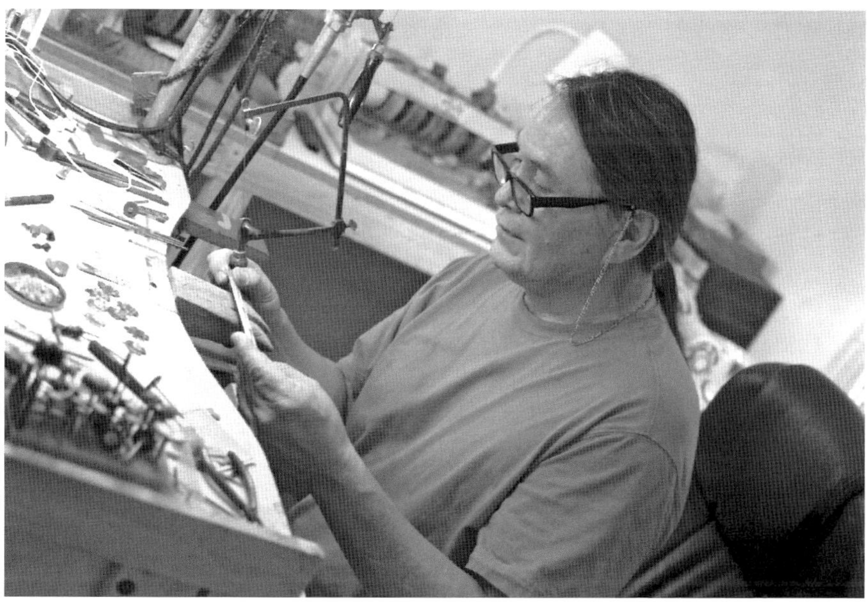

Ric Charlie files a gold bracelet at his workbench. *Photograph by Rory O'Neill Schmitt, all rights reserved.*

on his Ray Ban shades and holds onto the torch with this naked hands: no protective goggles, gloves or ear plugs. He holds onto the long handle of the crucible, moving the tool as he melts the gold and copper alloys. He sets up his tufa block with a clamping tool he has been using for forty years and quickly pours in the liquefied gold into the tufa cast. Next, he opens the tufa stone and removes the metal piece with pliers, dunking it in a pickling solution. A minute later, the piece is cool enough to touch, and he examines it for imperfections.

Next, he scrubs the pieces clean in the bathroom sink, adjacent to his home studio. He said, "You don't want dirty metal." He is making sure that the piece is not more difficult to work with in the future. After the casting, pickling and scrubbing, he does a lot of filing. In the background, he listens to classic rock and roll music or watches shows on his wall-mounted flat-screen TV. He spends several hours filing to create smooth edges and fixing imperfections. To cut out small circles of a rose gold cast, for instance, he uses a small saw with a wire; to make rounded sides, he uses a filing tool. After setting the diamonds, he pieces all of the different parts together to create one bracelet. One of his pieces of jewelry, such as the kind of bracelet described, takes approximately three weeks to create.

Yeibichais: Fear and Fascination

Aspects of Ric's Navajo culture, such as healing ceremonies and sand paintings, inspire many of his artworks. In particular, he often chooses Holy People, called *yeibichais*, as his subject matter. As a child, he was both fearful of and drawn to *yeibichais*. He shared:

> *I grew up in watching the ceremonies on the reservation, and the different ceremonies, the healing ceremonies that go on in a private residence, with the medicine man—I mean, a lot of that to me is part of me, and I try to add a little bit of childhood memories into my work but in my own way.*
>
> *Like the* yeibichais, *to me, they're the spiritual healers. I do a lot of them, and I've always been fascinated with them.*
>
> *As a kid, I mean, to me as a kid they were scary. Growing up, they'd come once or twice a year to gather gifts, like food...so you give out your*

> *offerings to them. You give...canned goods, you give...watermelon...The* yeibichais *would come and ask for offerings they could take back to the ceremony and be able to perform their ceremony.*
>
> *Growing up, as a kid, my grandparents and parents would always say, "If you're a bad boy,* yeibichais *gonna come around and whip you." Well, growing up, I was always a bad boy, I guess. I mean, I always thought that there was something I did wrong, I'm gonna get a whipping, so I tried to keep my distance from them. Still, at the same time, it fascinated me.*

Since Navajo custom prohibits portraying *yeibichais* realistically, Ric creates abstract representations, guided by his memories and feelings.

Additional Information

Ric has trained students in Flagstaff to carry on the traditional method of tufa-stone casting. Learning jewelry-making has given many of his students direction, as well as allowed them to support themselves and afford basic things, like school clothes. Many came from single-parent homes and struggled with the high living costs on the reservation. He said, "A lot of these kids got so much talent, but they don't know what to do or how to go about creating or starting a line of work. I was there teaching them my technique, which has taken me almost forty years to learn. I'm kind of proud of it, some of my kids. I'm actually, I'm proud of all my kids." Ric has introduced students to art galleries and juried shows at the Heard Museum. Some of his students have gone on to achieve great success.

Ric's artwork is in the permanent collection of the Heard Museum, where he also participates in the annual Heard Museum Indian Fair and Market. Like several other artists in this book, such as Jesse Monongya, Marlowe Katoney, Barbara Teller Ornelas and Ed Charlie, Ric headed to the 2015 Santa Fe Indian Market to sell several of his artworks and participate in competitions. When asked if he usually sold all of the jewelry he brought to the market, he said: "No, but that's a good thing. When you sell out, it means that you didn't have enough inventory."

Ric currently resides with his sweet sixteen-year-old dog in Goodyear, Arizona, a suburban area about an hour outside Scottsdale. When making art, he has an inspiring view of the Estrella Mountains. As carving involves

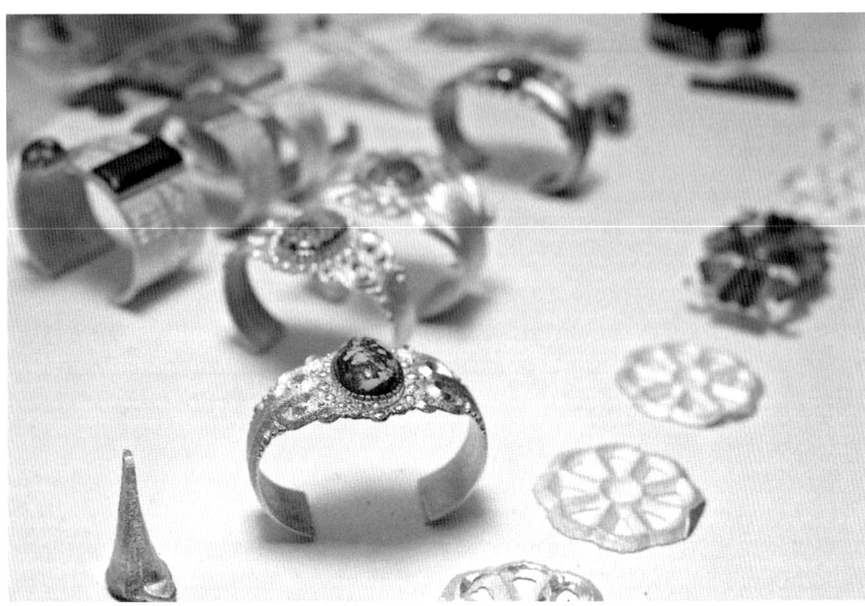

Ric Charlie has created an inventory of exceptional bracelets, which he brought with him to sell at the 2015 Santa Fe Indian Fair and Market. *Photograph by Rory O'Neill Schmitt, all rights reserved.*

very close examination and fine motor detail, he rests his eyes by taking a breath and looking outward to the mountains. He said, "My purpose in life is to do what I love to do: create art and make jewelry."

To view his works and learn more about this artist, viewers can go to his website, www.riccharlie.com.

6

EDWARD CHARLIE

Hails from Michigan

Emerging artist Edward Charlie hails from Harrisville, Michigan. Edward is Ric Charlie's younger half-brother. In the 1970s, their father, Thomas Charlie, moved to Detroit to seek employment as an electrician with the Big Three automotive industry. At an auto factory, he met Carol Williams, a drill press operator. Edward referred to his Caucasian mother affectionately as *bilagaana*, a Navajo slang term for "white people." Thomas and Carol married, and Edward was born on December 19, 1974.

Summers on the 'Rez

Carol's family encouraged Edward to explore his Navajo roots. He said, "My mom's grandparents were trying to help encourage me to learn more about it. Information was so limited. Just growing up in Michigan, there's not a lot of tribes up there...Trying to find information back in the media centers back then was impossible...Internet's changed everything now."

Edward learned about his Navajo heritage through spending summers with his dad's parents on the Navajo reservation in Arizona. He shared, "It was a completely different world. Coming from Michigan, [there was] farming and white people everywhere. In Arizona, they're more into sheepherding and weaving. I liked it. It was such a different experience in the way they [Navajos] live…Just living from what Mother Earth provides you."

As a child, Edward observed his grandmother create Navajo weavings. He said, "It was pretty fascinating to watch. She would do the whole spinning her own wool and making her own thread and everything." In the 1980s, she was a part of a collective women's weaving group that "put together Shima, which is one of the largest Navajo rugs ever made."

On the reservation, Edward was able to get to know his family from the Edgewater clan, including his stepgrandfather (who was a sheepherder), and his siblings: five brothers and three sisters. During the summertimes, he wasn't permitted to hear traditional storytelling. He explained, "The time I visited…my grandparents was in the summertime. They don't tell stories in the summertime because that's when the monsters are awake. Wintertime is when they sleep. So you can tell stories. When the summertime comes around, we don't tell the creation stories."

Edward continues to learn about his Navajo heritage to this day. He explained, "Through my art is the only way I've been able to find most of my information on my Navajo culture." In this stage in his life, he is "embracing it more and finding out and understanding their whole way of life." Ed explains that the message in his work is also his mantra: "Walk in beauty. There is beauty in everyone and everything."

Ed explained that due to his biracial heritage, he was often treated differently than others. It has been difficult for some Navajos to accept him. Since Navajo culture is matriarchal and his mother was not Navajo, many did not consider him to be Navajo. He stated, "I was treated like an outsider. It [has] gotten better now. I remember when I was coming out as a kid, I was treated…as a half-breed, in a way." Though Ed's family accepts him as a Navajo artist, it has taken awhile to be embraced by others in his culture. He noted that things are moving in a more positive direction.

Call to Become an Artist

Ed has always loved making art. At age three, he started created paintings and drawings. When Edward was eight, he learned how to do glass etchings. Later, at age ten, he began making jewelry. He had watched his brother, Ric, do tufa casting on the reservation and was amazed. He described the experience:

> *Well, the jewelry, when I first saw jewelry when I was ten, when I came out here* [to Arizona] *for the first time, it burned in my head. I've had the bug for it ever since then. That pretty much took precedence over any drawing or painting I was doing. That became more of my passion at that point. That's from meeting Ric, too. That's the first time I saw tufa casting, was with Ric. A ten-year-old boy watching somebody melt metal and fire. It was the coolest thing I'd ever seen!*

Prior to setting out on his own as a jeweler, Ed held various positions, including spending some time in the navy, bartending for eight years and doing construction work for four years. Edward moved to Flagstaff, Arizona, in 2003, upon the invitation of Ric to help him out with his jewelry business. He worked with his brother for several years, wherein he was able to learn the silversmithing craft through direct instruction and "just [through] doing it." He said, "I never thought I would be doing this for a living. I always thought I would just have a job. My idea when I moved down here was just to help Ric do his artwork. I had the abilities to do the things that he couldn't find other people to do. I'd never pursued it [before]—pushing my art to sell."

He explained that working full time as an artist can be extremely challenging. He said, "It's probably one of the hardest things I've ever done. Just trying to make a living at art is…I wouldn't recommend it to anybody. You put so much work into something, and it won't sell. You have to hold onto it. Then, nothing else sells. You're trying to scrounge after shows. You're trying to make ends meet. It's tough when you're not known yet."

Edward is inspired to pursue the life of an artist by his brother-in-law, Baje Whitethorne, who is a Navajo painter, jewelry maker and sculptor in Flagstaff. In addition, he is inspired by the legendary Charles Loloma, whom he described as "pretty much like the Godfather of jewelry." Ed is driven by his own need to make art. He said, "I just don't feel right if I don't do something everyday in art. I just feel like I need to keep creating. I feel like, even if I worked every day, I still wouldn't be able to accomplish all the stuff I wanted to do."

Though he focuses his creative energy primarily on making jewelry, Ed also paints. Recently, he sold an acrylic triptych painting of Monument Valley called *Beauty*. His painting process includes working from photographs as well as painting in nature. He explained: "I usually sketch them out from a photograph and see how they're going to be. I try to use that as the context but…once you start using the colors, it seems to go its own way—once you get the palette going."

Artistic Products and Processes

Edward describes his artistic processes as traditional. He noted, "Tufa casting is probably one of the most traditional mediums to work in for Navajos. Mostly, the forming work [shaping the pieces, whether doming them or making them into bracelets] that I do is more traditional."

Edward works in his outdoor studio tirelessly, often from the early morning until 9:00 p.m. His work area is under a pergola, which is common in Phoenix backyards, as it provides shade from the fierce sun. In the summertime, temperatures rise to 114 degrees, leading Ed to jump into the pool up to eight times a day.

To create a piece of jewelry, Edward first creates a mold. Using various dental carving tools, he carves contemporary native designs into tufa stone. Resembling pumice, tufa stone is made of compressed volcanic ash and is extremely heavy. Sometimes, he carves small holes to create a bumpy texture; the final product has a surface that is likened to a snakeskin.

Next, Ed smooths out the surface and then places another stone, which has a flat surface, on top of the carved tufa. He makes sure the two pieces

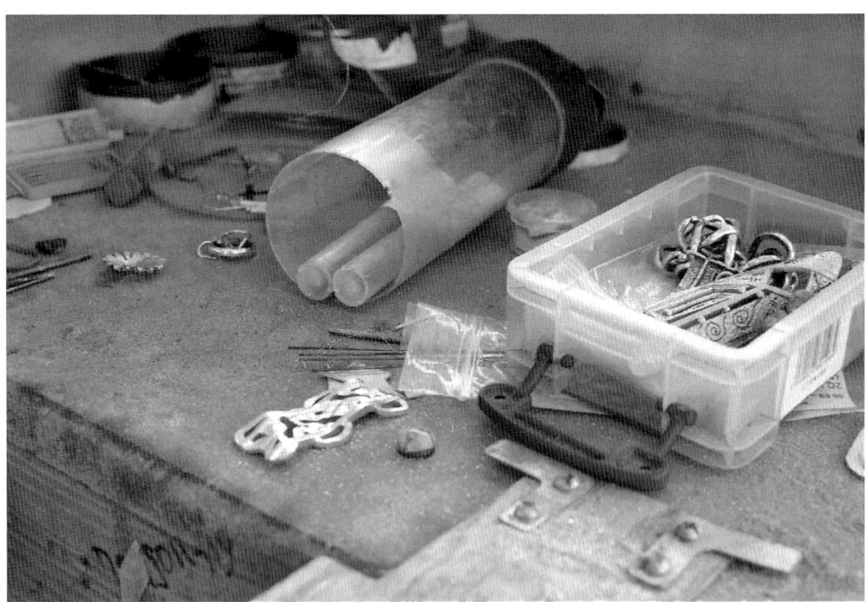

Atop Ed Charlie's workbench are jewelry pieces in process, as well as silver and turquoise materials and a plethora of tools. *Photograph by Rory O'Neill Schmitt, all rights reserved.*

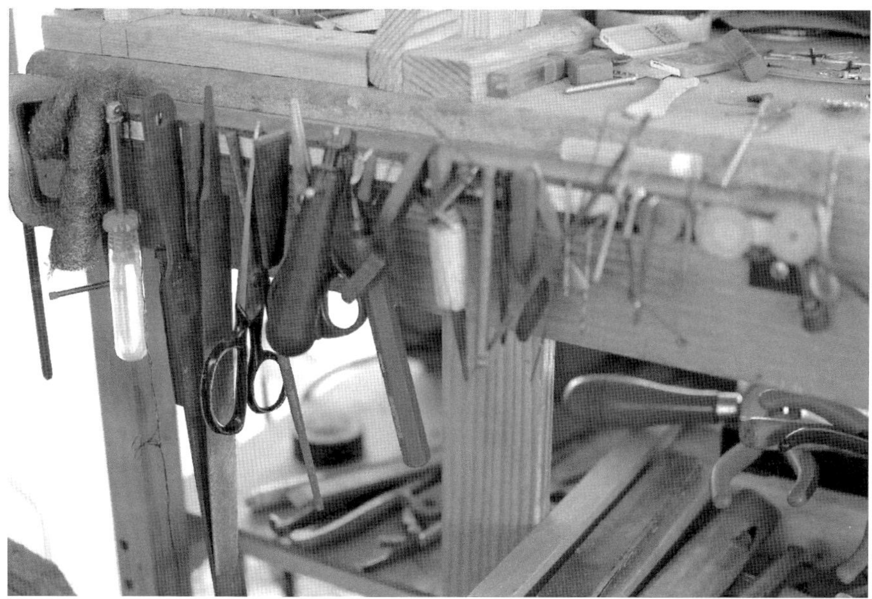

This jeweler's commitment to attaining precision in his art form and maintaining the highest standards requires that he have a variety of tools accessible. *Photograph by Rory O'Neill Schmitt, all rights reserved.*

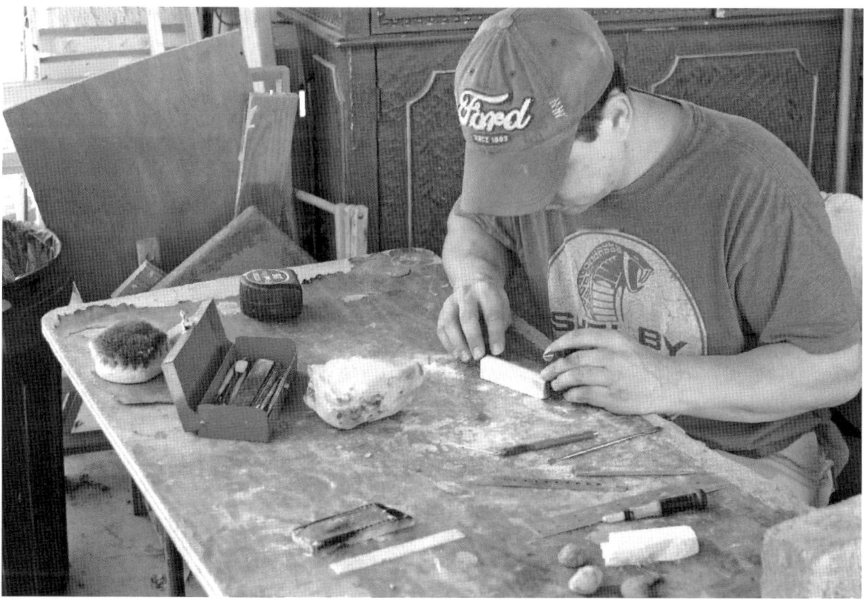

Ed Charlie carves designs into tufa stones using dental precision tools. *Photograph by Rory O'Neill Schmitt, all rights reserved.*

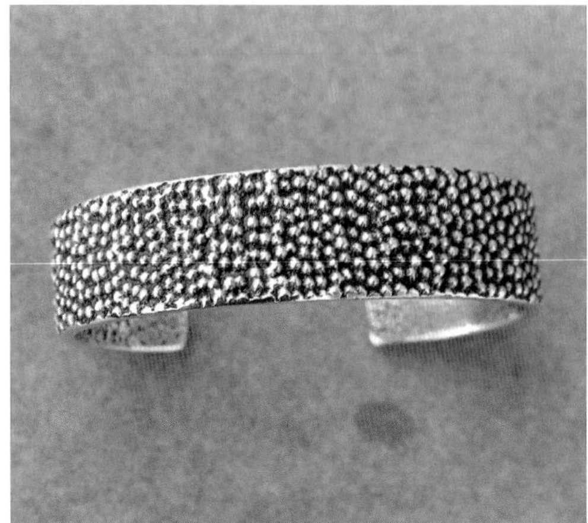

Left: This bracelet features the signature texture that Ed Charlie employs in his jewelry. The bumpy surface of this silver bracelet resembles snakes commonly found in Arizona deserts. *Photograph by Rory O'Neill Schmitt, all rights reserved.*

Below: The object on the left is a tufa cast, into which silver has previously been poured. The silver object on the right, which is the result of a tufa casting, will be later shaped by Ed Charlie to create a bracelet. *Photograph by Rory O'Neill Schmitt, all rights reserved.*

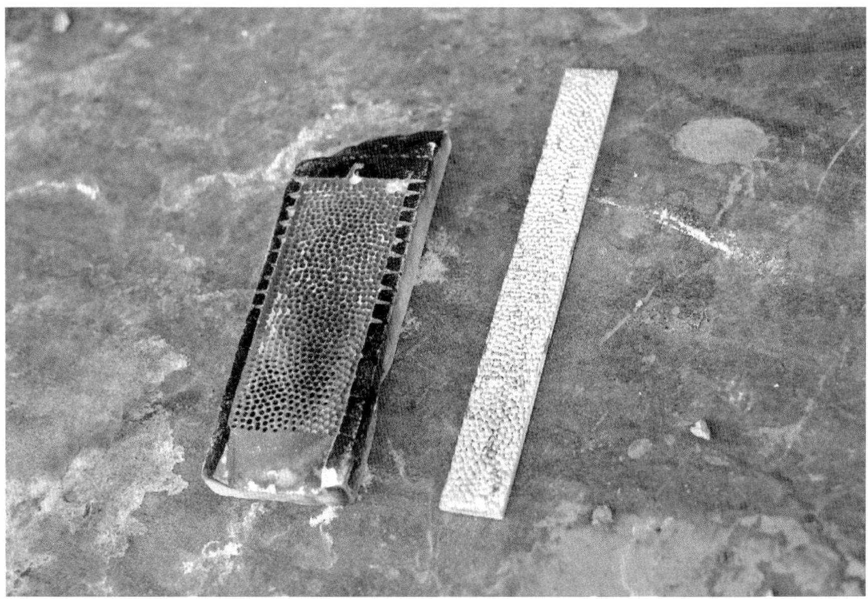

line up. He puts on his protective eyewear, long gloves and earplugs. He melts small beads of silver grains in a metal crucible with a Turbofiring tool. He sets up the tufa stones, standing on their edge, surrounded by cinderblock and brick. With the opening placed at the top, Ed pours the silver into the tufa mold. Then, he dips the silver in a pickling solution and lets it cool. He next rounds this flat silver piece to create a ring or another type of jewelry.

Using the tufa-casting method, Ed creates a variety of original jewelry pieces, including silver bracelets, bangles, belt buckles, bolo ties and broaches.

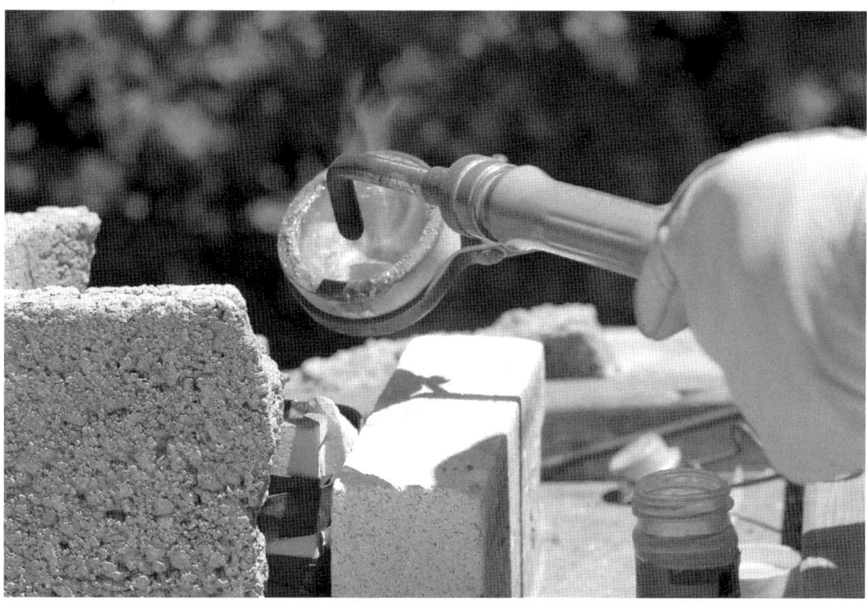

Ed Charlie shows the tufa-casting method, which involves using a gas-powered torch to melt the silver grains in a crucible. *Photograph by Rory O'Neill Schmitt, all rights reserved.*

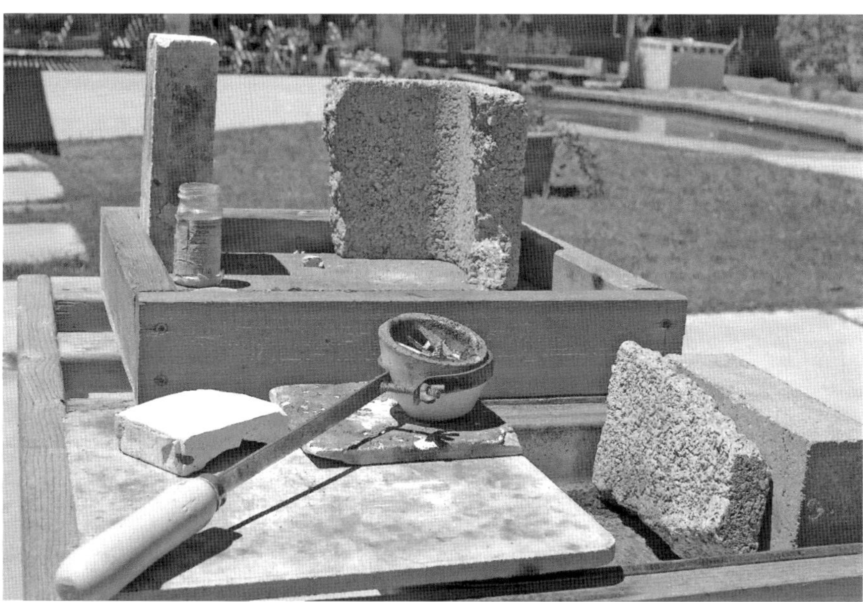

Prior to melting the silver to pour into his jewelry casts, Ed Charlie prepares the tufa-casting station. He combats the high heat of tufa cast pours even in the record temperatures of Phoenix summers. *Photograph by Rory O'Neill Schmitt, all rights reserved.*

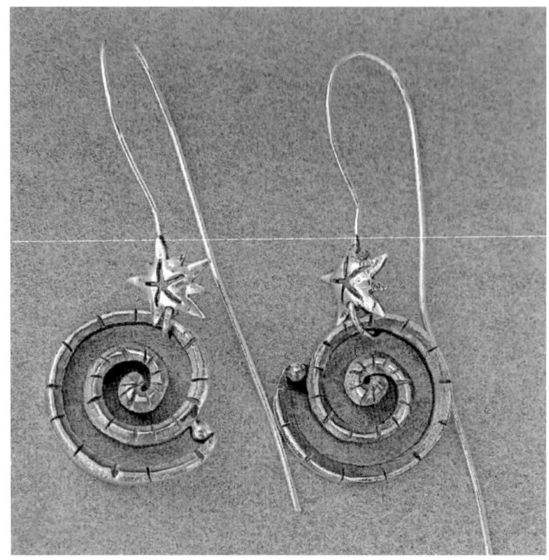

Left: These spiral-shaped dangling silver earrings are one example of Ed Charlie's more affordable pieces. *Photograph by Rory O'Neill Schmitt, all rights reserved.*

Middle: Ed Charlie wears one of his designs that features the dragonfly symbol. Depicted as a vertical line, crossed on the top by two horizontal lines, the dragonfly symbol often referenced water in Navajo traditions. *Photograph by Rory O'Neill Schmitt, all rights reserved.*

Bottom: Dragonfly images adorn this silver bracelet by Ed Charlie. *Photograph by Rory O'Neill Schmitt, all rights reserved.*

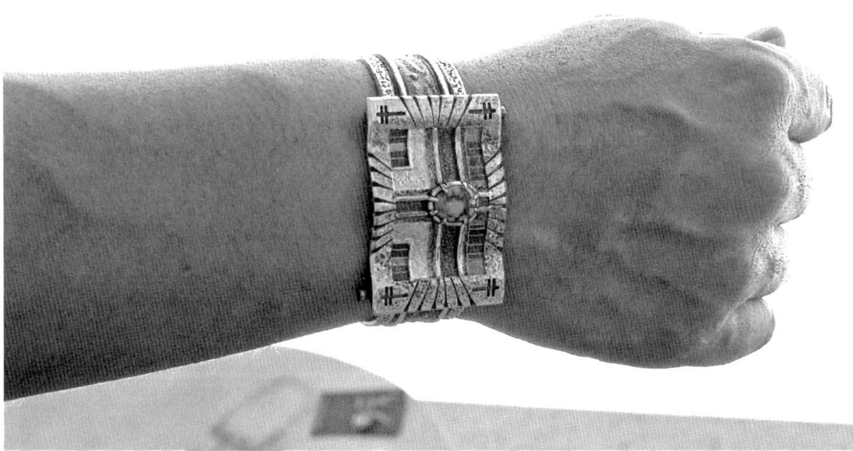

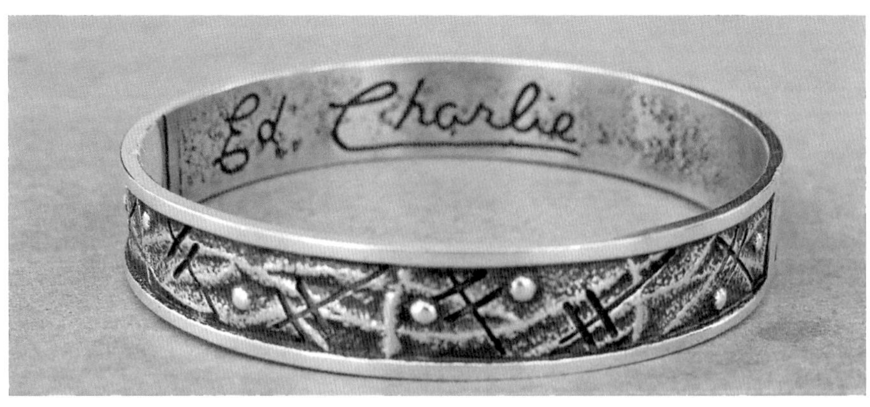

He also makes earrings, concho belts and pendants, and he incorporates turquoise, coral, lapis, citrine, sugilite and other semiprecious stones. On his jewelry, he often creates the dragonfly symbol, which has become quite popular among current collectors.

Accomplishments

In 2015, Edward was awarded Best of Show and Best Artist awards for his bracelet "Spider Woman" by the Indian Arts and Crafts Association (IACA), an institution that establishes the standards of American Indian art. Upon winning, he humbly shared, "I'm still in shock—shock and also a relief, in a way. It means that things will sell a lot easier now, hopefully. It's feast or famine being an artist until you're discovered. I guess. I haven't had that luxury yet."

Edward's previous awards also include the New Horizon Award for Innovation and Design at the Navajo Nation Fair (2012) and the Judge's Choice Award at the Heard Museum's Indian Market (2013). Currently, Edward's artwork is included in the exhibit "Turquoise, Water, Sky: The Stone and Its Meaning" at the Museum of Indian Arts and Culture in Santa Fe.

Edward is committed to serving his native community. He has worked with the Art of the People organization, which promotes native arts and culture and also provides scholarships for children. In 2012, he led demonstrations and taught painting techniques during the centennial celebration in Prescott, Arizona.

Edward encourages collectors to make sure they are informed about the jewelry they are purchasing and that it is authentic. They should also consider art purchases, whose values increase over time, as investments. In addition, the quality of the material is of utmost significance.

Collectors can purchase custom-made artwork through contacting the artist directly or through visiting the Heard Museum Gift Shop in Phoenix, the Autry Museum in Los Angeles and Wright's Gallery in Albuquerque.

Additional Information

Edward lives with his partner, Chelsea Ridout, in Phoenix, Arizona. Chelsea deeply believes in his talent and graciously supports his business, including managing communication with his gallery and the art world and coordinating events (such as the Heard Museum's Indian Fair and Market).

Edward is represented by River Trading Post in Old Town Scottsdale, Arizona (www.rivertradingpost.com). Gallerist Kathi Ouellet holds Ed's work in the highest regard. She stated:

> *I'm so proud of Ed. I've known him for years and have watched his work get better and better. His creativity, combined with his expert engineering, results in amazing work. He uses traditional themes in a contemporary way to enhance the story or the theme of the piece. His latest award, the 2015 IACA Artist of the Year, is well deserved, and I expect him to continually evolve and become one of the most sought-after master craftsmen in the world of Indian art.*

7
BARBARA TELLER ORNELAS

Seven Generations of Weavers

While on a piñon-picking expedition in the mountains, a mother gave birth to her daughter one month early. On November 26, 1954, Barbara Teller Ornelas was born in Montrose, Colorado, to Navajo parents, Ruth Shorty Begay and Sam Teller. Along with her two sisters, Roseann and Lynda, and two brothers, Ernest and Earl, she was reared in Two Grey Hills, New Mexico on the Navajo reservation.

When she and her siblings would get into trouble, Barbara explained that her father would "ship us off to my grandmother's [Nellie's] house" in White Rock. For Barbara, spending time there was: "Probably the best times I've had because I learned how it was, the old ways with my grandparents." Barbara's childhood memories include: "My grandfather was a storyteller. Instead of television, he used to tell us stories at nighttime. He used to use a flashlight and use [his] hands as puppets. We would see these living scenes on the ceilings of a hogan at nighttime."

Like many of her Navajo peers, Barbara went to boarding school. From kindergarten to sixth grade, she attended Toadlena Boarding School in Toadlena, New Mexico, and for junior high and high school, she attended boarding school in Aztec, New Mexico. Following high school graduation in 1974, Barbara moved to Phoenix for business school. She has lived in Arizona ever since. She said, "Even though I wasn't born and raised here, I feel like this is my home."

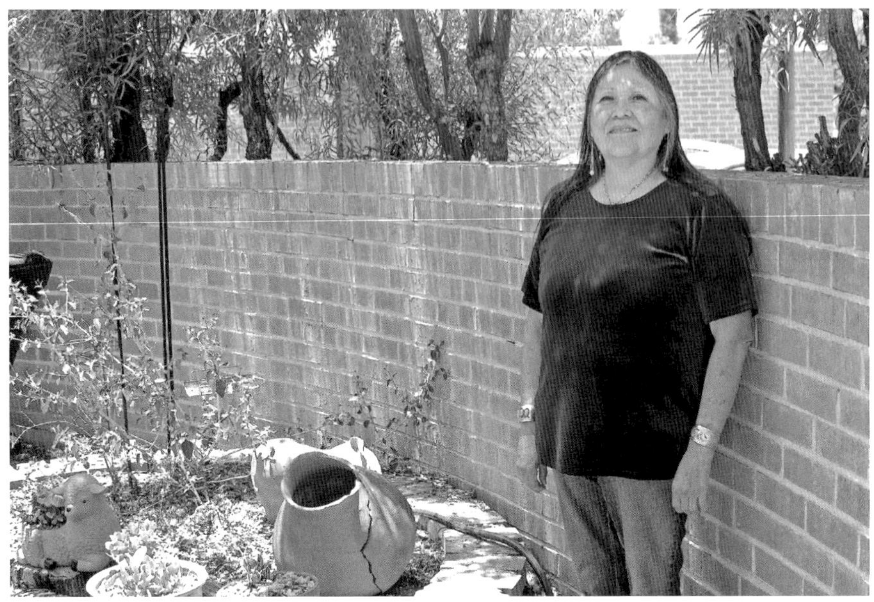

Master Navajo weaver Barbara Teller Ornelas stands proudly outside her home in Tucson, Arizona. *Photograph by Rory O'Neill Schmitt, all rights reserved.*

When asked how she transitioned from being a business student to an artist, Barbara replied, "I was already an artist. My art is learned from generation to generation…My art is passed down in my family." Barbara's recorded family history has seven generations of Navajo weavers. The first generation was her great-great-grandmother Asdzaa Tabaaha. The second generation was her great-grandmother Denetsonie Bitsi. The third generation included her paternal grandmother, Nellie Peshlakai Teller (1901–1965), who created Two-Faced rugs, saddle blankets and twill weaves. She described Nellie: "She was more experimental, and she was more open to things. She was a weaver, but she also did dyeing wool. She did pottery, and she did a lot of things that were different from what my maternal grandmother was doing." Barbara's maternal grandmother, Susie Tom (1903–1985), wove in the Two Grey Hills style.

The fourth generation included her mother, Ruth Teller (1928–2014), and an aunt, Margaret Yazzie (1930–). Accomplished Two Grey Hills weavers, their artworks are referred to as tapestries rather than weavings due to their high weft count. Their artworks can be found in national and international collections. Barbara's mother feared that younger generations would not continue the weaving tradition, leading this art form to die. Therefore, she encouraged her daughters and grandchildren to weave. Barbara and her two sisters—Roseann Teller Lee (1945–1996) and Lynda Teller Pete (1958–)—became the fifth generation of weavers. Barbara began learning weaving around the age of five. And by age ten, she had sold her first rug.

Barbara described the process of learning Navajo weaving:

> *I learned the legends and the stories and the myths of Navajo weaving from both of my grandmothers. I learned the basic weavings from my mother, and I learned techniques and troubleshooting from my sister Roseanne…*
>
> *There was always weaving in my family. It didn't matter what years we went to my aunt's* [Margaret Yazzie's] *house. She had, like, five weavings standing in her living room. The only really good memories I have of my maternal grandmother is* [of] *her sitting in front of her weaving all the time.*

Barbara's father, Sam, was a trader at Two Grey Hills Trading Post for over thirty years. Traders there had influenced weavers in the region to create what would become the classic Two Grey Hills style. This style is defined by the use of hand-carded, hand-spun and natural-colored wool and includes unique geometric designs, featuring a double diamond pattern that represented the mountains of the Two Grey Hills region. Barbara remembers her grandmothers and aunt weaving in the Two Grey Hills style behind the trading post, where they could view the actual two gray hills. Speaking the native Diné language throughout her life, Ruth taught herself English so that she could speak to tourists about her weavings. Barbara learned demonstration techniques from watching her mother's interactions.

Barbara taught her own two children how to weave. Sierra Nizhoni Teller Ornelas (born in 1981) and Michael Paul Teller Ornelas (born in 1985) have their weavings in the permanent collections of the Arizona State Museum and the Heard Museum. Sierra resides in Los Angeles and works as a TV writer. In her spare time, she weaves on the loom in her office. In 2004, Sierra created the documentary *A Loom with a View: Modern Navajo Weavers*, which chronicled the weavers in her family: Margaret Yazzie, Barbara Teller Ornelas and Michael Teller Ornelas. Michael has a degree in computer science from the University of Arizona and worked for the Arizona State Museum in Tucson.

The influx of successful Navajo male weavers has decreased the gender stereotype for this art form. Michael began weaving around age four. Michael's portfolio documents his artworks and his early weaving training.

A family snapshot shows Michael as a toddler by the loom as his mother weaves. Michael uses a variety of styles that he integrates into his pieces. For example, one twelve- by eight-inch weaving is composed of red, black and white stripes while a smaller eight- by eight-inch weaving was created with Two Grey Hills colors. Barbara notes that some of his weavings with geometric shapes were inspired by the period pieces Michael would see at the Arizona State Museum. Michael often travels with Barbara to shows and sells his weavings at the Santa Fe Indian Market and the Heard Museum Indian Fair and Market (where he won Best of Show in the Youth Division in 2003).

In the seventh generation, the weaving prospect in the family is Roseann's granddaughter Roxanne Rose Lee (born in 2000), whom both Barbara and her sister Lynda have helped to teach.

Artistic Processes

Barbara's weavings take on their own personalities. She preplans the designs only when she is planning a very large piece. The color and the nature of the wool influence the weavings that comes to be, as she combines colors of different fleeces to create different shades of brown and gray. The wool preparation process can take about one month, but Barbara creates enough yarn to last one year. In the past, she prepared wool from her aunt Margaret's sheep. Since her aunt is no longer able to care for sheep, Barbara finds wool from others. Currently, she uses Cordale, Rambouillet and Lincoln sheep; she buys wool that is already clean and processed but not spun.

Barbara creates a separate foundation of equally spaced vertical yarns (this is called the warp) on the loom. Then, she weaves in yarn (this is referred to as the weft) to create a pattern. Navajo tapestries are different from rugs. They are woven tighter: 80 threads per running inch define the weft count of a tapestry. Barbara's tapestries have 100 to 130 weft threads per inch. The quality of her Navajo tapestries is comparable to Persian rugs.

Barbara follows many weaving traditions, one of which is to have a peaceful mindset when weaving. She acknowledged spirits and feelings associated with the Navajo weavings. She said, "They have no blankets or rugs without spirits in them. I was always told never to be angry, never to be upset because of moods, never to send bad moods and their spirits. I had to learn to [be] calm…because sometimes your weaving will take on how

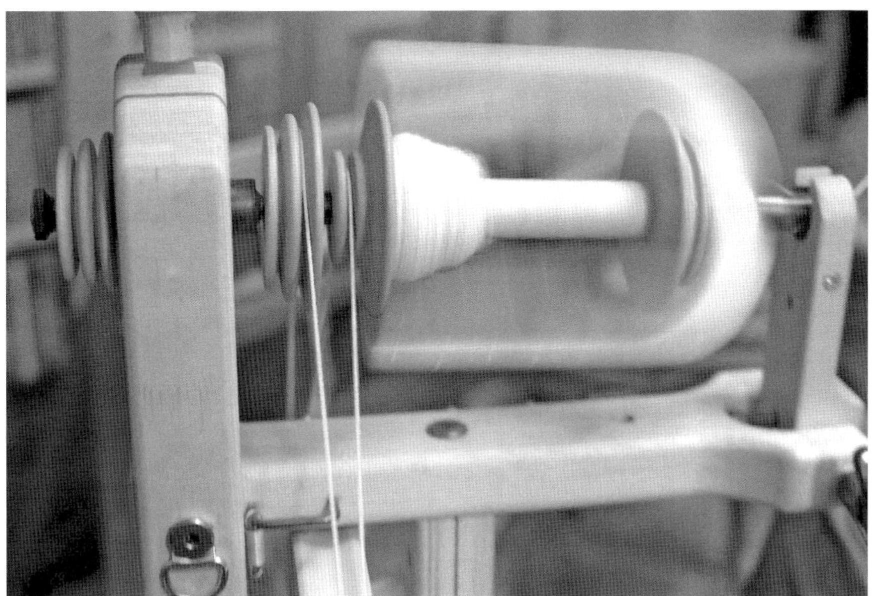

Committed to preserving cultural traditions in weaving, Barbara Teller Ornelas prepares her own wool. *Photograph by Rory O'Neill Schmitt, all rights reserved.*

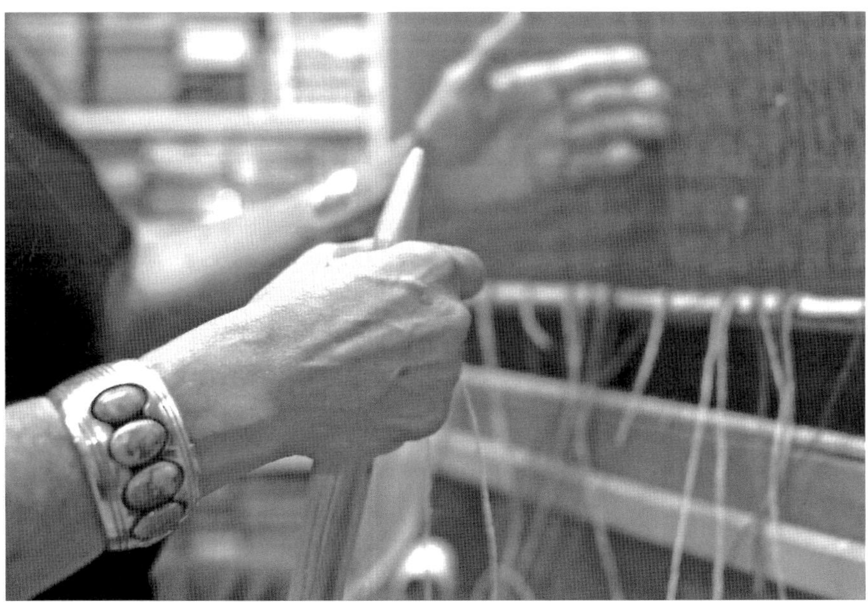

A close-up of the artist's hands shows Barbara Teller Ornelas's mastery over the tools involved in creating Navajo tapestries of high weft counts. *Photograph by Rory Schmitt, all rights reserved.*

you feel or your attitude." Maintaining a positive attitude is crucial, as the weavings carry her feelings.

Barbara is also experimental in her processes. She shared, "I think, being an artist, you have to be both. You have to honor your traditions and what you learned that's traditional, but you also have to challenge yourself and try to do challenging things to just push the limits."

Barbara works in a variety of styles, combining the double diamond designs of the Two Grey Hills style with the pastel colors of the Burnt Water style. She also creates Ganado-style weavings, using bright red aniline dye colors. She admits that critics have not always favored her innovative weaving ideas. One rug featured a string of turquoise stones. Referred to as the "edge," this strand traditionally represents the Navajo weavers' path: a line weavers put in to honor Spider Woman. Along with using pastel hues in Two Grey Hills style, this weaving was referred to as a Miami Vice Navajo rug.

Early in her career, Barbara confronted boundaries of Navajo weaving. She explained that previous generations of weavers were confined to weave according to their region's particular style. She explained:

> *You couldn't cross styles because traders and the gallery owners would tell you, "You're only a Two Grey Hills weaver. You should not be weaving anything else."*
>
> *That's where I came from. I kind of broke barriers because I had customers asking me, ""Can you make me a piece with Two Grey Hill colors? Or Burnt Water colors...?"*
>
> *I started doing other things.*
>
> *Even with my mom—she got upset, saying that "You shouldn't be doing this because you're a Two Grey Hill weaver."*
>
> *I'm like, "Yeah, but I need to do this to feed my family."*
>
> *It also...opened doors to where I could work with different colors and work with different patterns. It gave me a whole new outlet on weaving—not just from my grandmother's time to my mom's time, where they only did Two Grey Hills and everything was set in stone how they did things. I kind of bucked the system with doing that."*

These days, Navajo weavers are not pigeonholed to a regional style. The new generation of weavers has more options. She explained:

> *Nowadays, it's really cool because my kids are benefitting from that. They get to do whatever they want, whatever style they want, and they're not*

categorized within their certain style of weaving. It means they're literally free to do whatever they want.

One thing that really struck me was one time, we had an art show. Somebody asked my son, "What kind of weaving is this?"

He goes, "It's Michael Ornelas style."

I'm like, wow, that's pretty cool.

Barbara is open to learning new weaving styles. Recently, she started to learn the twill technique. Her grandmother Nellie used this technique but unfortunately passed away before she was able to teach her. Currently, Barbara is also pondering doing a collaborative weaving with her son.

Barbara is a leader in evolving the weaving art form. She is dedicated to her goal "to have people view Navajo weavers as artists." During the late 1970s and early 1980s, Barbara approached galleries to sell her artwork. She battled weaving being labeled as craft and not fine art. She explained the stigma she encountered as an American Indian weaver:

I bypassed galleries and trading posts and started going to museums and art shows to sell my pieces, which was unheard of for a Navajo weaver to do back in the day…They told me to get back to the reservation and sell it there.

[They'd say,] *"Maybe we'll buy it off the truck…"*

It was very heartbreaking to hear, but I think it made me more determined. They're not gonna put me in my place…Yeah, and they used to make fun of me because I had a portfolio. I had pictures of me and my weavings in the book. I had business cards. They thought that was one of the funniest things ever…

I would call myself an artist, and they would say, "No, you're just a weaver."

Some galleries' refusal to recognize her as an artist made her more determined. She had the dignity and grace to overcome obstacles and garner respect for Navajo weavers as talented, intelligent, creative and unique artists.

The Big One

In the 1980s, Barbara and her sister Roseann Teller Lee were experiencing difficulty selling their weavings, even though Roseann was one of the best Two Grey Hill tapestry weavers of the time. Barbara explained:

> *Navajo weaving wasn't really selling anymore. It was hard to find buyers for our pieces then.*
>
> *My sister would finish a piece, and we'd sit in the trading post and sell it. The guy was telling us that "nobody's interested in buying these weavings anymore. Something needs to happen."*

When they returned home, the sisters brainstormed ideas. Their mother suggested doing a very large rug, and Barbara told her, "That's been done before. People make large rugs all the time." Ruth explained that this type of weaving had not been done in their style before. Roseann and Barbara set off on their collaboration. They created the weaving in their parents' Newcomb home; their father offered his toolshed as workspace. Their mother observed the weaving process to ensure straightness and symmetry. She taught them the importance of discipline and perfection in the weaving art.

The first step in making the weaving was a nine-month process of preparing the wool. Barbara completed the carding, which involved combing the fleece between two wood boards set with rows of metal teeth. Each color of the design was blended through the carding. She used dyed black wool for the background and mixed the black wool with white to achieve various shades of gray. Next, she spun the wool into a fine yarn. The sisters used thousands of yards of wool for this tapestry. Barbara explained, "It took us…two and half years of actual weaving time." In 1984, they warped the loom and took down the finished rug from the loom three years later. It was one of the largest Navajo weavings to date. Their tapestry, affectionately referred to as the "Big One," measured five feet by eight feet, ten inches. The rug features exceptional design and mastery of technique. They created the tapestry in Two Grey Hills style, using natural-colored wool from white and brown sheep.

Barbara and Lynda entered the weaving into the Santa Fe Indian Market competition. It won two Best of Show awards at there (1987 and 1991) and one Best of Show award at the Heard Museum Guild Indian Fair and Market (1996). Later, it was sold for $60,000, a price that shattered records.

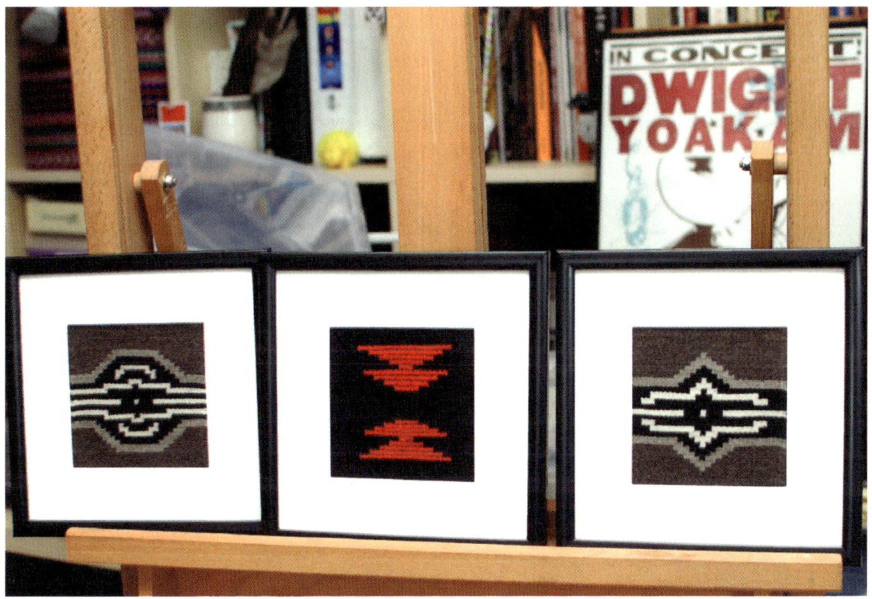

Emerging artist Michael Teller Ornelas creates weavings inspired by Navajo period pieces at the Arizona State Museum in Tucson. *Photograph by Rory O'Neill Schmitt, all rights reserved.*

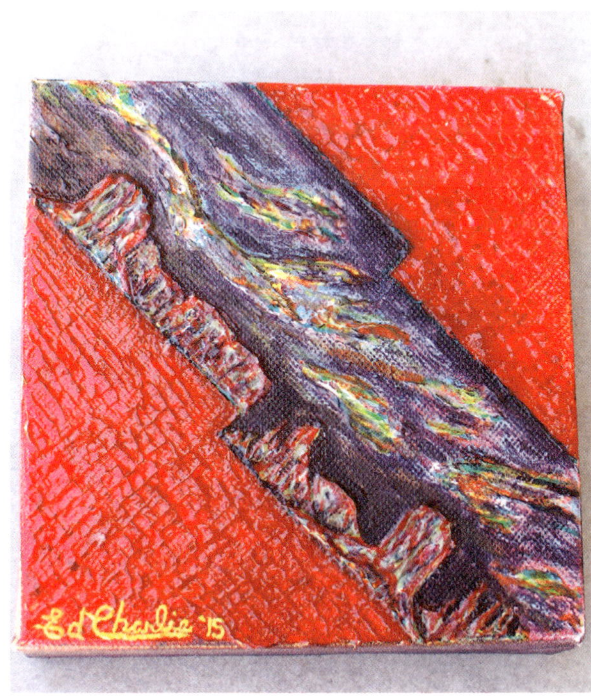

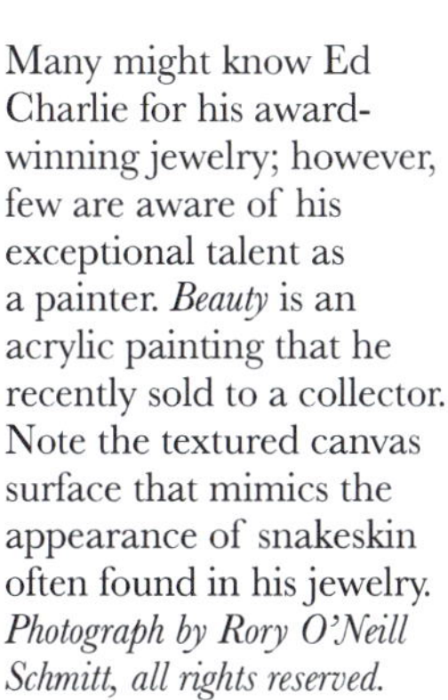

Many might know Ed Charlie for his award-winning jewelry; however, few are aware of his exceptional talent as a painter. *Beauty* is an acrylic painting that he recently sold to a collector. Note the textured canvas surface that mimics the appearance of snakeskin often found in his jewelry. *Photograph by Rory O'Neill Schmitt, all rights reserved.*

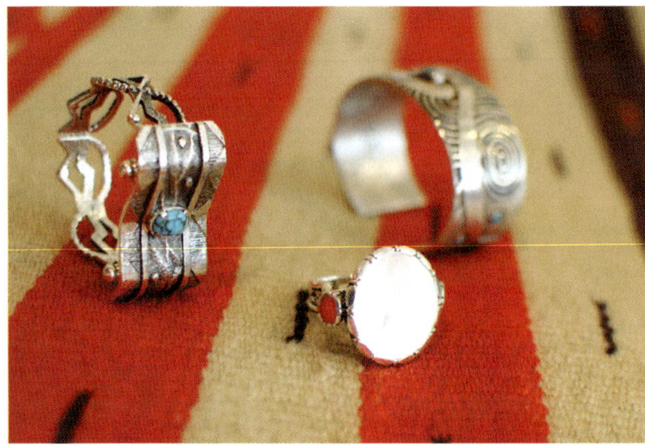

Three silver jewelry pieces displayed at River Trading Post, a gallery located in Scottsdale, Arizona, reflect the range of styles and materials of jeweler Ed Charlie. *Photograph by Rory O'Neill Schmitt, all rights reserved.*

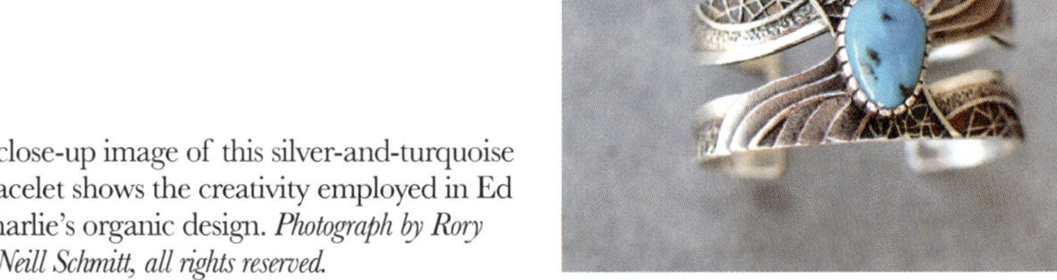

A close-up image of this silver-and-turquoise bracelet shows the creativity employed in Ed Charlie's organic design. *Photograph by Rory O'Neill Schmitt, all rights reserved.*

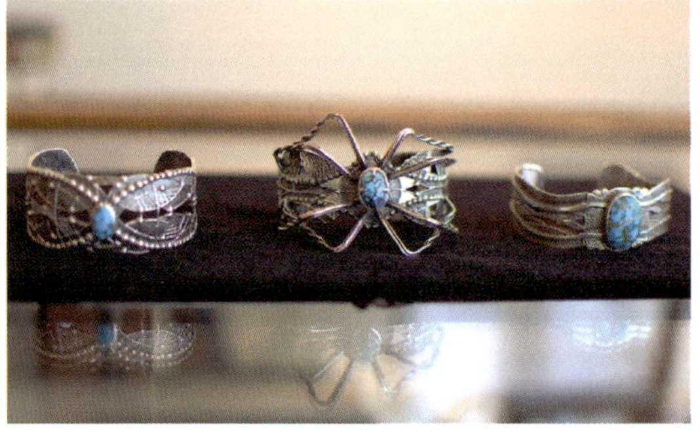

Three silver-and-turquoise bracelets exemplify the artistic range of jeweler Ed Charlie. *Photograph by Rory O'Neill Schmitt, all rights reserved.*

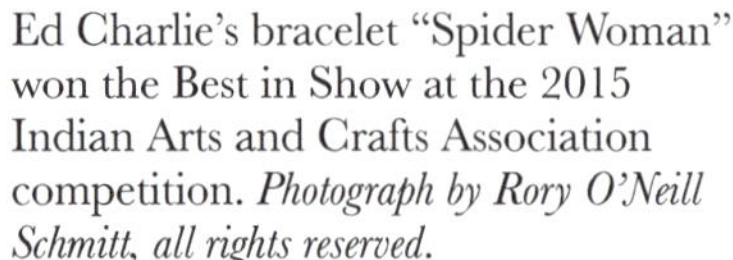

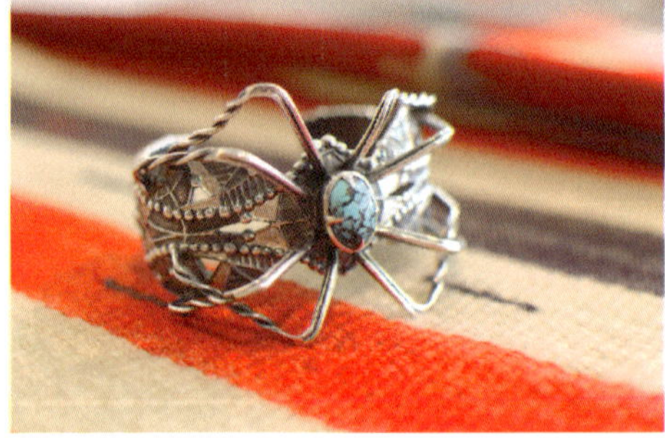

Ed Charlie's bracelet "Spider Woman" won the Best in Show at the 2015 Indian Arts and Crafts Association competition. *Photograph by Rory O'Neill Schmitt, all rights reserved.*

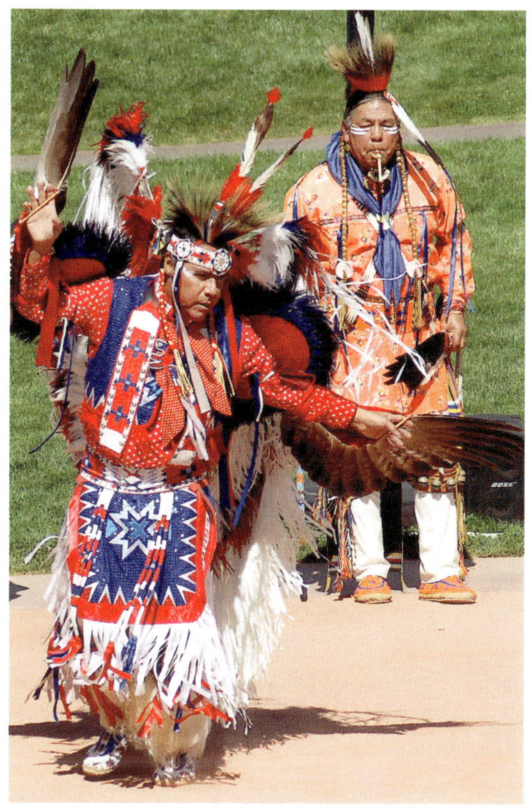

Left: An Eagle dancer performance at the 2015 Heard Museum Guild Indian Fair and Market in Phoenix, Arizona. *Photograph by Rory O'Neill Schmitt, all rights reserved.*

Below: Visiting my in-laws' home in Snowflake, Arizona, introduced me to a different way of life, one where people remain deeply connected to the land. There, vast, open spaces are dotted with junipers, prickly pears and yucca. *Photograph by Rory O'Neill Schmitt, all rights reserved.*

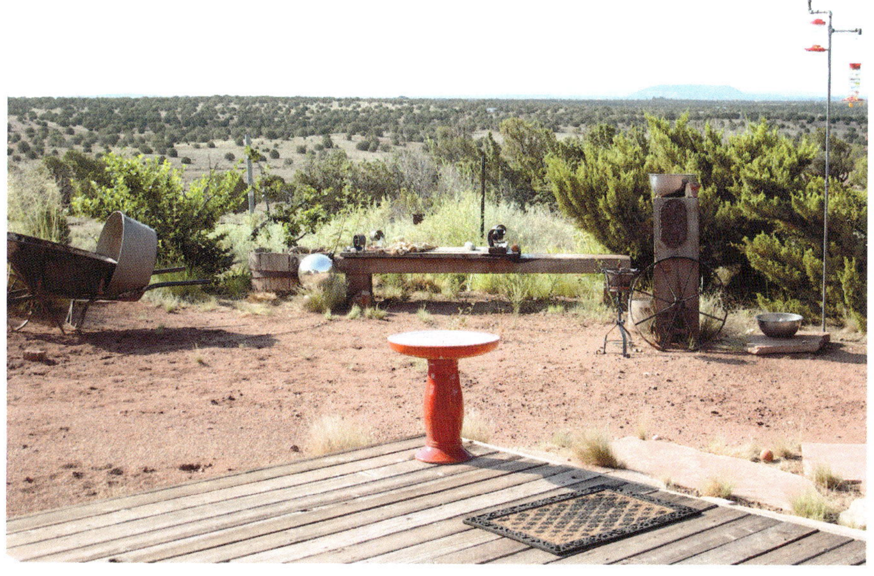

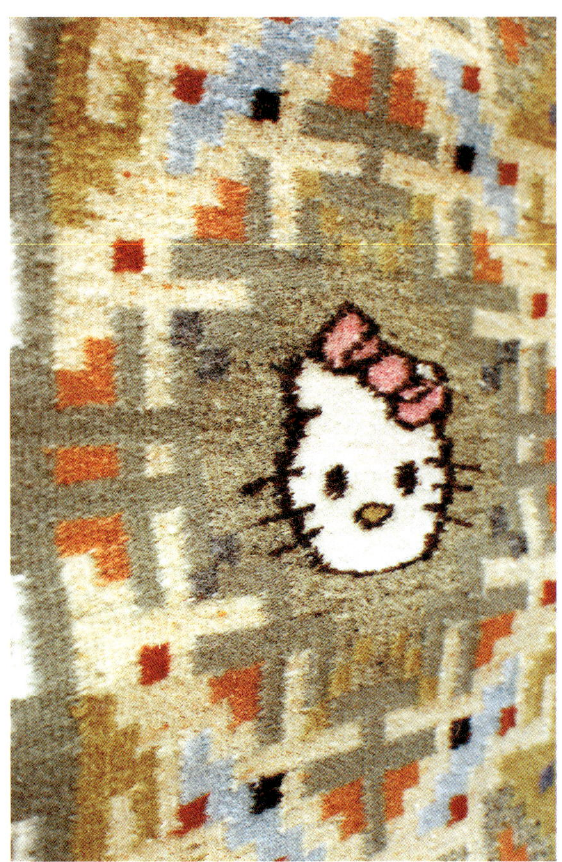

Left: In this artwork featuring Hello Kitty, Marlowe Katoney fuses Navajo weaving traditions and designs with popular culture. The artist participated in the 2015 Heard Museum Guild Indian Fair and Market. *Photograph by Rory O'Neill Schmitt, all rights reserved.*

Below: The personal workbench of leading jeweler Jesse Monongya contains precious stones in a spectrum of brilliant colors and shows a work-in-progress bracelet at center. *Photograph by Rory O'Neill Schmitt, all rights reserved.*

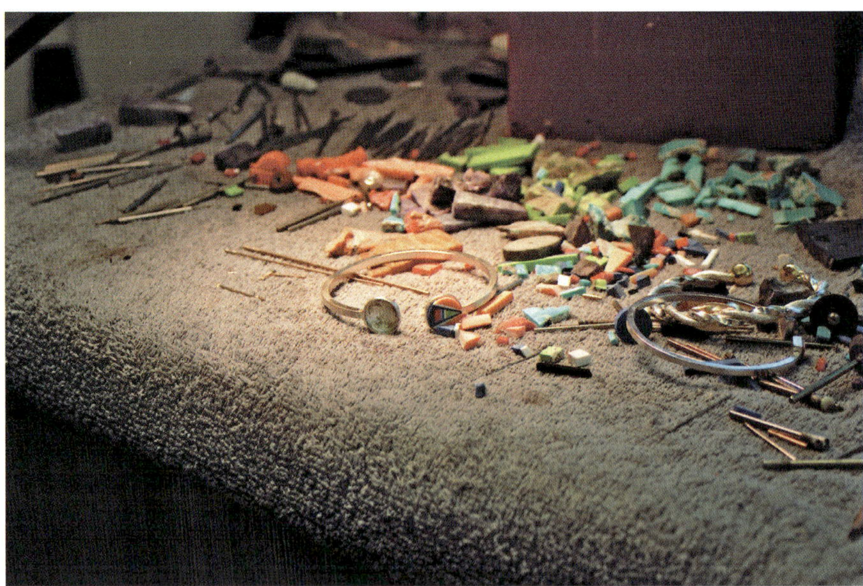

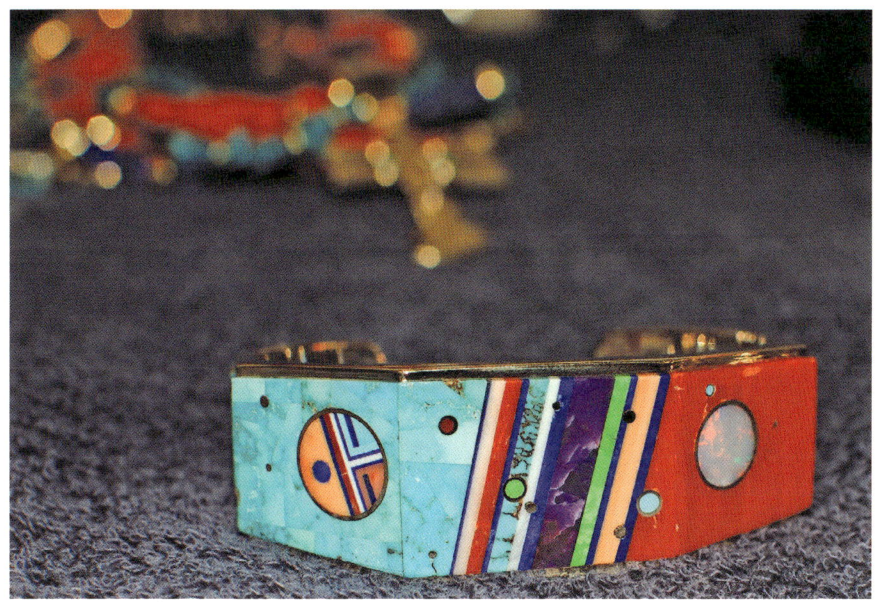

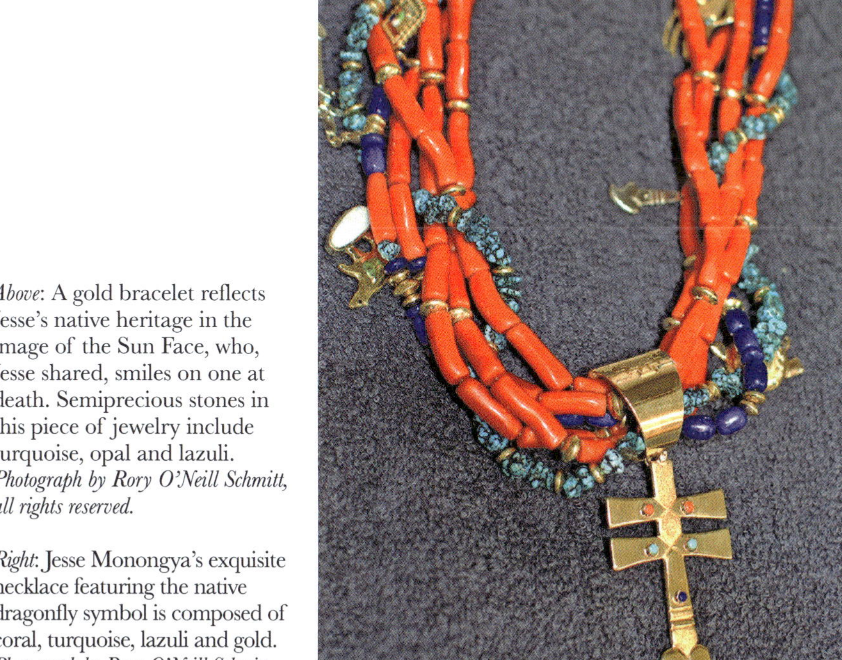

Above: A gold bracelet reflects Jesse's native heritage in the image of the Sun Face, who, Jesse shared, smiles on one at death. Semiprecious stones in this piece of jewelry include turquoise, opal and lazuli. *Photograph by Rory O'Neill Schmitt, all rights reserved.*

Right: Jesse Monongya's exquisite necklace featuring the native dragonfly symbol is composed of coral, turquoise, lazuli and gold. *Photograph by Rory O'Neill Schmitt, all rights reserved.*

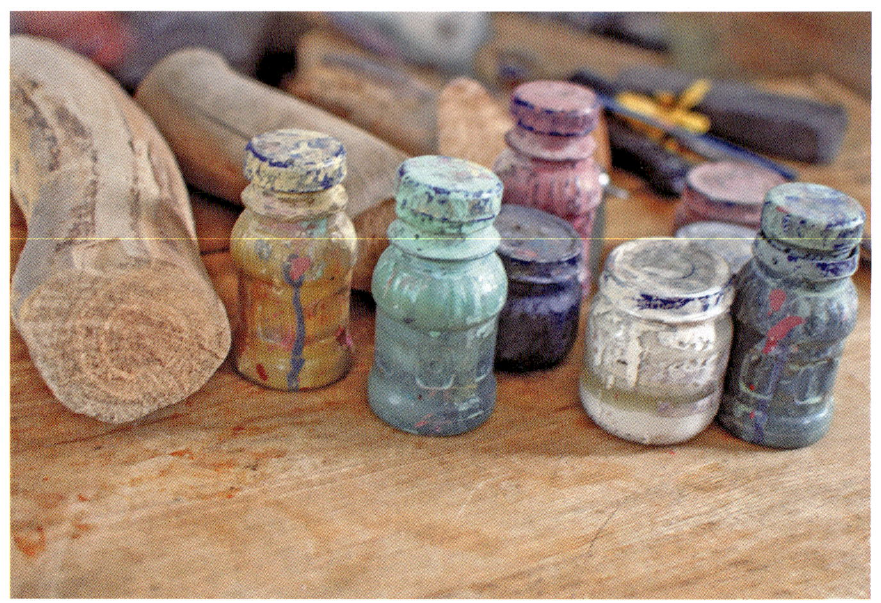

Artistic materials for Manuel Chavarria's katsina doll carvings include cottonwood root and paints. *Photograph by Rory O'Neill Schmitt, all rights reserved.*

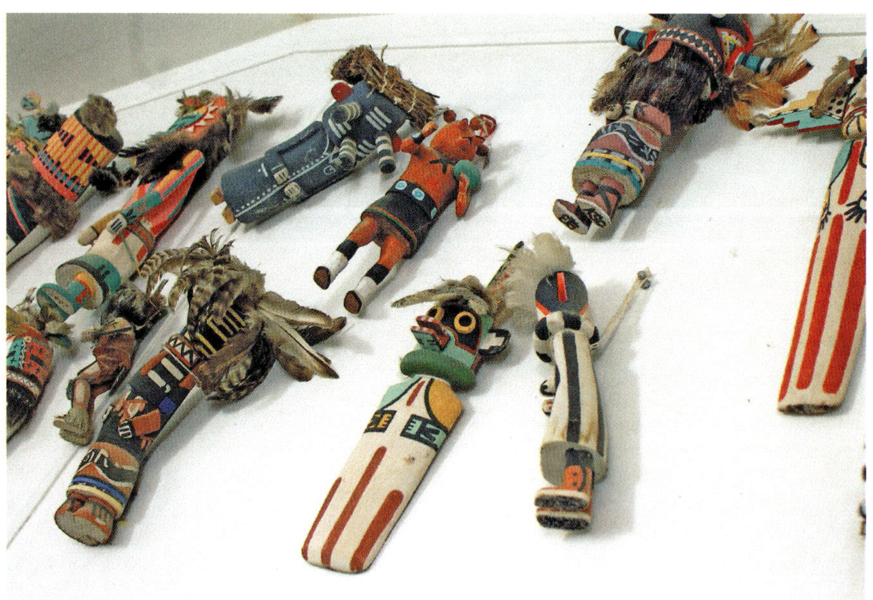

Children learn about katsinas by being exposed to katsina dolls, which are often displayed in the family's home (as in this photograph of Manuel Chavarria's home) and serve as a reminder of the specific teachings. *Photograph by Rory O'Neill Schmitt, all rights reserved.*

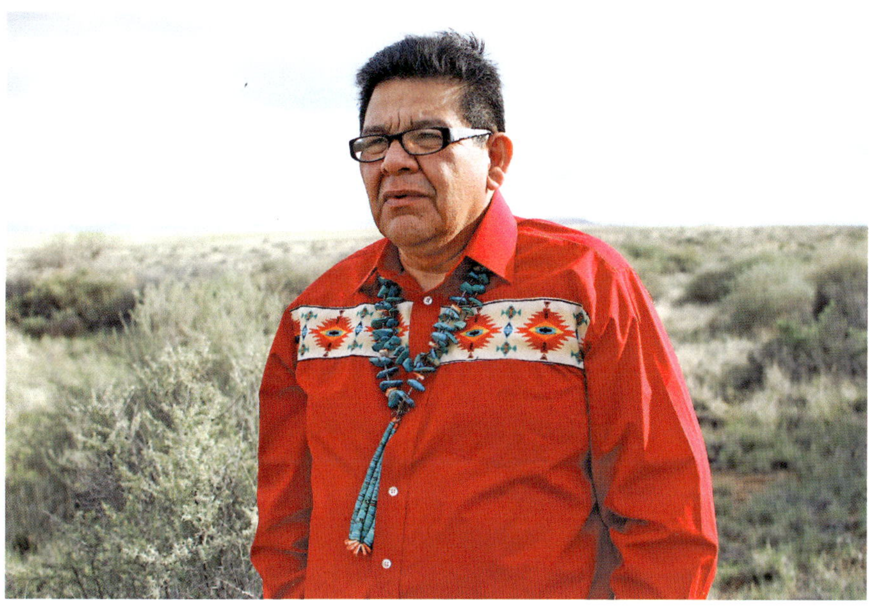

Artist Manuel Chavarria is pictured here outside his home on the Hopi reservation in Polacca, Arizona. *Photograph by Rory O'Neill Schmitt, all rights reserved.*

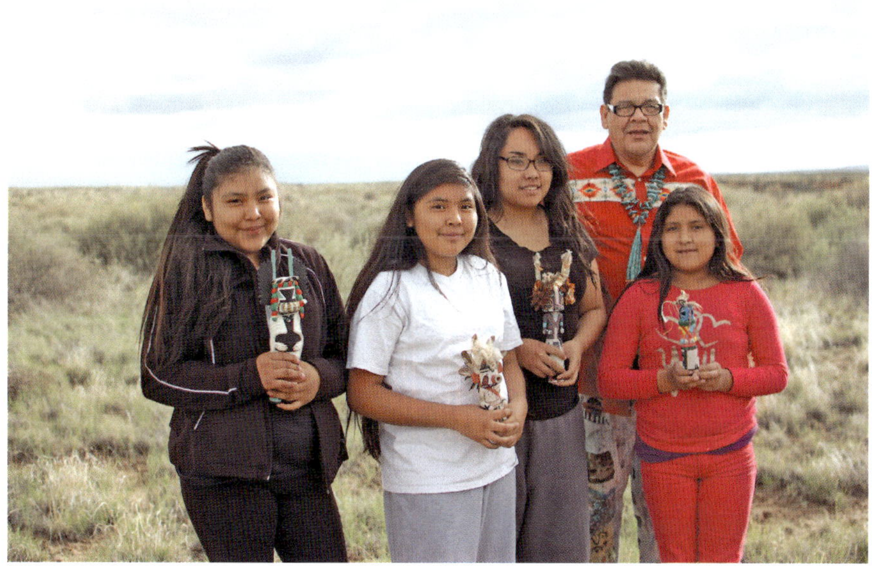

Manuel Chavarria's granddaughters hold their favorite katsina dolls outside the family home. *Photograph by Rory O'Neill Schmitt, all rights reserved.*

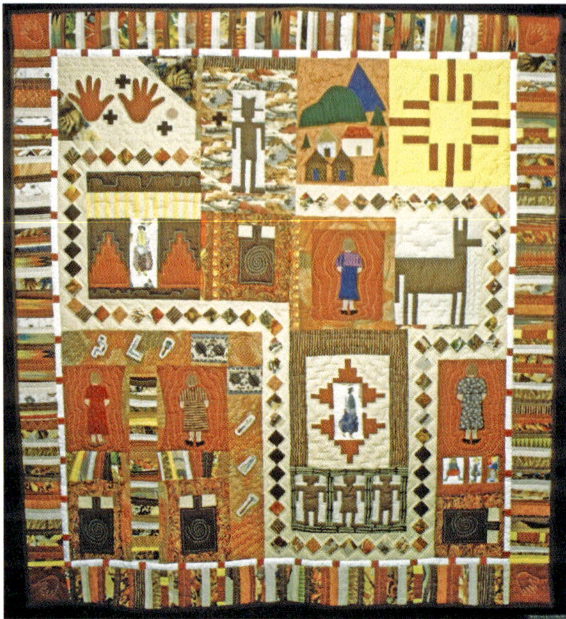

Left: "Charlie Wood Maze" (2000) is Margaret Wood's eightieth quilt. For this piece, Margaret Wood used the theme of the Pima maze, in which a person tries to find his way along a path, to depict the biography of her father. *Courtesy of Margaret Wood, all rights reserved.*

Below: In "Helen Mae Watchman Wood Maze" (2008), Margaret Wood depicts her mother's life through emphasizing places, including the hogan, homes and apartment where Helen resided. *Courtesy of Margaret Wood, all rights reserved.*

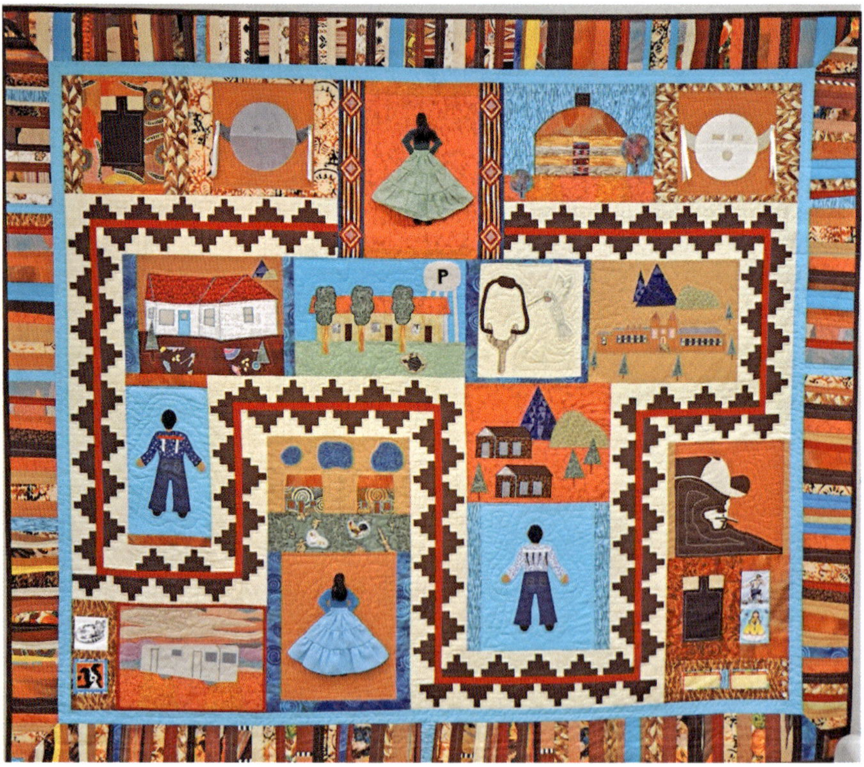

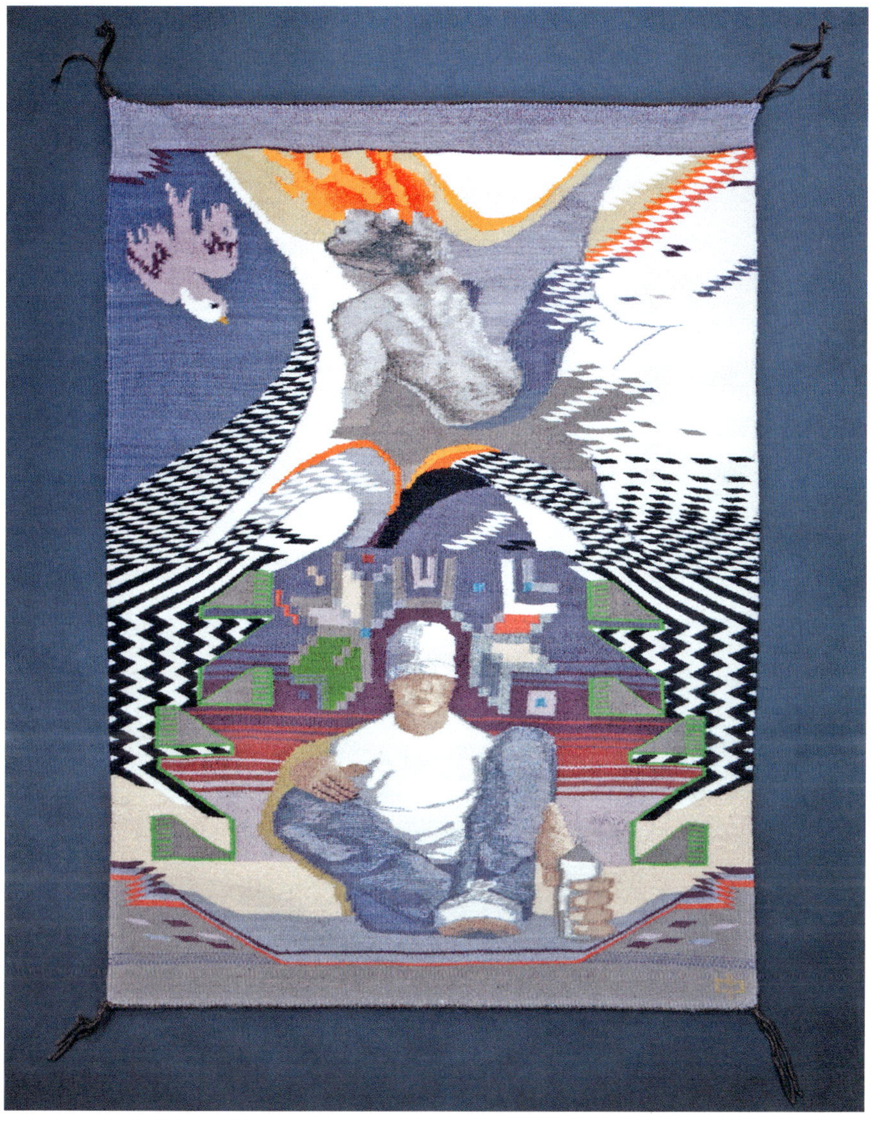

"The Acquisition" is a pictorial weaving created by Marlowe Katoney of a modern youth with spray paint. *Courtesy of Marlowe Katoney, all rights reserved.*

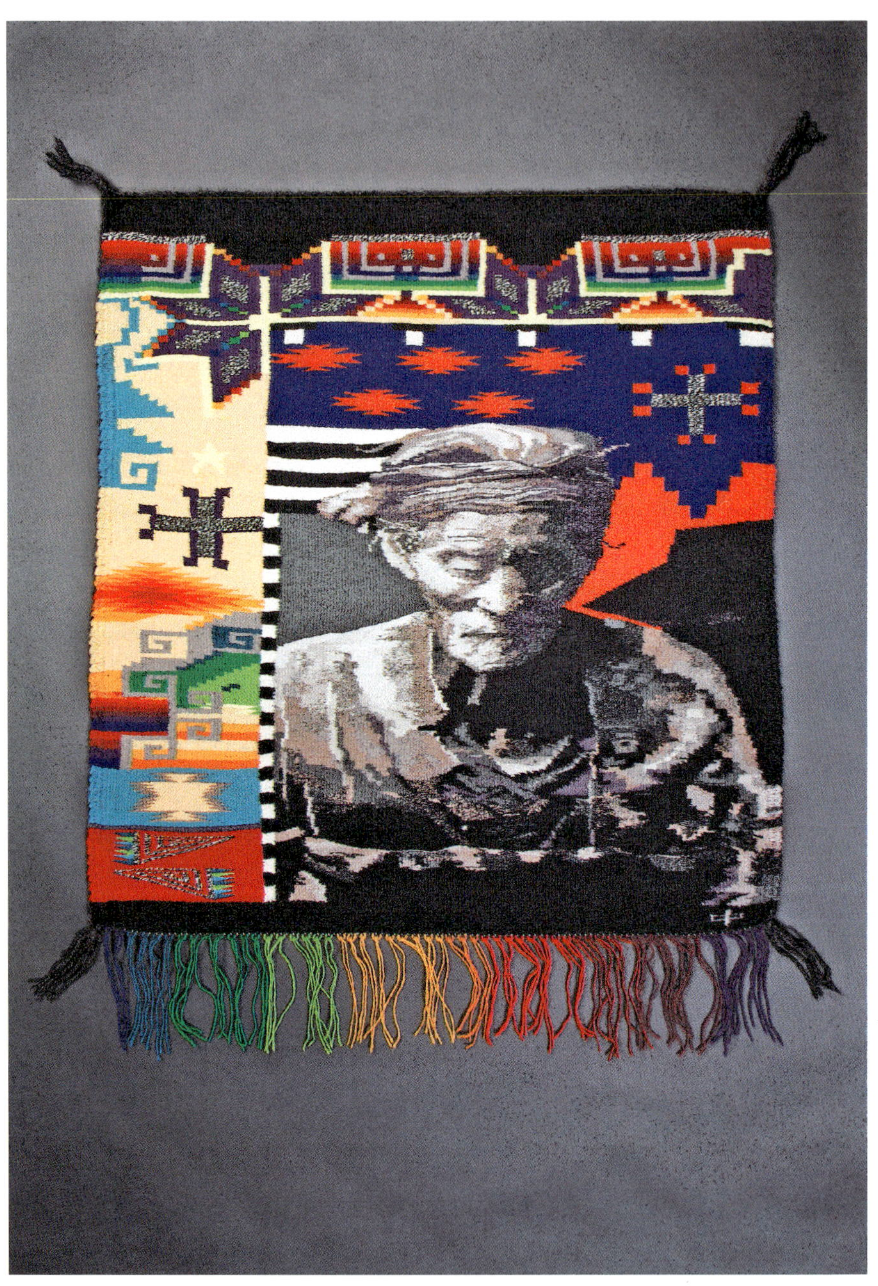

In his first weaving, "Survivor," Marlowe Katoney depicts a Navajo survivor of the Long Walk. The artist explained that Navajos have endured difficult struggles in order to survive. *Courtesy of Marlowe Katoney, all rights reserved.*

Right: This close-up shot of a recent weaving by Marlowe Katoney shows the details in a portrait of a woman's face. Indeed, weaving and painting share common techniques. *Photograph by Rory O'Neill Schmitt, all rights reserved.*

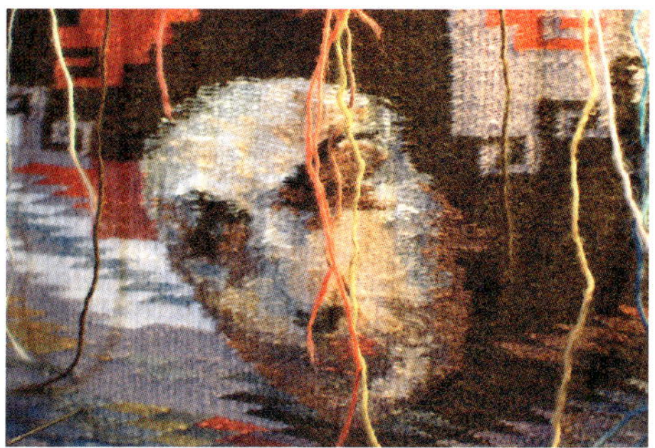

Below: "Winter Apparition" is a pictorial weaving, featuring creations from nature, such as a bird and a rose, as well as geometric shapes and designs. *Courtesy of Marlowe Katoney, all rights reserved.*

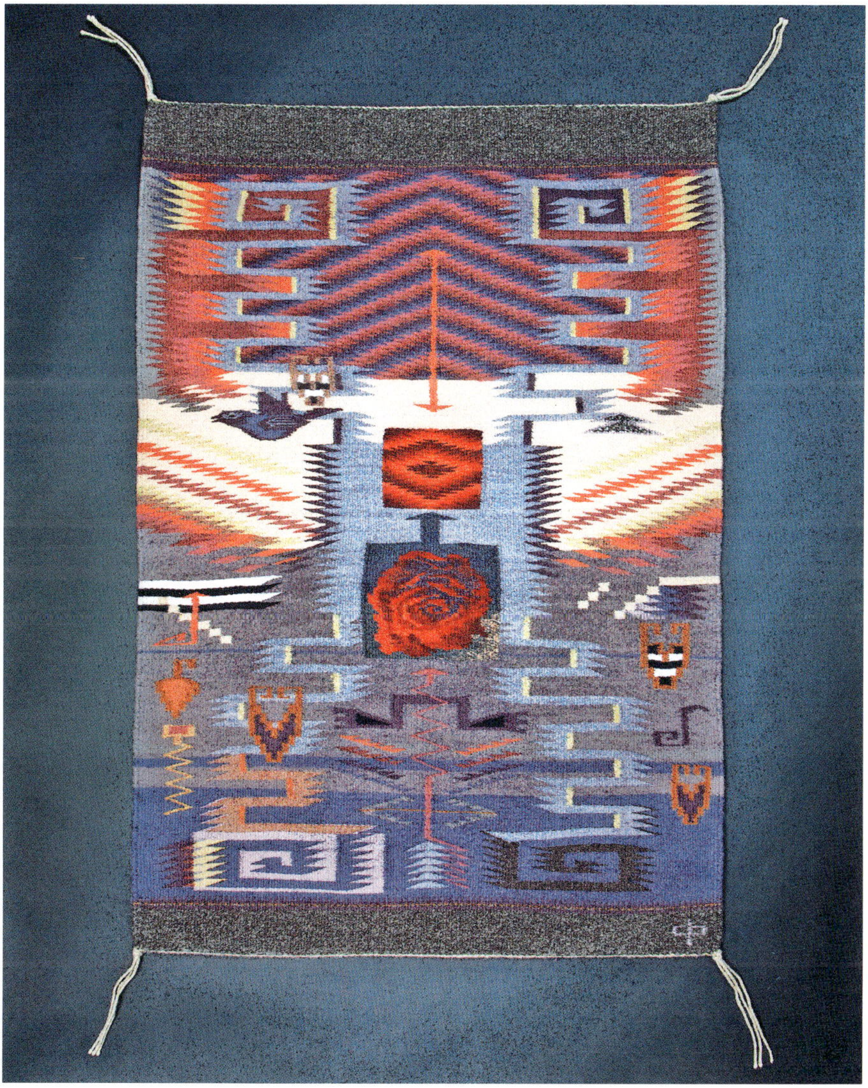

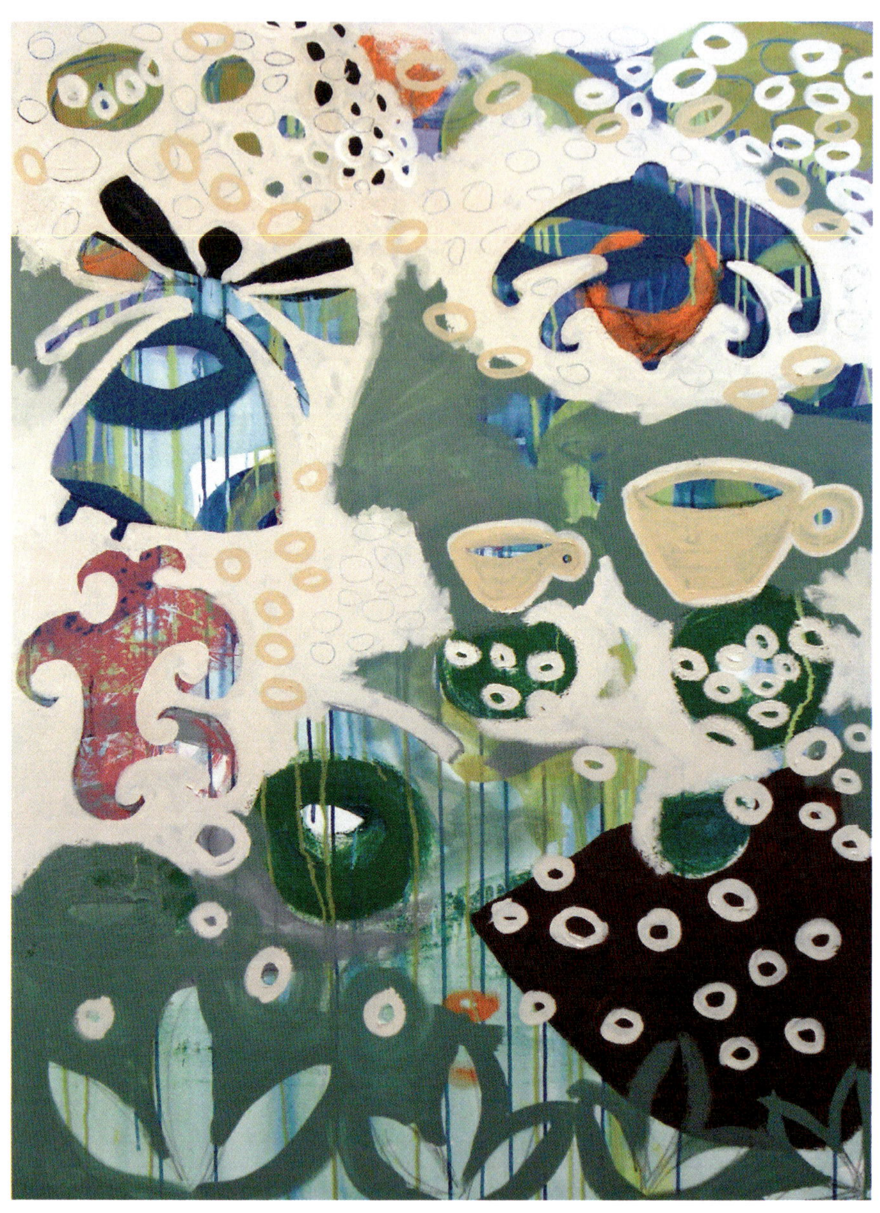

Melanie Yazzie creates floating organic shapes in a spectrum of colors in this playful design for "Spring Time at Red Lake II." *Courtesy of Glenn Green Galleries, all rights reserved.*

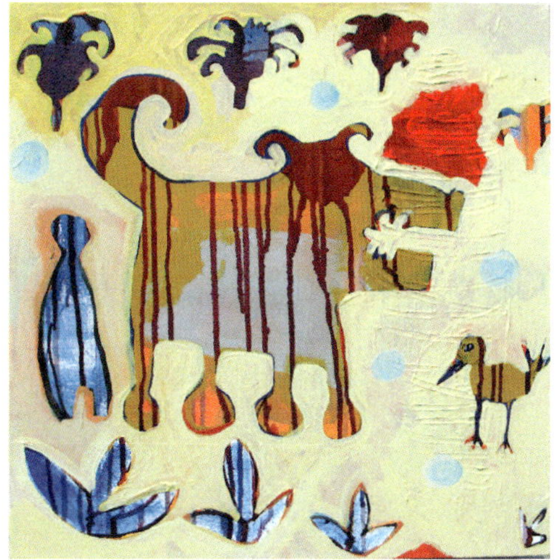

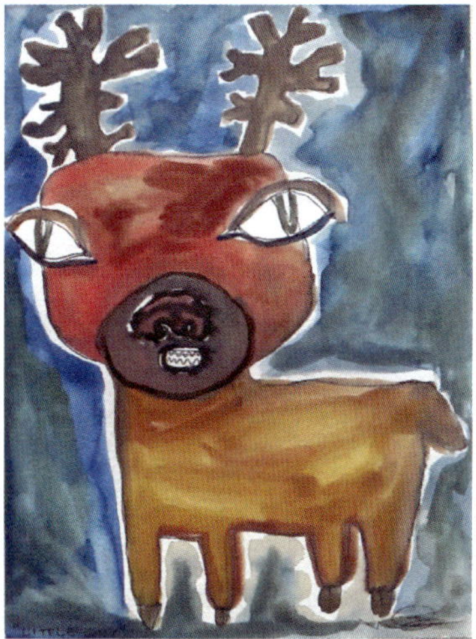

Left: Melanie Yazzie's artwork often includes animal imagery, as in this painting, *Following Grandpa*. *Courtesy of Glenn Green Galleries, all rights reserved.*

Right: For *Little Guy*, Melanie Yazzie used guache watercolor on paper. *Courtesy of Glenn Green Galleries, all rights reserved.*

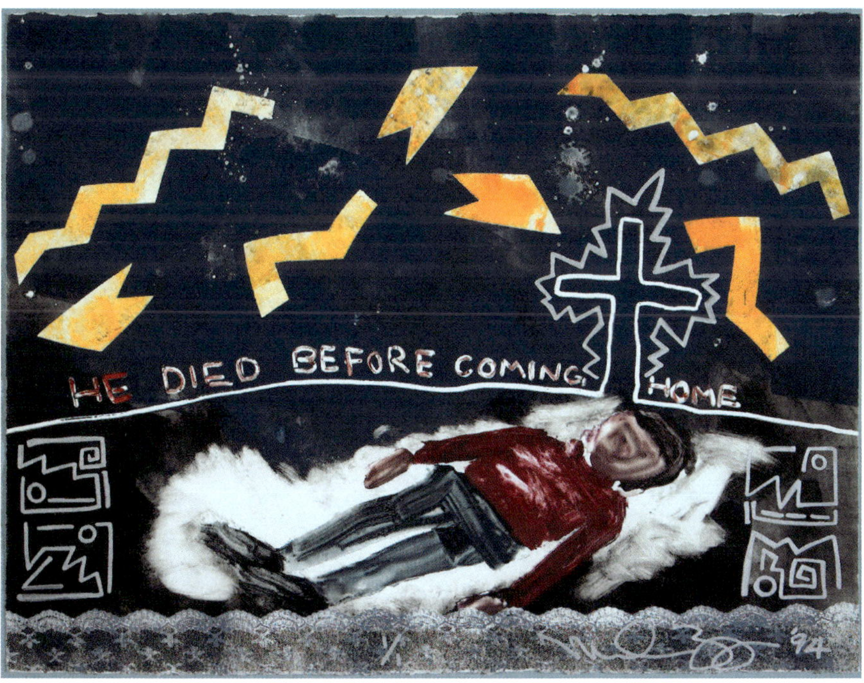

"He Died Before Coming Home" is a print that Melanie Yazzie created in 1994. *Courtesy of Melanie Yazzie, all rights reserved.*

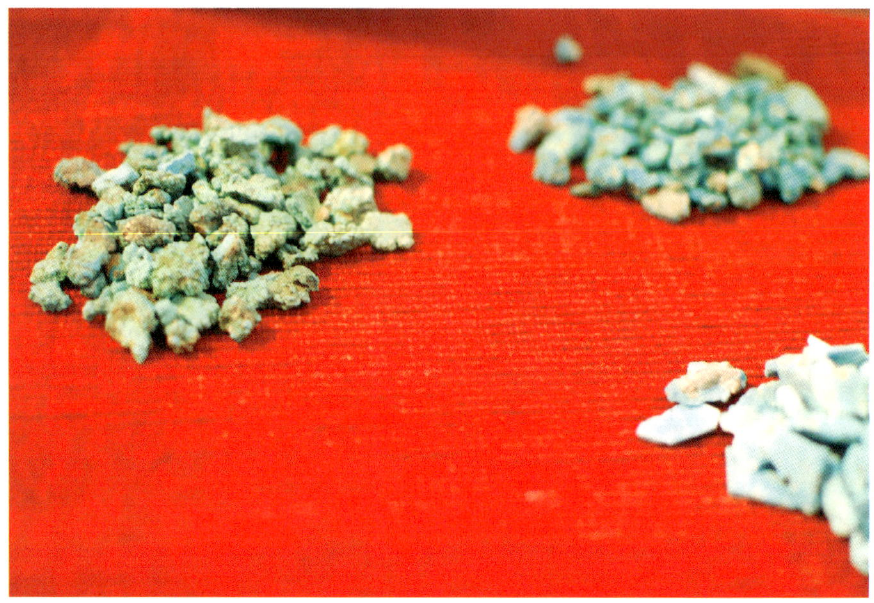

Turquoise comes in a variety of rich colors and matrices. Piki Wadsworth uses turquoise from the Sleeping Beauty, Castle Dome, Morenci and Red Mountain mines. *Photograph by Rory O'Neill Schmitt, all rights reserved.*

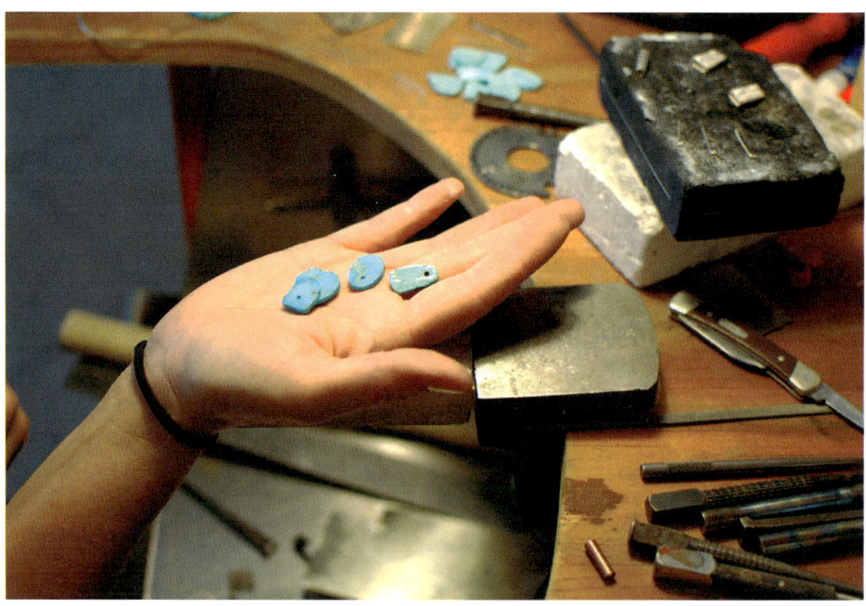

Piki Wadsworth holds turquoise beads that she has shaped, polished and drilled. *Photograph by Rory O'Neill Schmitt, all rights reserved.*

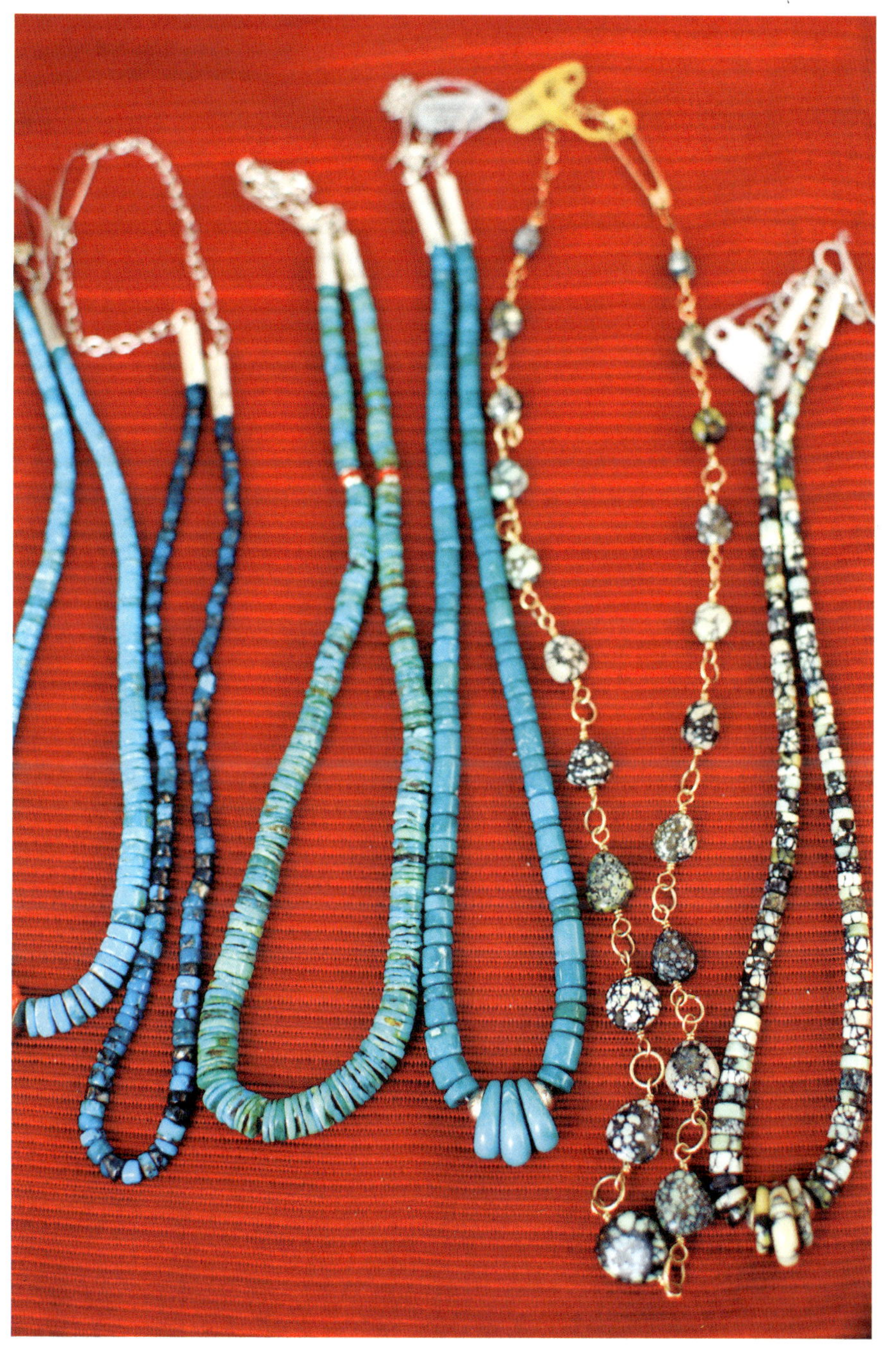

This photograph of five necklaces by Piki Wadsworth shows the complex range of turquoise employed in her jewelry. Notice the diverse shapes, sizes, colors and matrices of the turquoise stones. *Photograph by Rory O'Neill Schmitt, all rights reserved.*

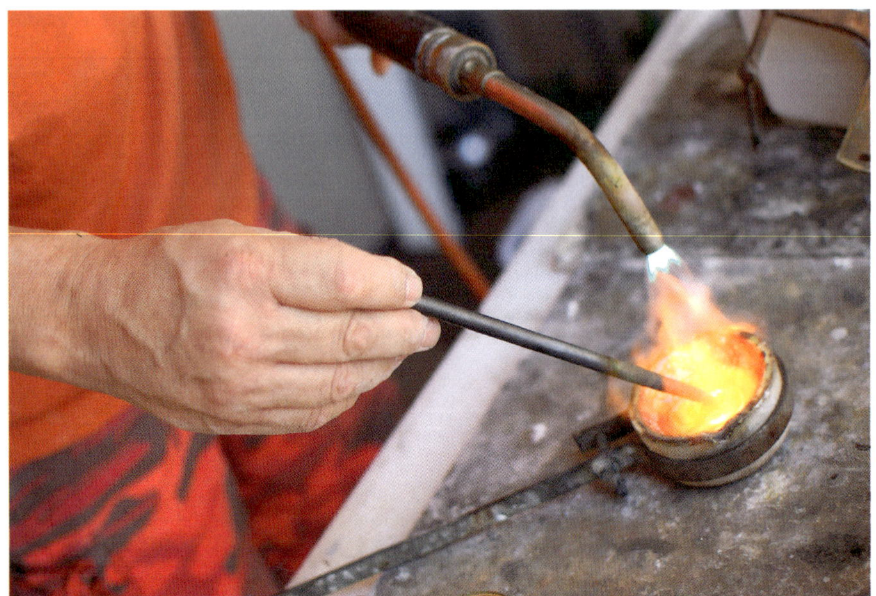

With his left hand, Ric Charlie uses a torch to melt the gold in a crucible while, with his right hand, he stirs the liquid to create uniformity. *Photograph by Rory O'Neill Schmitt, all rights reserved.*

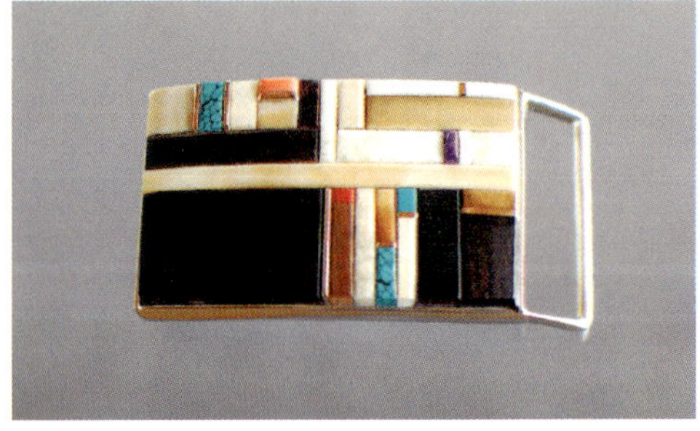

Verma Nequatewa creates exquisite mosaics of stone in her jewelry pieces, as in this pictured belt buckle. *Photograph by Rory O'Neill Schmitt, all rights reserved.*

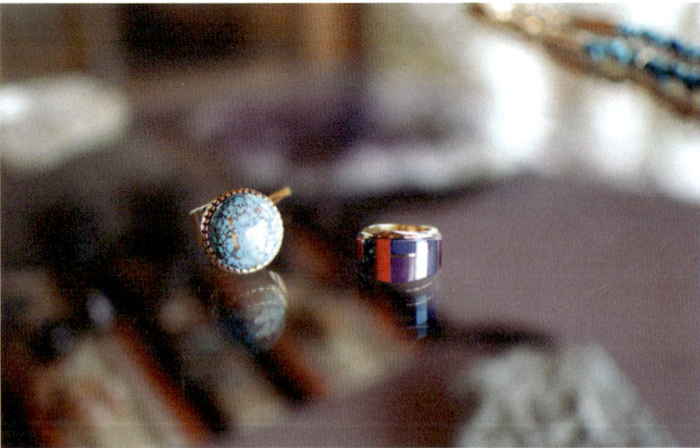

Two rings by Verma Nequatewa sit atop a jewelry display case in her studio in Hotevilla, Arizona. *Photograph by Rory O'Neill Schmitt, all rights reserved.*

IN THE STUDIO WITH BARBARA

Barbara's studio is an approximate ten- by fifteen-foot room in her Tucson home. The space shows Barbara's deep commitment to Navajo weaving, as well as her personality. Details include a shelf with tiny lamb figurines and a magnet on the file cabinet that says, "Yay for Sheep!" Indeed, weaving is integral to Navajo culture and identity. Barbara said, "I think, to me, being Navajo and weaving is almost the same thing. We are told that sheep is life, that we live and die by our flock. We use the sheep as a way to trade for food, a way to have food, and then we use the pelts and the fleece to weave beautiful blankets."

A floor-to-ceiling shelf holds huge plastic clear tubs of wool that she will prepare. She has three looms set up in her studio: To the right is a giant blue, white and black striped weaving in progress set up on a loom. To the left side of the room is a newly set up smaller loom. Centrally located is the loom, set up on an easel, and on it is an exceptional two- by three-and-a-half-foot black, white and gray tapestry. Each part of the process of creating this weaving, done by hand, required an exceptional amount of care; and therefore, the weaving is anticipated to sell for the price of $18,000.

To allow precision in weaving, Barbara directs the lighting: She has two lamps clamped to her easel, as well as a bright overhead florescent light. Sitting on a pillow on a pink-cushioned chair, Barbara works from the bottom up. Her design process involves math skills to ensure the pattern lines up. While weaving, she focuses on one square at a time: she weaves the right side and then copies the left side so that it is symmetrical.

Outside Barbara's studio window, the hum of carpentry equipment can be heard as she weaves. A nephew (Roseann's son), Terry Lee, creates weaving tools, such as weaving combs, battens and looms. He also embellishes the tools by doing wood-burning. For example, as Barbara is a fan of Dwight Yoakum, he drew a cowboy hat on her weaving comb and wrote in cursive, "Dwight."

EDUCATING THE WORLD ABOUT NAVAJO WEAVING AND WEAVERS THROUGH WORKSHOPS

In addition to teaching her children, Barbara Teller Ornelas has taught others, some of whom have become award-winning weavers. With her sister

Lynda Teller Pete, Barbara leads exceptional Navajo weaving workshops. In 2015, Barbara and Lynda instructed sixteen workshops in cities all over the country. Students come from all over the world to attend these workshops; they travel from such places as Nova Scotia, England, Russia and Japan. Barbara and Lynda teach students how to develop weaving skills on their small looms, including basic stripes and a bit of patterning. Sometimes, students are master weavers but want to learn Navajo weaving. Barbara explains that she often learns from her students and finds ways to her speed up her own processes.

Instructing at Idyllwild Adult Arts Center has been a special tradition for Barbara and Lynda. For the past eighteen summers, they have taught beginner and intermediate Navajo weaving within Idyllwild's Native American Arts Program. This program, north of Palm Springs, has adult workshops in the native arts for all levels of experience in such areas as Navajo weaving, Navajo jewelry, Hopi jewelry, Hopi-Tewa pottery, glass blowing and native basketry. The Idyllwild Adult Arts Center provides scholarships for American Indian students. This summer, Barbara and Lynda's thirteen-year-old grandniece, Roxanne, was awarded a scholarship to attend the program.

Due to Arizona's extreme summer heat, Barbara and Lynda drive at night to California, bringing the small looms, commercial wools, weaving combs and tools. (Driving during the daytime can expose the wool to excessive heat, causing damage. Barbara says, "I pile it all up in my Jeep." Barbara cares for her materials and supplies, protecting them like a herder caring for her flock. She brings the materials and the knowledge with her to all parts of the world, weaving into others' lives a richer understanding of Navajo culture.

When asked if there is any controversy about teaching nonnatives Navajo weaving, Barbara explained that she is trying to have others gain an awareness of what is involved in Navajo weaving and what it is like to be Navajo weaver. Some collectors want to understand Navajo weaving better and may initially view weaving as easy and say, "I can do that." After taking her class, one collector student said, "I'm never going to say that ever again. If I hear someone say that, I'm going to kick them!" Students come to realize why weavings are so valuable. This art form requires expert math skills, planning and problem-solving abilities, an eye for innovative design and a commitment to maintain the utmost standards and a mastery of the craft.

What Weaving Means for Her

Traditionally, Navajo women were the weavers in the family. Barbara explained that rearing children and creating weavings have commonalities. She stated:

> *I always remember a story that Grandmother told me about how, when you first set up your work it's like you're giving birth to a child. As you're weaving, it's like watching your child grow. Then, when you're finished with your weaving, it's like this new child generated from your work. You need to give lessons to them and then send them off into the world.*
>
> *That's basically how I feel...I call them my "babies"...When people come to admire my work, I tell them, "These are my babies."*

The loving act of supporting a weaving so that it becomes an artwork is the essence of being an artist for Barbara. Her dedication to making sure her weavings develop into high-quality tapestries is like that of a tireless mother, devoted every day to her child. She nurtures an idea into a highly complex, innovative work of art. In addition, Barbara notes that Navajo weavings preserve and reflect Navajo history. She shared:

> *I was always told that Navajo weaving holds your family together...*
>
> *We can tell the history of Navajo people just by seeing certain kinds of weavings that came before Bosque Redondo. Then, there were weavings that came during Bosque Redondo, and then weaving that came after that. Then, the weavings that were made when the railroads came in, then when the trading posts came in.*
>
> *When you look at Navajo weavings, you're really looking at Navajo history and what is going on, what's been going on in our families, in our culture."*

Additional Information

Barbara Teller Ornelas was named a Living Legend at Gallup Ceremonial (2015), an honor that her relative Jesse Monongya has won in past. (Barbara's maternal great-grandmother was the sister of Jesse Monongya's grandmother.) She has received numerous awards and honors, including winning Best of Show at the Santa Fe Indian Market (1991) and later serving as a judge there (1992). From 1986 to 1987, she was an artist in residence at the Heard Museum. Since 1983, Barbara has also served as a lecturer at museums. She presented on Navajo weaving at the British Museum in London in the 1980s.

Collectors commission her work, but individuals can also buy tapestries directly from Barbara at two shows each year. She described some collectors' experiences: "People come up to me and say, 'Oh, I bought this rug, and I just couldn't help myself.' It's not the prettiest rug, but somehow they felt something like a connection. I would tell them, 'You didn't pick that rug. That rug picked you.'"

Viewers are drawn to the spirits and feelings of Barbara's weavings. She explained, "People are always asking me, 'Do the patterns mean anything? Do they have any meaning?' I tell them, 'There really isn't. It's more of a feeling that you get when you do your weaving.'"

Family Connections: Lynda Teller Pete

Barbara's sister Lynda Teller Pete is also an exceptional weaver. She shared family memories of growing up on the Navajo reservation and learning how to weave. Lynda remembers spending summertime in Newcomb, New Mexico, where her mother is from, and spending wintertime at Two Grey Hills trading post, where her father worked. She described her father as a compassionate community member. He was the only Navajo-speaker at the trading post, so many members of the community would seek his assistance. Lynda shared: "My father actually was there to write letters for people, for people [who] didn't know how to write. He made phone calls for people. He drove people to the doctor. He had the only vehicle around in a pretty wide radius. A lot of people went to the trading post for help, and he was there to give a lot of his time to the community, as well as the trading post."

Lynda also recalled his work selling Navajo weavings to visitors from all over the world, including Germany and Japan, because "everybody wanted to go to the famous Two Grey Hills trading post." As a child, Lynda thought that this experience was the regular way of life. As an adult, she came to a different realization. She said:

> *I was surprised when I did finally go to school and learned that not all Navajo kids came from weaving families. That there were kids* [who]

came from ranching families, from farming families, silversmithing, basket-making, pottery-making...For me, that was kind of foreign, and I had no idea. I thought everybody knew how to weave...My mom started off teaching me how to do the Two Grey Hills type of weaving, and in the area where I'm from, most everybody learned how to do Two Grey Hill weaving. All my aunts, all my cousins, everybody that I knew in my little community, everybody did Two Grey Hill weaving.

Lynda learned how to do Two Grey Hills weaving from her mother, Ruth Begay Teller, around age six. She remembers weaving with her sister Barbara: "My father built this loom. There were two looms, and he had them braced together on top. My sister and I, we would sit facing each other. That was good for days that little kids are getting along, but we don't always get along when you're younger. Whenever I used to bug my sister Barbara my mom used to come and put a sheet between the two looms so that we wouldn't see each other. I would pick up my weaving tools and still poke at her through the wood."

As children, the Tellers learned prayer songs associated with weaving. Lynda explained, "There are no universal Navajo prayers...Every family has their own prayers; they have their own songs." Ruth also instructed her children about the complex considerations of designing weavings. Lynda said:

"I always thought that the hardest part about that whole thing was learning the design phase. I would ask my mom, "Can I do my own thing?" She would say, "Well, only if it fits." I never knew what that meant: "Only if it fits."

After I finally figured out what I was doing and learning more about design and color combinations and things, [I realized] *it's all about math. And that's what she meant: "If it fits." You got to count your work; you got to count your steps. You have to count everything. Not everything is going to fit.*

...Now, when I teach weaving, it's all about the math. I had to drum it into the student's head that we have this...You're going to grasp your design, you've got to count your work, you've got to count your turnarounds...You got to know how much is going to pack down if you have a soft hand, if you have a heavy hand. There's so many variables that go into weaving, that sure if you were the best mathematician in the world, you could really figure stuff out with your designs and stuff.

Ruth Teller supported Lynda in attending college at Arizona State University. After she earned her bachelor's degree in criminal justice, Lynda told her family: "Weaving is really, really hard…So, now that I have a college degree, I don't want to weave anymore. I am going to find a job."

She moved to Colorado, where she began her twenty-eight-year career devoted to the Department of Labor. After her sister Roseann passed away in 1996, Lynda decided on a life change. She said: "I started thinking about who the historian would be, because my sister was the historian. She was the keeper of all our stories and all of our things surrounding the weaving. She was the one [who] kept it for everyone. I started worrying about what's going to happen now. That's really how I got back into it. My mom gave me some of my sister's tools, and it helped with the grieving process, using her tools…It gave me a sense of balance, I think. It really helped with the grief process."

Around the year 2000, Barbara invited Lynda to assist her with teaching weaving at the Idlywild Summer Arts. Soon after, Lynda decided she wanted to do weaving full time. Lynda has been instrumental in developing curriculum, handouts and instruction techniques in order to streamline the learning process.

Weaving is at the heart of their family. Lynda explained what weaving means to her. She said, "It keeps our family together. It gives us a sense of purpose. It's tradition, it's a sense of pride, it's a sense of vision, hope, unity." Today, Lynda weaves in different styles, including contemporary and period pieces. She is also frequently in the process of making a Two Grey Hills weaving. Lynda sells her weavings at Santa Fe Indian Market. Collectors also commission pieces by contacting the artists at www.navajorugweavers.com.

8

MARLOWE KATONEY

WINSLOW, ARIZONA

Marlowe Katoney was born in Flagstaff, Arizona, in 1976 to Navajo parents Pearl and Wilson Katoney. He grew up in northern Arizona in Winslow. His family includes artists (his grandmothers were weavers and his cousin and uncle were silversmiths) and railroaders (his grandfather, father and uncle).

Marlowe showed an early interest in visual art and artistic processes. As a boy, he would watch his maternal grandmother weave. And he often observed his father drawing in his free time. Marlowe enjoyed studying his dad's *Southwest Art* and *Arizona Highways* magazines, where he discovered inspirational Hopi jeweler Charles Loloma.

AN ARTIST'S PATH

While studying at Winslow High School, Marlowe focused his research project on Charles Loloma. With his mother, Marlowe traveled to Loloma's home, located on the Third Mesa of the Hopi reservation. Though Loloma had died just years before in 1991, Marlowe learned more about him through speaking with one of his nieces (who also is a jeweler), Verma Nequatewa.

Marlowe learned that before becoming a master jeweler, Loloma worked as a painter and potter. This knowledge would serve as a parallel in his life, as

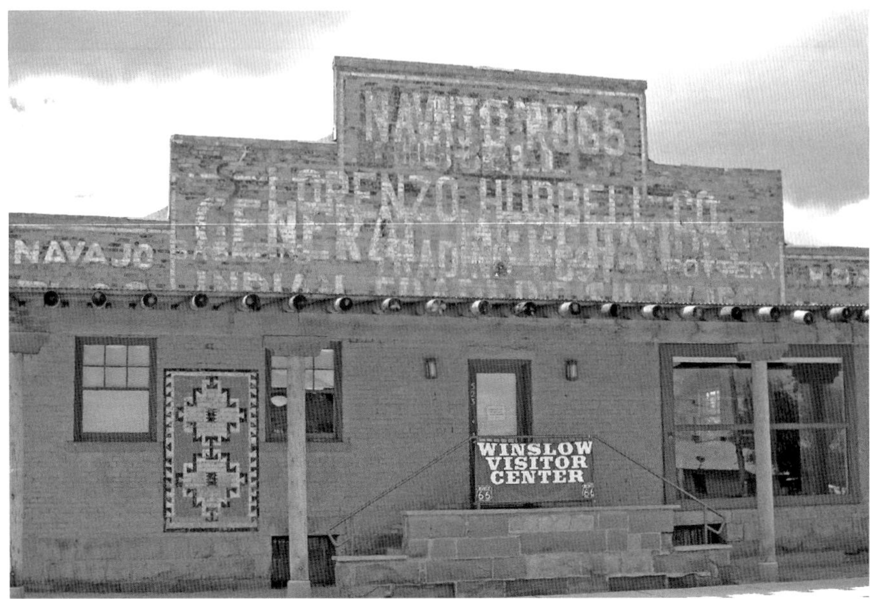

The Winslow Visitor Center, located on Second Street, promotes community events and area attractions. *Photograph by Rory O'Neill Schmitt, all rights reserved.*

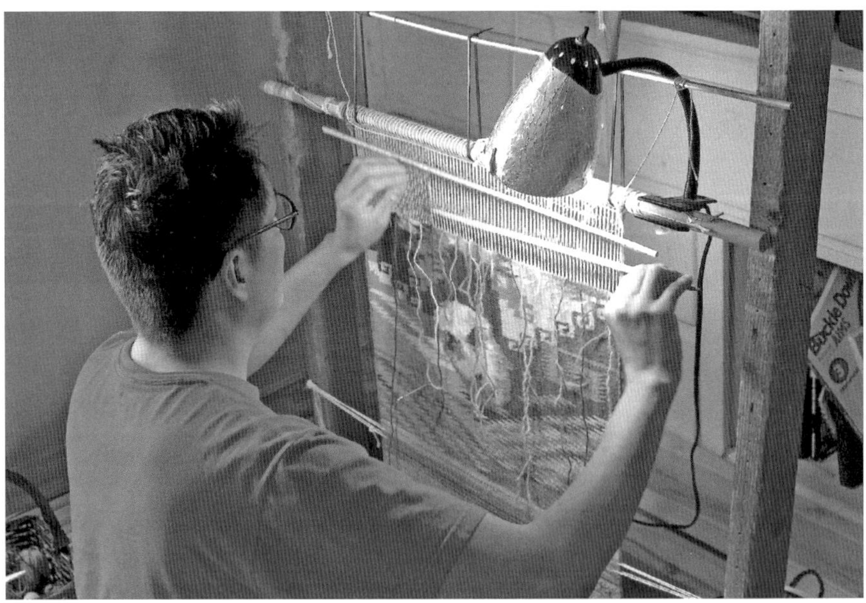

In this photograph, Marlowe Katoney is working on a weaving to be displayed in a contemporary fiber art exhibit in Brooklyn. *Photograph by Rory O'Neill Schmitt, all rights reserved.*

Marlowe studied pottery and painting prior to pursuing his path as a Navajo weaver. Marlowe said:

> *I really wanted to go into making jewelry because I loved Charles Loloma's work, I researched his background, what he did before he became a jeweler. I knew that he became a painter, and he was a potter before making jewelry. Those are things that I recognized in his work because of the texture, the process and how he incorporates the abstract into his work.*
>
> *In high school, I took up painting, and I did pottery work because I wanted to gain that experience. I wanted to see what he had seen because I knew that he had studied with Fred Kabotie from a really early age. I wanted to see what he experienced.*

Marlowe attended the University of Arizona in Tucson from 1995 to 1999 and studied painting, two-dimensional design and sculpture. Many of Marlowe's weavings include storm patterns, inspired by traditional Navajo designs. The expansive landscapes of Arizona frequently inspire him and serve as a focus in several of his artworks, as well. He shared, "Growing up in northern Arizona, I was always surrounded by landscape. That was the focus of…my artwork." He said, "A lot of my paintings, which are abstract, are landscape-based, and I guess you could say organically based."

When he realized that no other family member on his mother's side was continuing the art of weaving, Marlowe transitioned to create weavings in 2009. Weaving is a form of tapestry-making, an ancient hand-weaving technique wherein the artist weaves small areas using various colors to make images or patterns. Marlowe applied his painter skills to the weaving medium, which is very similar to painting, though with wool; however, to create particular details or gestures in a weaving can take much more time and involve more complicated processes than creating a similar result using paint. Both mediums require careful planning of composition, selection of colors, decision making about symbolism and reflections on cultural and personal meanings.

Incorporating the Contemporary into a Traditional Form

Like other Navajo artists before him, Marlowe integrates his experiences into his weavings. He explained that native artists have been including elements from their environments for ages. He said:

> *A lot of weavers will probably tell you, and even textile scholars who have studied Navajo rug weaving,* [it] *is the popular culture, whether it was in the turn of the century, like in 1920s…or even 1950s through the 1990s…When you see a lot of artwork, whether it's rug weaving or not, it has always played a particular role in what Navajos are doing, or what Native Americans are doing, as far as the products we might pick up at the grocery store, or in 1925, something that somebody may have picked up at the trading post. You see how those things are implemented.*
>
> *I think, unknowingly, a lot of Native Americans incorporate it in there, but that really makes a statement about that particular time. For me right now, those are things that are part of the popular culture with young Native Americans, because you see those things on clothing, you see that sort of thing on television. It's something that speaks about what's going on right now with Native Americans.*

In one weaving, called "The Acquisition," Marlowe composed an image of a young man wearing baggy jeans, a T-shirt and a baseball cap. He is casually seated with his head down. This figure reflects a similar portrait in a mural he created while studying at the University of Arizona. Indeed, Marlowe's weavings bring a contemporary spin on the traditional weaving medium. The figure is a regular guy, sitting on the street, perhaps similar to a person he has seen before.

Marlowe explained that he is inspired by environments he witnesses in his day-to-day life. He said, "When you paint, or whenever you make any type of artwork, you're always compelled to work in the familiar, whether it's social situations or your environment and how you interact with it. Somehow, that's always incorporated into your work."

SURVIVOR

Marlowe tells history through his textiles. In his first pictorial weaving, "Survivor," he references the Long Walk. The central black, white and gray figure with a forlorn expression is a Navajo survivor of the walk to Bosque Redondo. Contrasting with this figure are bright colors along the weaving's border. The vivid framing references Navajo creation mythology, as rainbows were a means of providing transportation for the Holy People.

Navajos have had to endure through difficult struggles in order to survive. To deal with suffering, Marlowe explained that many Native people turned to creating weavings. During the Long Walk, Navajo weavers were unable to take their yarn with them. Therefore, they adapted to their situation. They deconstructed the Mexican blankets they were given; they reused the yarn to create weavings with even sharper details. As creating art sustained many Navajos before him, so it does also for Marlowe.

Popular Culture

In his artworks, Marlowe incorporates traditional Navajo cultural symbols and images from popular culture, such as video games and cartoons. For example, recent weavings have included the Navajo tree of life and Hello Kitty. In "Angry Birds Tree of Life," he references the tree of life, which is represented as a corn stalk growing out of a wedding basket. Often, birds are included. This Navajo image symbolizes the joining of the bride's and groom's families. In this weaving, Marlowe's creatures resemble the touch-screen characters from the Angry Birds video game. Fourteen red birds, each with a unique facial expression, sit on leafless branches of a tree, which resembles the traditional design for the Navajo tree of life. The idea for this twenty-three- by twenty-six-inch weaving came from Marlowe's experience of visiting his aunt's garden and becoming frustrated that all of the produce had been picked.

Exhibitions

Marlowe has exhibited his artwork throughout the United States, including at the 1Spot Gallery in Phoenix (2015), Heard Museum (2013–14), Phoenix Art Museum (2013), Studio 53 Fine Art Gallery (2013) and the Amerind Museum and Research Center (2012–13). In 2011, his weavings were auctioned at Maxwell Museum and Canyonlands Natural History Association. Marlowe has also served as a demonstrator at the Heard Museum Indian Fair and Market (2013–15) and the Museum of Northern Arizona Marketplace (2012).

Marlowe's awards and honors include Rollin and Mary Ella King Fellowship, School for Advanced Research of the American Experience (2015), Honorable Mention at the Museum of Northern Arizona Navajo

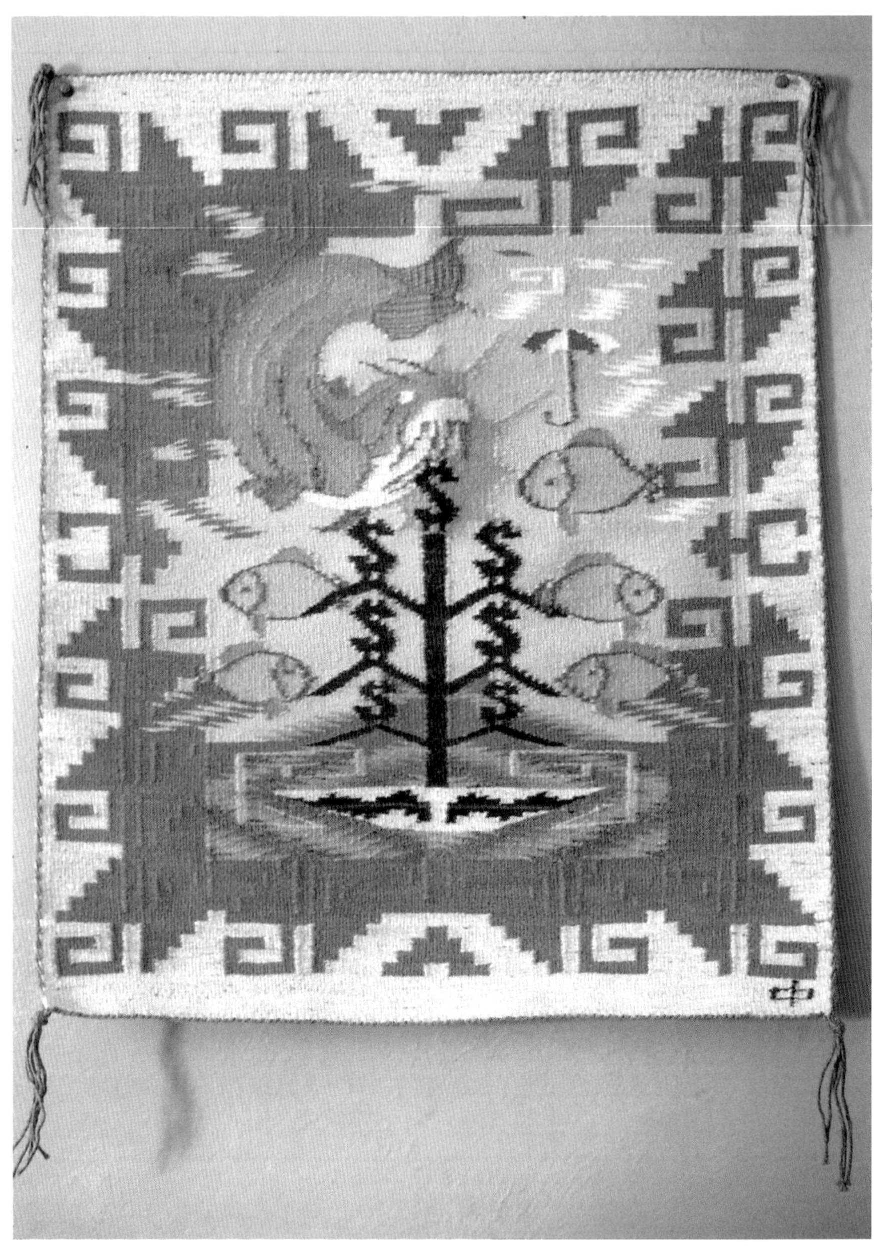

This contemporary pictorial weaving, "Tree of Life: American Epic" by Marlowe Katoney, includes the Navajo tree of life symbol, as well as traditional geometric designs. Within the tree, Marlowe has placed dollar signs to comment on the complex issues involved in capitalism. In the lower right corner, the artist has signed his name with a symbol, 中, which is also the Chinese character for middle. *Photograph by Rory O'Neill Schmitt, all* rights reserved.

Show (2014, 2013 and 2012), Spirit Award Museum at the Northern Arizona Navajo Show (2012), Idyllwild Native American Arts Summer Program Scholarship (2012) and Honorable Mention at the Gallup Ceremonial (1994).

An Advocate for American Indians

Marlowe is an advocate for embracing contemporary artworks emerging from native artists today. Sometimes, he is frustrated when art critics make statements about an artwork or jewelry piece like, "Well, it doesn't look Native American. It doesn't look anything like it should."

Marlowe's artworks can be called a Navajo rug, tapestry, weaving, textile or fiber art. Perhaps, the labeling of Navajo art form as rugs, rather than tapestries, has led to and perpetuated the label as a craft that fits certain parameters defining a American Indian art standard instead of high art. In fact, another artist in this book, Barbara Teller Ornelas, had early struggles with being recognized *only* as a weaver (and not as an artist) by galleries.

Contemporary native artists are tirelessly working to expand beyond the bounds of what has been previously accepted as native art forms. They are setting a standard for themselves. Marlowe said:

> *I think that right now, in Native American art, what we're doing right now…We're really trying to set a standard for ourselves in art society. I think that we're trying to find a place in art, in general.*
>
> *I really see it in a lot of artists, young artists, artists my age, artists who are coming up in the world as painters. It's really difficult because you see a lot of art critics outside of the Native American art circle. And they see what we're doing as a craft and only a craft, not as an art.*

Marlowe wants to make a change. As Charles Loloma forged a new standard for jewelry, Marlowe aims at transforming expectations for weaving as a contemporary fine art form. He shared, "I hope at some point, I can make a change. It doesn't matter who's doing what. When the artist is Native American and they're producing art, there is a statement that's being made about our culture at that particular time."

Marlowe also feels that a bigger issue is misconception of Native Americans by nonnatives. He shared that during college,

> *in the dorm, there were students from the Midwest and from back East. They had people that they knew* [who] *had claimed to be Native American, who probably were, but when they came out here to the Southwest they had seen Navajos, Tohono O'odham, Apache Native Americans. It was very obvious to them that we were Native American by our experience.*
>
> *A lot of them…always questioned me. They would say, "Wow. We didn't know that there were real Native Americans like you out there. We just thought they weren't around or…lived somewhere way out in the boonies and didn't have any connection with modern society."*

Marlowe advocates for the need for the education system to teach students about contemporary American Indians.

Additional Information

Marlowe currently resides in Winslow, Arizona, and works full-time as a weaver. The shops at the Heard Museum and Museum of Northern Arizona sell his artwork. To purchase his artwork, individuals may also contact him via his website, www.marlowekatoney.com.

9
MARGARET WOOD

Early Education and Influences

Margaret Wood was born to parents Helen Mae Watchman Wood (Navajo) and Charlie Wood (Seminole), in 1950 at the Indian Hospital in Parker, Arizona, which is located along the Colorado River. Throughout her childhood, she lived in towns across northern Arizona, including Flagstaff and Tuba City.

In 1968, Margaret received a full scholarship from the Navajo Nation to attend Arizona State University; in 1971, she earned her bachelor's degree in elementary education from ASU. Later, Margaret was awarded another full scholarship to attend graduate school at the University of Denver; in 1973, she earned her master's degree in library science. Though she was employed as a teacher (1971–72) and a librarian (1973–78), Margaret was drawn to become an artist. Perhaps this artistic identity was influenced by her grandmother and an aunt who wove Navajo rugs; her two brothers, who did silversmithing; her cousins who created paintings; and another aunt (who is currently the family matriarch) who makes quilts.

Undoubtedly, the biggest influence on Margaret was her mother, Helen Mae Watchman Wood, who taught her how to sew. Margaret said, "She had an old Singer. Starting [when I was] age nine, she let me play with it. When things got hopelessly thread-bound, she would step in and clear my mess and re-thread it, and off I would go." Margaret began by making doll clothes and then progressed to making simple patterns and her own clothing.

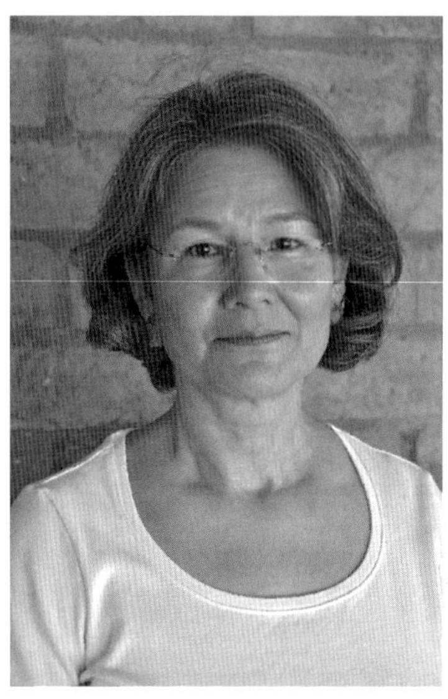

This photograph features Navajo fiber artist Margaret Wood, who resides in Phoenix, Arizona. *Courtesy of Margaret Wood, all rights reserved.*

Fashion Designer

An important childhood memory that Margaret connects to her future career occurred when Helen created a blouse out of Seminole patchwork fabric, which mimicked a man's baseball jacket. Margaret would also create modern adaptations of traditional Native American clothing designs. While working as a first grade teacher on the Navajo reservation, she would often wear her original clothing that was inspired by traditional designs. Her goal was to encourage her students to learn about, as well as take pride in their heritage.

From 1974 to 1975, Margaret wrote her book, *Native American Fashions: Modern Adaptations of Traditional Designs*. Van Nostrand Reinhold published the first edition of this book in 1981, and she had a second edition printed in 1997. In 1980, she started her own fashion company, Native American Fashions, Inc., which produced clothing based on modern adaptions of traditional designs.

Quilt Maker

In the 1970s, Margaret admired the winning quilt at the Heard Museum art fair, which was created by a San Carlos Apache artist. However, Margaret was disappointed when, the following year, the same person won with a very similar design. The new judges had not reviewed the previous year's winners. When she told her husband, Tom Galbraith, that the quilt lacked creativity, he challenged her: "Why don't you do something original for next year?" Margaret responded, "Well, I'm going to." She took on her husband's challenge and made her first quilt at age twenty-seven. The following year, her silk quilt, which depicted a Navajo wedding basket, won an honorable mention.

While working as a fashion designer, Margaret produced quilts as a sideline of her business. After thirty years, she decided to redirect the focus of her creative outlets. She stated, "I felt a great sense of release of not having to do the clothes. I got much more excited about the quilts." Her self-perception had transformed: "Until about 1990, I called myself a fashion designer who did quilts. In about 1990, I realized I really enjoyed the quilts more…I started calling myself a quilter who did some clothing…That was my career."

Creative Process

Working from home, Margaret sketches her artistic ideas in a notebook, a practice that began when she and her husband became engaged. She participates in a "ripening process," in which she adds to the original sketches. Her ideas build on top of one another to create a concept that holds deep meanings for her. After reviewing her design sketches, she selects a quilt project. She often works on multiple quilts at the same time. Margaret is flowing with creativity and inspiration. She remarked, "I still have a two-inch-wide file of quilt ideas, so I'll never finish in my lifetime."

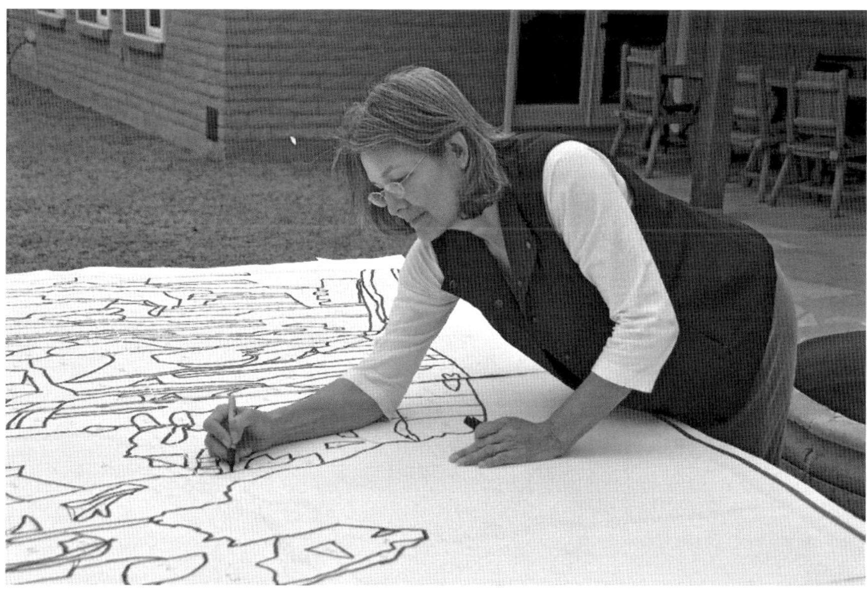

Prior to sewing her quilts, Margaret Wood creates large sketches of her designs. *Courtesy of Margaret Wood, all rights reserved.*

Margaret notes that viewers can look at her quilts and appreciate them. She would like for her artwork to be able to stand alone visually. However, in order to deepen viewers' understanding of her personal quilts, she includes a long fabric label on the back of the quilt that contains more information about the artwork. She said, "Someone can look at the quilt without knowing all of that and enjoy it, but…after they read the label, then they have a whole different point of the quilt."

Indian/Woman

Margaret's first quilts were composed of geometric designs that were inspired by Navajo rugs and baskets. Later, she integrated personal stories into her quilts. One event from her life inspired her twenty-third quilt, "Indian/Woman," constructed in 1991.

While working with her fashion company, she received a telephone call from Arizona State University inviting her to participate in an event promoting minority women in business. She explained, "The working title [of the quilt] was 'Freeway Flash' because on the way home—I am a bit of a clothes horse—I started thinking: 'How would I have dressed? Did they want me to look like an Indian woman, or did they want me to look like a business person?'"

She envisioned a life-sized quilt of the back of an American Indian woman dressed half in traditional wear and half in a business suit. Margaret lay on the floor and her husband traced the outline of her body, so that the proportions would be correct. To the head of the figure, Margaret attached a dark brown long hair wig, which she had in her closet from her college days.

The eighty-three- by fifty-six-inch quilt is composed of navy and cream colors, as well as Navajo colors representing the cardinal directions: black onyx (north), white shell (east), turquoise (south) and yellow abalone shell (west). In addition, since the number four is significant in Navajo mythology, elements in the quilt are repeated in fours. On each of the four corners, she appliqued Navajo weaving prints. Diverse materials for the quilt include cotton, ultrasuede, wool, polyester and metal.

Margaret interpreted the artwork: "It's difficult being an Indian woman. It feels like you're straddling two cultures. You're trying to be faithful to your Indian culture and your Indian family, but most of us live in the dominant Anglo culture, where we work and have to get along with Anglo people." She

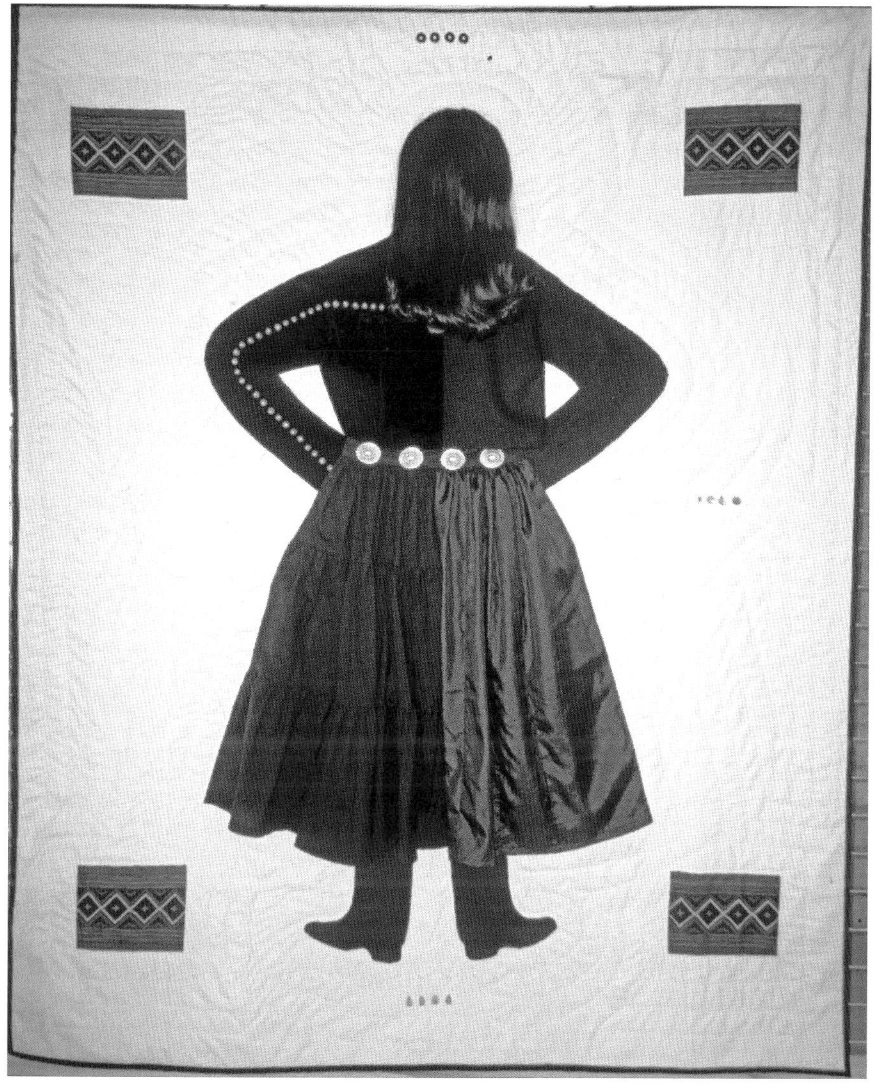

In "Indian/Woman 1" (1991), Margaret Wood depicts her struggles with navigating American Indian and Anglo cultures. *Courtesy of Margaret Wood, all rights reserved.*

explained that many American Indian women's challenges are amplified as they move between worlds; they often adjust their language and manners to adapt to these worlds.

For several years, she talked about the figure in the artwork as if it was someone else. Then, in 1999, she realized, "Oh my God. That's me. It literally was me because I had to trace my body. I didn't make

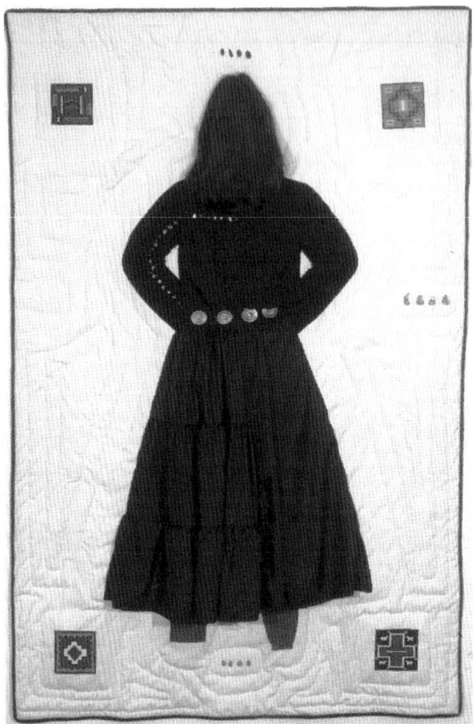

"Indian/Woman 2" is an autobiographical quilt by Margaret Wood, in which she uses diverse materials, including a human-hair wig. *Courtesy of Margaret Wood, all rights reserved.*

the connection for almost ten years. And it was embarrassing that it had taken me that long. After that, the geometrics [in quilts] weren't so interesting. I have done more personal stories of things that really are touching closer to who I am." Margaret has created additional biographical quilts, including one of herself, Indian Woman 2; a quilt about her father, Charlie Wood Maze (2000); and one about her mother, Helen Mae Watchman Wood Maze (2008). Learning more about the lives of her parents plays an integral role in comprehending these artworks.

Charlie Wood (1913–1997) hailed from southeastern Oklahoma. He was of Seminole ancestry and belonged to the Tiger or Mountain Lion clan. Helen Mae Watchman Wood (1920–1964) was Navajo and belonged to the Towering House clan. Helen was raised on the Navajo reservation in Fort Defiance, Arizona.

Helen and Charlie met on Route 66 in Flagstaff. They married in 1944, and in 1949, they moved to Poston in order to homestead with other Navajo and Hopi families. Helen taught first grade at Poston Elementary School, and Charlie worked as a carpenter. Later, they moved to Tuba City, where Helen continued to work as a teacher and Charlie worked as a carpenter. Charlie and Helen had three children together: Ronald Cully Wood, Margaret Ann Wood and Charles Wood Jr. In 1962, Helen became ill and was forced to quit teaching. A stroke, resulting from surgery, led to her sudden death two years later.

Charlie Wood's Maze

Margaret's eightieth quilt was constructed from 1995 to 2000. This journey quilt is approximately sixty-four by fifty inches and is composed of rust-colored fabrics that Margaret collected over a decade. The design is loosely based on the Pima maze, an iconic symbol found on baskets and jewelry referring to a Pima-Maricopa legend. On a person's journey, he may experience negative events but is still able to find balance.

The theme of this artwork is a person trying to find his way along a path. Viewers can identify the pathway and view each image that is tied to his life. Charlie's path starts as distinct but becomes muddier and more confusing. On Charlie's pathway, Margaret placed significant artistic symbols, representing instances in his life: his six wives (Ernie, Ruby, Helen, Betty, Margaret and Colleen); a Stetson hat; a bottle of whiskey; the colors of Lucky Strikes cigarettes; an *X* to mark the placement of the radiation treatment for his larynx cancer; and helping, healing hands. The quilt's design also includes a diamond-shaped Seminole piecework graphic, which represents stepping stones of her father's journey.

During the creation process, the artist struggled with whether she should sell it, as it held deeply personal meanings for her. Margaret decided she could work on two similar quilts so that she could sell one and keep one in her family.

Helen Mae Watchman Wood's Maze

Created in 2008 and measuring about seventy-one by eighty-three inches, the Helen Mae Watchman Wood Maze is composed of rust, tan, brown and turquoise colors. Mixed media includes human hair, cotton velveteen, polyester, ribbons and shell buttons.

This quilt's story moves clockwise along a Navajo wedding basket stair-step path. Margaret emphasizes places, including the hogan, homes and apartment where Helen resided. In 1944, Helen was one of the first Navajo individuals to graduate from Arizona State College (now called Northern Arizona University). Margaret placed an image of the Old Main to represent this point in her mother's life. Additional significant images are the sun and moon (representative of Navajo mythology) and Helen's husband and children. Lastly, a bottle of whiskey represents both Helen's and Charlie's struggles with alcoholism.

Monument Valley

Arizona geography inspires Margaret's quilting adventures. Currently, she is creating an art installation of six full-sized quilts depicting one face of a monolith in Monument Valley. Her process is as follows: She creates patterns based on her husband's eight- by ten-inch photographs. Then, she breaks down the photographs into units on a clear acrylic sheet. She enlarges the sheet several times, makes multiple copies and uses the copies for a time-consuming appliqué process. The approximate dimensions of the quilts are ninety by seventy-five inches. Thus far, Margaret has completed three quilts. She is working around Rain God Mesa, located in the center of Monument Valley.

Exhibitions and Service

An innovative fiber artist, Margaret reinterprets American Indian traditions through her quilts. She has exhibited in museums and art galleries across the United States, including "Lov'n Arizona" at the Phoenix Airport Museum (2012–13); "Quilt Stories" at the Riverside Metropolitan Museum, Riverside, California (2008–09); "Native Quilters of the Southwest: Arizona, New Mexico, Utah, Colorado" at the Navajo Nation Museum, Window Rock, Arizona (2005); "Timeless Vision: A Juried Exhibition of Fine Contemporary Craft" at Yavapai College Art Gallery, Prescott, Arizona (2004); "Stiches in Time: Quilts from the Riverside Municipal Museum" (2003); "Changing Hands: Art without Reservation" at the Museum of Fine Art, Santa Fe, New Mexico (2003), and the American Craft Museum, New York (2002); "The Art of Western Living" at the Desert Caballeros Western Museum, Prescott, Arizona (2001–02); "Native American Quilts from the Southwest: Tradition, Creativity and Inspiration" at the Institute of American Indian Arts, Santa Fe, New Mexico (1998–99); and "Expressions of Spirit: Contemporary American Indian Art" at the Wheelwright Museum, Santa Fe, New Mexico (1995).

Margaret's artwork was included with over forty American Indian and Native Hawaiian artists in the Smithsonian Institution exhibition "To Honor and Comfort: Native Quilting Traditions" from 1997 to 2001. This exhibit traveled to the Smithsonian National Museum of the American Indian, New York; Heard Museum, Phoenix, Arizona; the Museum of International Folk

Art, Santa Fe, New Mexico; and the Bishop Museum, Honolulu, Hawaii. In addition, her work was featured in the "Head, Heart, and Hands" exhibit, which was shown at the Kentucky Art and Craft Gallery, Louisville (1998), and the American Craft Museum, New York (1999).

Margaret has also co-curated exhibitions, including "American Indian Women Artists: Beyond Craft," at the Riverside Metropolitan Museum (2011) and "Fashion Fusion" at the Heard Museum (1999). Currently, she lectures and conducts workshops, including a lecture on the history of American Indian clothing, as well as workshops on Seminole patchwork techniques.

Margaret has supported her local community as a volunteer for the Arizona Commission of the Arts, the Phoenix Arts Commission and the Phoenix Indian Center and as the volunteer executive director of an American Indian art service organization, Atlatl (1990–91). For the past ten years, she has been an active member of the Phoenix Indian Medical Center Auxiliary in Phoenix, Arizona.

Additional Information

Additional information about the artist can be found at her website, www.margaretwood.net. Margaret's quilts can be purchased through the artist, as well as at the Navajo Spirit boutique in Gallup, New Mexico.

Part III

Contemporary Hopi Artists

10
THE HOPI TRIBE

WHO ARE THE HOPIS?

As descendants of cliff-dwelling Anasazi and Sinagua peoples, Hopis trace their history in Arizona back two thousand years. Hopis are a Puebloan culture and are the sole Pueblo tribe in Arizona (nineteen Pueblo tribes exist in New Mexico). Hopi ancestors *Hisatsinom*, or "People of Long Ago," recorded their history of migration as petroglyphs in the Southwest. They chipped drawings into sandstone cliffs and faces of rocks. Their homeland, in northeastern Arizona's Colorado Plateau, is called *tuuwanasavi*, meaning "Land at the Center," and features sandstone canyons and mesas, dotted with juniper and cedar trees.

Hopi peoples have been referred to as the *Moki* or *Moqui*; however, many refer to themselves as *Hopitu*, meaning "Peaceful People." Hopi values include respect and humility, and Hopis are deeply committed to caring for others and the earth. They believe in goodness and beauty and are extremely connected to preserving the culture of their community. Many Hopis speak their native Uto-Aztecan language. Some contemporary schools, such as the Hopi School, encourage the preservation of the Hopi culture. Its curricular foundation is Hopi philosophy.

The driving force behind Hopi culture is religion. Many Hopis believe that all things in nature have a spirit or soul. The Hopi Path of Life, *Hopivotskwani*, is a union of humans with the natural world. Hopi religion places emphasis

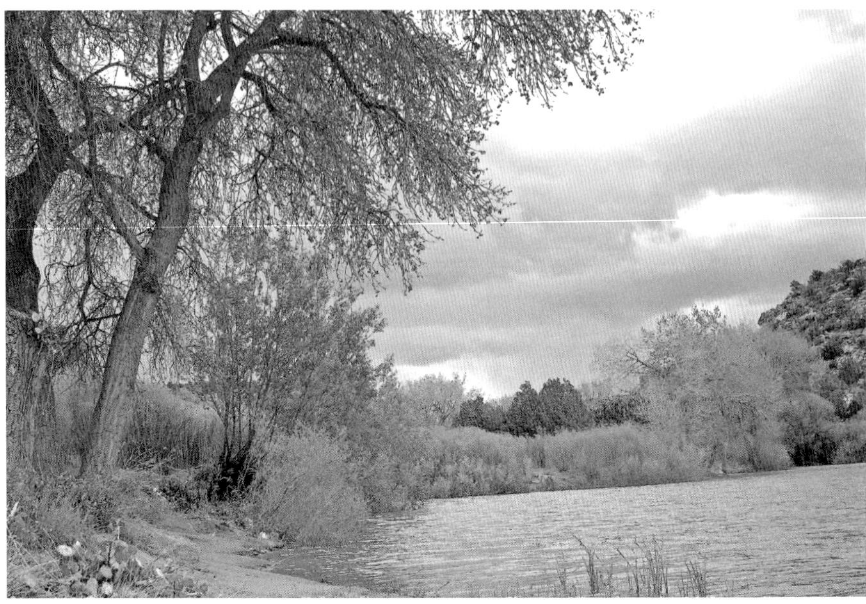

On the Hopi reservation, peaceful areas invite individuals to sit and enjoy nature. This picture shows the natural vegetation and water found in this semiarid desert region. *Photograph by Rory O'Neill Schmitt, all rights reserved.*

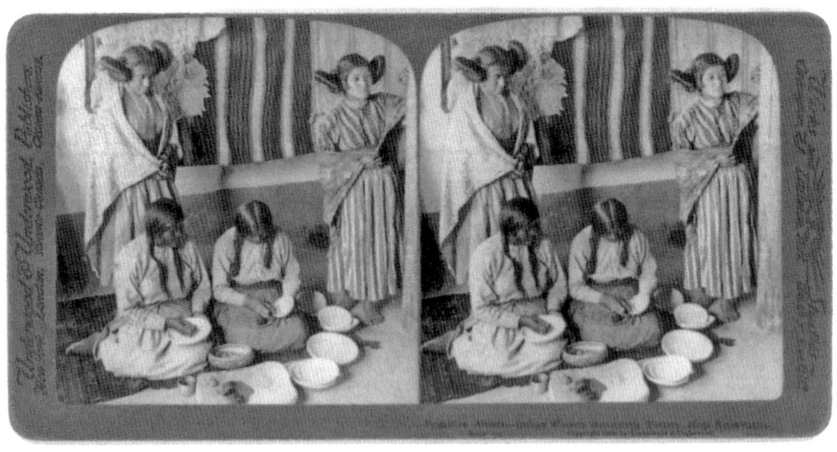

The two Hopi figures standing (in background) wear squash-blossom hairstyles. In the foreground, two Hopi women create pottery. "Primitive Artists–Indian Women Decorating Pottery, Hopi Reservation, Arizona" was created by Underwood & Underwood in 1903. *Courtesy of the Library of Congress, all rights reserved.*

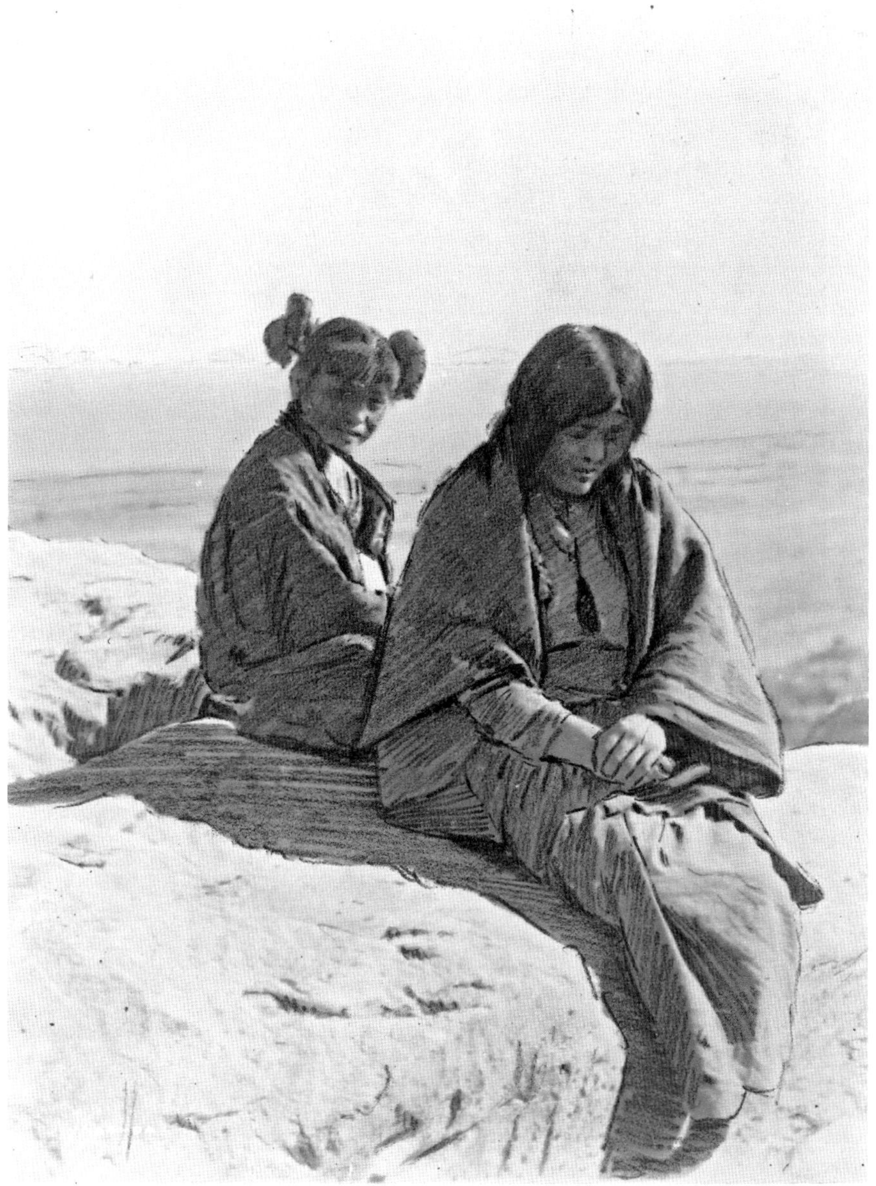

In 1905, Edward Curtis photographed two Hopi women seated on a cliff and titled the photograph "Maiden and Matron." *Courtesy of the Library of Congress, all rights reserved.*

on the changing seasons, to which the cycle of ceremonies is connected. In a special underground chamber, called a *kiva*, Hopis hold religious rituals and participants wear special traditional textiles. Some villages permit non-Hopi people to attend select ceremonies. Hopis pray for rain, for the crops to grow and for the well-being of all of the living.

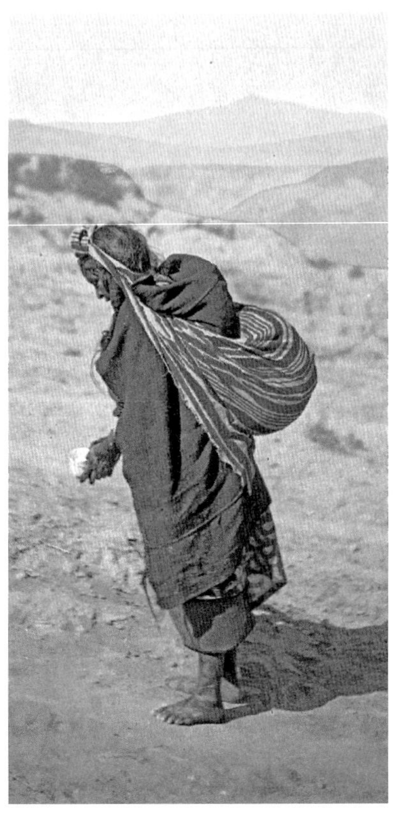

"Patient Toil, Moki Pueblos, Arizona" was published by the Detroit Photographic Co. between 1898 and 1905. *Courtesy of the Library of Congress, all rights reserved.*

Hopis have a clanship system. A clan is considered a family, as it has common ancestors who are linked through their migration stories and matrilineal lines. Each of the thirty-four clans of the Hopi people holds particular duties, and each person has specific responsibilities. In their matrilineal society, gender often dictates responsibilities. When a woman and man marry, the husband moves to live near his wife's clan, and he also has some responsibility to his own clan mother. Women own the homes and gardens, and men take care of the herds and farms. Though residing in the semiarid desert, which receives about eight to ten inches of annual rainfall, Hopis are master farmers. Many grow beans, melons, cotton and corn. Corn is staple food and has special ceremonial significance. Different kinds of corn—such as blue, white and yellow—are traditionally used in Hopi ceremonies. For example, in Walpi village, blue corn is used at the child's naming ceremony.

As their homeland, or Hopiland, was somewhat isolated geographically, Hopis have been able to practice their own religious life. Though Franciscans established missions in Hopi villages during the Spanish colonial period of the 1600s, Spanish influence did not seep into their culture. Rather, Hopis overthrew their Spanish oppressors and drove them back to Mexico in the Pueblo Revolt of 1680. Fearing retaliation, Hopis retreated to the three mesa tops to become more defensible.

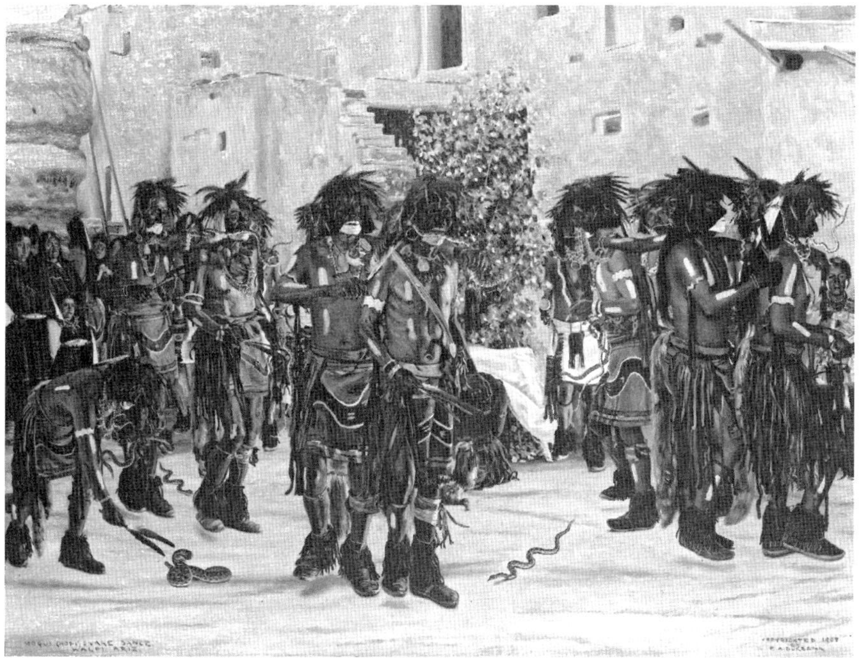

"Moqui (Hopi) Snake Dance, Walpi, Arizona" was created in 1909 by Elbridge Ayer Burbank. *Courtesy of Library of Congress, all rights reserved.*

Figure 3: A Hopi Tribe Timeline

AD 1000	Hopis' ancestors, Hisatsinom, migrate to northeast Arizona. They are farmers.
1300s	Hopis become skilled weavers, using cotton.
1500s	One of the oldest cities in the United States (that is still in existence), Old Oraibi, is established in 1550. Spanish arrived.

1600s	Franciscans establish missions in Hopi villages. Hopis overthrow Spanish in the Pueblo Revolt of 1680.
1700s	Hopis experience conflicts with neighbors and struggle to maintain their homeland.
1800s	The federal government sets aside land for the Hopis by executive order in 1882.
1900s	Hopis experience land disputes with Navajos. In the 1970s, the government of the United States establishes the Joint Use Area and Partitioned Lands.
2000s	Around seven thousand people reside in Hopi villages today.

In their history, Hopis had conflicts with nomadic Navajos, who were migrating south and were scavenging and raiding on horses. Navajos took food, material goods and Hopi women and children, which created considerable animosity between the groups. After the signing of the Treaty of Hidalgo in 1848, the U.S. government took control of the Hopi-Navajo conflict. The army attempted to eliminate Navajos, which they considered to be a problem, eventually leading to the Long Walk to the Bosque Redondo concentration camp years later. In 1882, Congress sought to resolve the Navajo-Hopi conflict by designating an Executive Order Reservation for Hopi; however, some Navajos continued to settle on the Hopi reservation. More of their homeland was later returned to the Hopi people. In the 1970s, the government of the United States established the Joint Use Area and Partitioned Lands; however, many Hopis considered this land allotment inadequate; Hopis were given only a fraction of their ancestral homeland while the Navajo lands were expanded. The land conflict continues to be a sensitive issue for many Hopis. The Navajo Nation bounds the Hopis' 2,500-square-mile reservation on all sides.

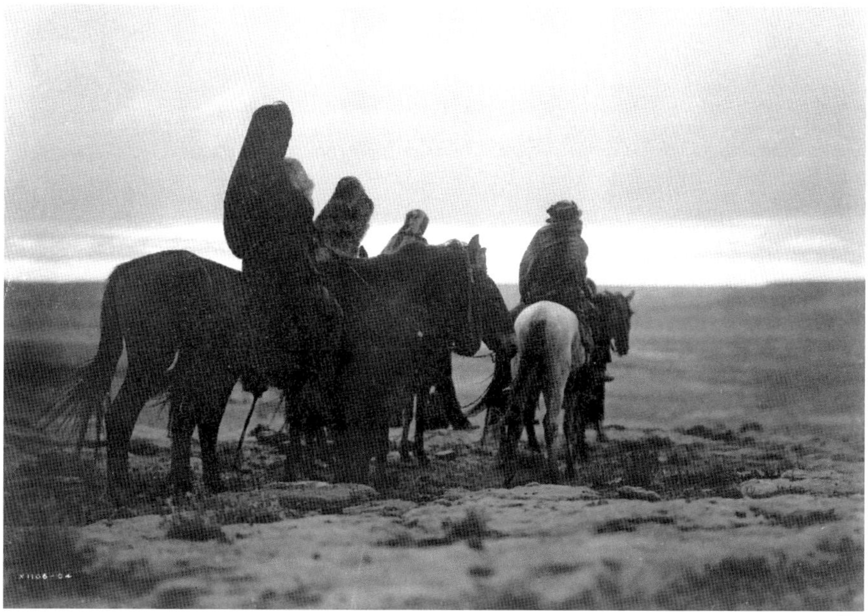

In 1905, Edward Curtis created "The Dawn of Day." In the photograph, a group of Hopis on horseback look out toward the horizon. *Courtesy of Library of Congress, all rights reserved.*

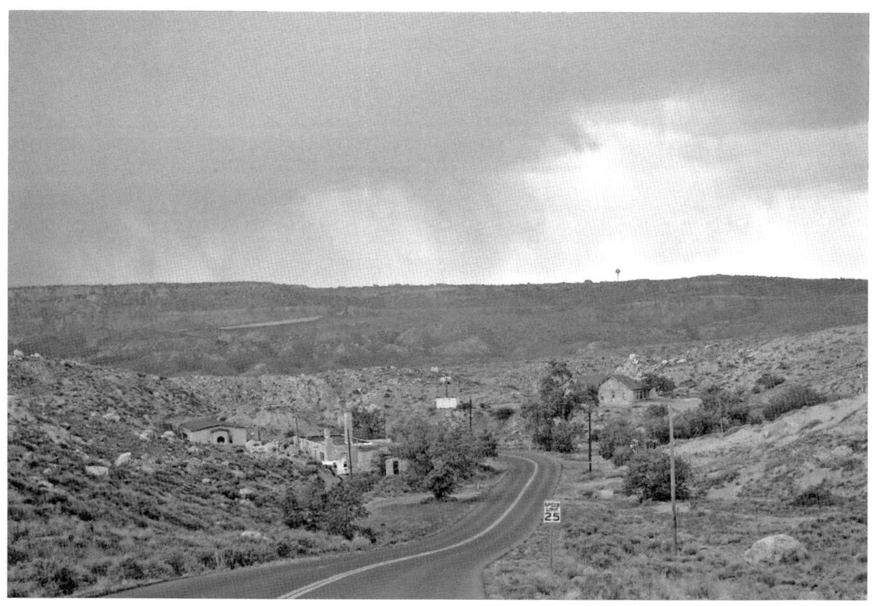

A main road on the Hopi reservation winds through the towns and up the mesas in the distance. *Photograph by Rory O'Neill Schmitt, all rights reserved.*

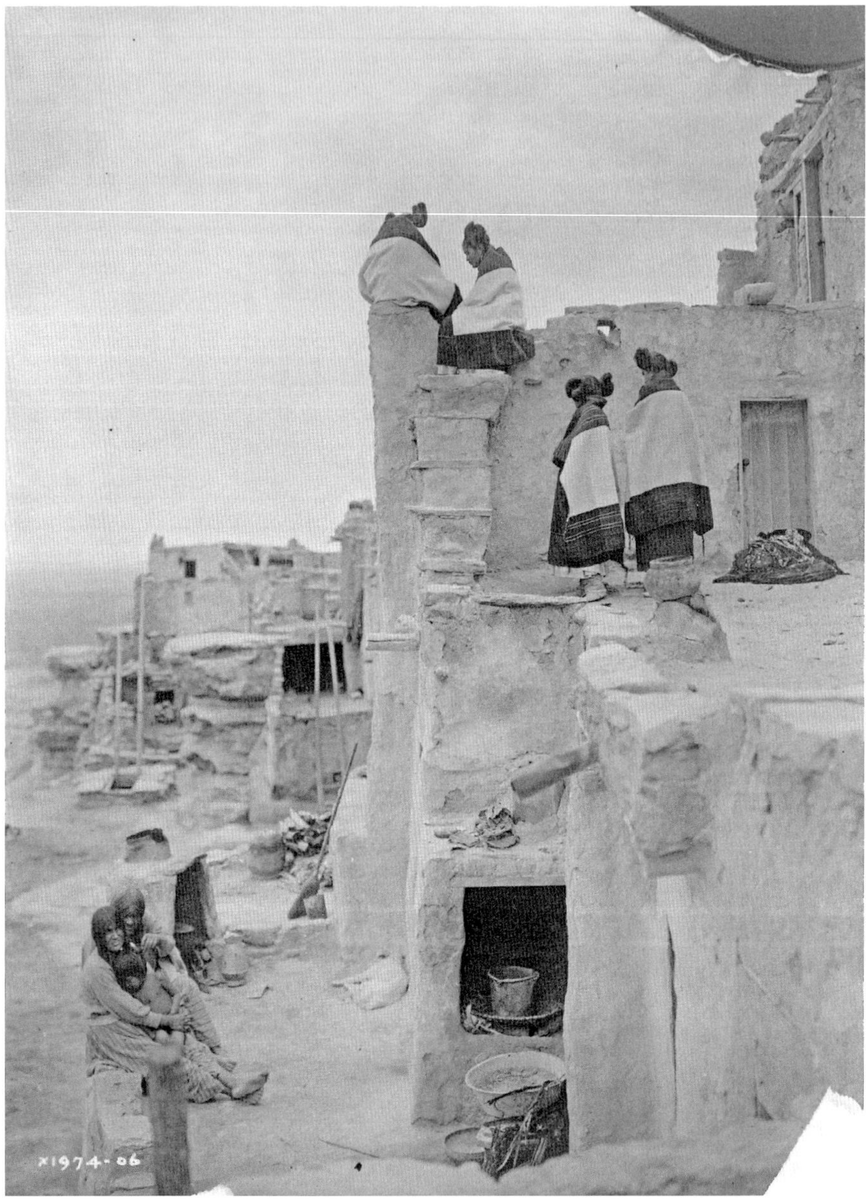

This 1906 photograph, "On the Housetop—Hopi," shows mesa-top living environments in Hopiland. The photograph was created by legendary artist Edward Curtis (1868–1952). *Courtesy of Library of Congress, all rights reserved.*

On the Hopi reservation, located exclusively in Arizona, about seven thousand people reside today. Many make their livings from farming and herding while others create and sell artworks to support their incomes.

HOPI ART

Throughout their history, Hopi peoples have created artwork; however, there is no equivalent word for "art" in the Hopi lexicon. Art forms include weaving, pottery and basketry. Traditionally, there has been a gender basis for the types of crafts created by Hopis. Since the 1300s, men created the cotton textile weavings and carved katsina dolls. They wove ceremonial garments, such as sashes, wedding robes, belts, and leggings. They also created a manta, a women's traditional black dress. When the Spanish introduced sheep, Hopi weavers began to use wool.

While Hopi men create weavings, Hopi women make pottery and baskets. There is a regional basis for women's crafts that continues to be in place:

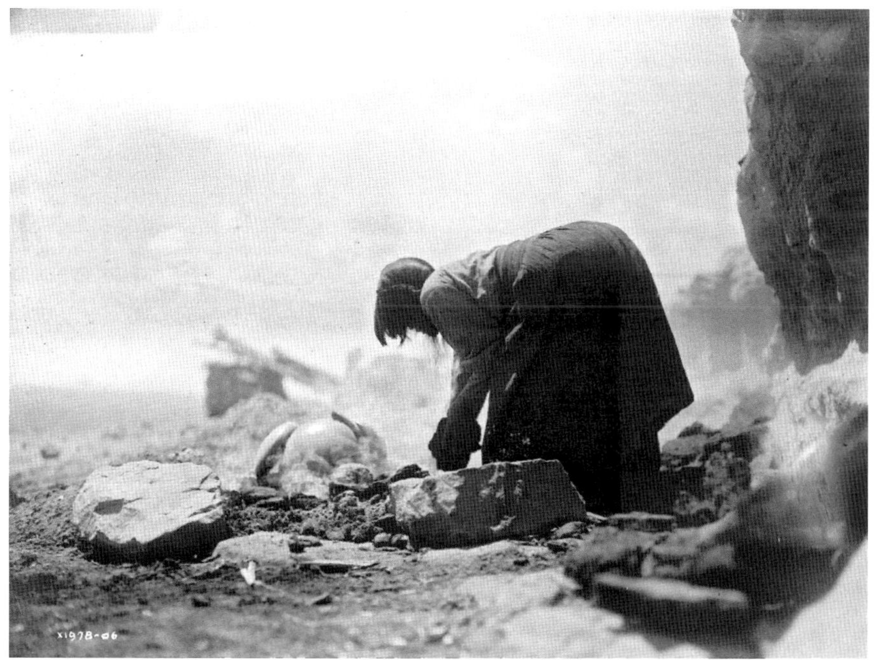

In 1906, Edward Curtis photographed this Hopi potter building her kiln. The potter, Nampeyo, is known for reinvigorating this art form. *Courtesy of the Library of Congress, all rights reserved.*

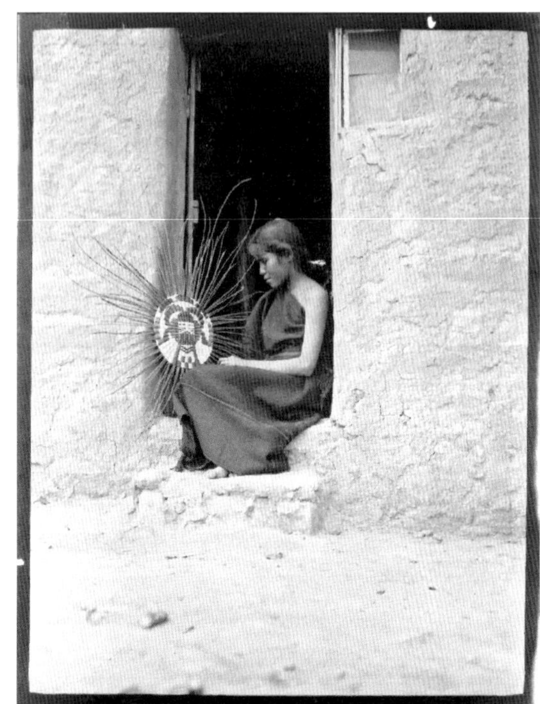

Right: "A Hopi Basket Weaver" was published by the Detroit Publishing Co. in 1910. *Courtesy of Library of Congress, all rights reserved.*

Below: Edward Curtis photographed a Hopi female potter in 1900. *Courtesy of the Library of Congress, all rights reserved.*

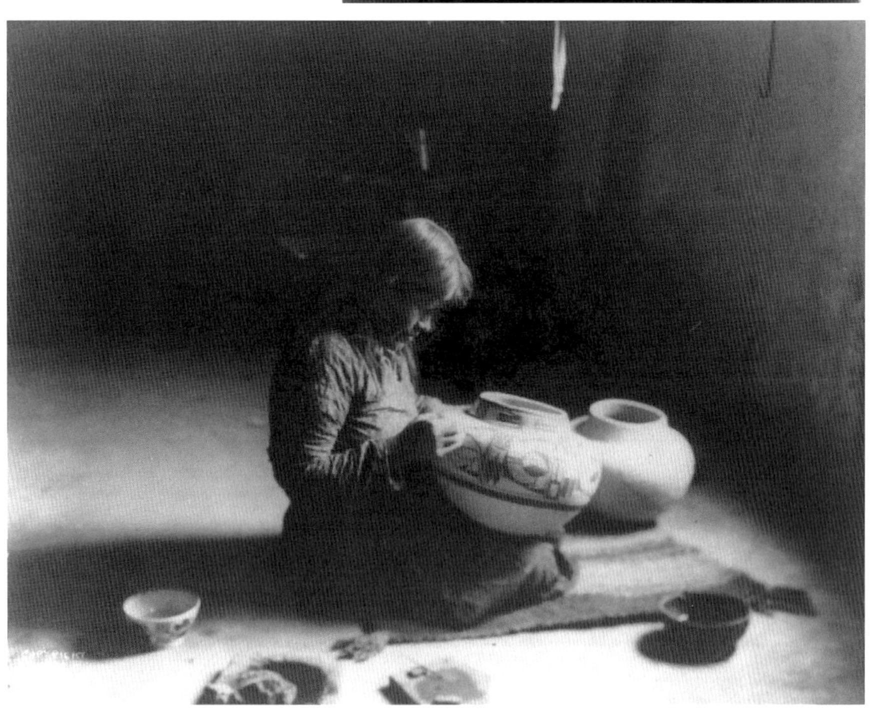

On the First Mesa, women make pottery. On the Second Mesa and Third Mesa, women create baskets. On the Second Mesa, women craft coiled plaques; on the Third Mesa, they construct wicker plaques, some of which have elaborate patterning and geometrics. Many plaited baskets are used as sifters while wicker and coiled baskets are utilized as ceremonial trays.

The renaissance of fine pottery was attributed to Nampeyo (1859–1942), a Tewa-Hopi woman of the First Mesa. An excavation at Sikyatki, a fifteenth-century site, led to the discovery of superior wares of craftsmanship and design. Sikyatki Polychrome (1300–1600) had been the height of Hopi ceramic arts. Prehistoric potsherds were technically excellent and beautifully decorated, featuring flamboyant decoration with flowing designs and conventionalized life forms. Nampeyo compared the poor quality of turn-of-the-century pottery to these prehistoric styles. She developed a new style based on fragments of black-on-yellow pottery found at the ancient site. These ceramics influenced pottery in the late twentieth century to today, with such design features as birds, wings and feathers. Nampeyo's family dynasty has made First Mesa the exclusive center for creating traditional pottery.

As this book features katsina doll carvers and contemporary jewelers, the following section examines those two mediums in further detail.

Katsinas and Katsina Dolls

Katsinas play an important role in Hopi religion. Katsinas, or *katsinam*, are ever-watchful invisible spirit beings. These spiritual essences live in nature, where they listen for the people's humble prayers and songs. Katsinas reveal themselves to the Hopi people through nature, in such forms as eagles, corn, trees and clouds. In public plazas and kivas, these benevolent spirit beings visit ceremonies as masked dancers to support Hopis' prayers for health and rain. Over 250 katsinas exist, each identified by an individual name, and they depict animals such as hummingbirds, deer or imagined creatures from December to July. The *Niman Tikive* is the going-home ceremony. Katsinas take the people's prayers with them and go to their spiritual home in the San Francisco Peaks.

While katsinas distribute bows and arrows to boys during dances, they give katsina dolls to girls. A katsina doll, or *tihu*, is a reward for virtuous behavior. These special objects are a rite of passage for girls, who receive them until they are initiated around the age of eight or nine.

A katsina doll is made in the likeness of the katsina; they are carved, painted, adorned and clothed to show the katsina's specific roles. They are teaching tools that reinforce the beliefs of the Hopis; children learn about katsinas by being exposed to the katsina dolls. They are often displayed in the family's home and serve as a reminder of the specific teachings. A katsina doll is also *paaho 3*, a prayer offering for the child. Each represents a blessing for growth, health and fertility. These objects are mostly made from cottonwood roots, which embody spiritual prayers for growth.

Traditionally, the carving of katsina dolls is taught to men, who receive special katsina initiation rituals. The initiated have privileged knowledge about the carvings, which is passed down from generation to generation. Boys learned weaving from their male relatives: father, grandfathers and uncles. As carving dolls has spiritual importance, the carver's mind must be positive so that the *tihu* has positive energy.

Evidence of katsina dolls can be found in decorations on pottery, in petroglyphs, and in murals painted on kiva walls, some of which date back to 1300. As more non-Hopis witnessed katsina ceremonies during the 1800s, interest in these katsina dolls grew. However, misunderstandings about katsina dolls increased, as well. Outsiders perceived katsina dolls as toys and talismans.

Originally, the body design of a katsina doll was a simple representation of the katsina. The focus was on the facial features and head, and the katsina doll appeared stiff and not lifelike. Old-Style katsina dolls were singly carved from cottonwood root with minimal carved ornamentation, using a few simple tools. Carvers used plant-based and traditional clay pigments in earth tones. They adorned katsina dolls with feathers of nonmigratory birds, as well as leather, strings, fur and hair.

As the art form evolved in the later nineteenth and early twentieth centuries, more attention was placed on the body, legs and arms as separate parts. As more and more technology became available, artists created realistic details using finer tools. They carved katsina dolls in refined positions, resembling motion, action or dance. Carvers also used brightly colored commercial paints, such as watercolors, acrylics, poster paints and stains. Katsina dolls became complex, highly stylized sculptures. Most recently, per collectors' requests, some carvers have begun signing their name or clan symbol to their works.

Jewelry

For ages, Hopis have celebrated beauty and honored nature through the creation of objects for rituals and body adornment. Designs added pleasure to the experience of using and wearing items. Prehistoric Hopi jewelry, such as strings of beads, bracelets and ear pendants, was made of bone, turquoise, stone, wood and leather. Hopis also incorporated seashells, which they traded from the Mexico, Texas and California regions. It wasn't until the arrival of the Spanish in the 1500s that the Hopis began to use metal in their jewelry. Later, in the 1890s, Hopis learned silversmithing from a neighboring tribe, the Zuni (Zunis had learned silversmithing from the Navajo about twenty years prior). Many Hopi silversmiths used the Navajo silver-turquoise style of jewelry.

Following World War II, Paul Saufkie and Fred Kabotie organized a GI training program, which was an eighteen-month program in jewelry-making on the Hopi reservation. Hopi jewelers learned the overlay technique and further developed their own unique Hopi jewelry style. In overlay, the jeweler cuts a design into a thin sheet of silver, blackens it for accent and then places it onto a solid piece of sheet silver. Hopi jewelers highly refined the overlay process and infused traditional Hopi pottery images into the designs.

Legendary Hopi Artists

Fred Kabotie

Fred Kabotie (1900–1986) grew up on the Hopi reservation in Shungopavi, Oraibi and Hotevilla, where his family encouraged him to celebrate their Hopi culture. Creative even as a child, Fred sketched katsinas on rocks and walls of abandoned buildings with charcoals. At the time, Hopi and the American federal government relations were strained. While "friendlies" were American Indians who complied with assimilation efforts, "hostiles" were those who fought to maintain their native ways of life. As a child, Fred Kabotie was forced to go to an Indian boarding school in Santa Fe, as American Indian assimilation was a goal of the federal government. If Hopi children didn't go to school voluntarily, police officers took them by force. Fred's parents wanted to maintain their traditional values. His father was jailed because he avoided sending his children to boarding school.

While at Santa Fe Indian School, unsympathetic school personnel taught Fred to discard his Hopi beliefs, become Christian, participate in a regimented life, learn practical vocations and speak English. However, the wife of the school superintendent, Elizabeth DeHuff, encouraged Fred to paint whatever he wished with watercolors. He painted memories of his Hopi homeland, including the katsinas. Later, Fred illustrated books she wrote, such as *Taytay's Tales: Collected and Retold* (1922).

Fred developed his talents as a painter, and his artwork was later exhibited in several museums. In the 1930s, commissioned to create murals in the Watchtower of the Grand Canyon National Park, Fred painted traditional Hopi symbols and scenes. He influenced later artists, who came to use the Kabotie Style of adding perspectives. He would paint a splash of dark color under the feet of figures, defining a sense of space. In his complete village painting scenes, he scattered figures in different positions, thus breaking up the composition of severe lines of repetitive dances.

Fred's commitment to his Hopi community can be seen in his acts of service. He instructed art at the Oraibi School on the reservation for twenty-two years (1937–59), organized the Hopi Silvercraft Cooperative Guild (1940s) and served on the Hopi Cultural Center Board of Directors as president (1960s).

Charles Loloma

Fred Kabotie trained Charles Loloma (1921–1991), who would become another legendary Hopi artist. Charles grew up in Hotevilla on the Third Mesa and attended high school at the Phoenix Indian School. He always loved creating artwork, including composing drawings, watercolors and murals. Following his deployment in World War II, Charles returned home and used the GI Bill benefit to study at Alfred University, the leading university for ceramics. He was the only American Indian student there at the time. While there, he learned many components of pottery, drawing, design and marketing. Charles's processes as a potter, such as creating unusual surface treatments and using experimental glazes, seamlessly translated to the jewelry methods he would use in the future.

Charles's sculptural jewelry is crafted of exotic stones, wood and rare gems pieced together like a puzzle. His Hopi homeland inspired architectural shapes in his jewelry. When constructing these jewelry pieces with mosaics of stone, he would consider how it would look from above, below and sides, as well as the inside. He noted the importance that the wearer brings to the piece.

Known as the most famous American Indian jeweler of his time, Charles continues to be an influential artist to many. Loloma paved a path for contemporary artists to overcome rejection in the 1950s that thought untraditional work wasn't "Indian enough." According to author Louis Jacka, Loloma was "readily acknowledged as the grand master and leader in contemporary jewelry art." Charles was a Hopi jeweler who transformed expectations of what Hopi jewelry should look like.

Closing

This chapter introduced the history, art and culture of the Hopi peoples. Like other native artists, Hopi artists remain committed to celebrating their culture and creating works in beautiful ways. The following chapters pay tribute to exemplary Hopi living artists who transform expectations of original art: jewelers Verma Nequatewa and Piki Wadsworth, katsina doll carver Manuel Chavarria Jr. and glass blower and poet Ramson Lomatewama.

11

VERMA NEQUATEWA

At Home on Third Mesa

As you drive to the Hopi reservation, you can see the mesas, small mountains with flat tops. Roads are more like narrow, windy lanes. Turning your head to the left or right, you can look off the mesas and down into the canyons and see small stone houses and remnants of past buildings. It is beauty, breath-taking beauty. Here, there are no gas stations or rest stops. Road markers are used as the addresses for homes. There's a simplicity of life with the lack of retail stores—less distraction, less focus on consumption and consumerism.

Verma Nequatewa's property in Hotevilla consists of several small brown buildings with purple trims overlooking a cliff of Third Mesa. Large solar panels can be seen from the highway, marking her home. To this day, many homes on the Hopi reservation do not have electricity. Verma explained that she installed solar paneling as not everyone on their mesa wanted electricity and preferred to live the lifestyle the people had used for hundreds of years. Her land consists of her personal residence, which is connected to her studio, a workshop, storage and an office for her husband, Bob Rhodes. There's a patio outside her studio with a jaw-dropping view. Looking out over the expansive canyon, you can't help but realize how large the world is and how small you are.

Coming from a large family of eight children, Verma was born in Hotevilla on September 11, 1949, to Hopi parents Wilson and Peggy Kaye. Coming from an artistic family, Verma's mother wove wicker plaques and her father carved katsina dolls. Deeply immersed in Hopi tradition, Verma has always followed Hopi ways of life daily.

Around the year 1966, when she was a teenager, Verma began apprenticing with her uncle (her mother's brother) Charles Loloma. For over two decades (1966–91), she worked alongside this esteemed jeweler as an apprentice, an assistant, a co-worker and a collaborator. She described:

> *He would maybe construct the piece, the metal section of it, do something. And, then I would maybe do the inlay work. At first, it was a mosaic and it was pretty rugged at the time but that was the learning part. So,* [while] *working together, he would kind of watch me* [and say,] *"Okay, well maybe* [add] *a little color or something."*
>
> …[And, we would go] *just back and forth. We had our benches next to each other."*

Verma wore an exquisite bracelet inlaid with dark blue lapis from Afghanistan and turquoise from Arizona. She explained that this collaborative artwork, which she had created with Charles Loloma, was "both of ours." He remains close to her.

Verma was drawn to follow in her uncle's footsteps. He was a trailblazer in the field of Hopi jewelry, as his cutting-edge style differed from traditional Hopi overlay techniques. Charles straddled two worlds: participating in clan responsibilities in Hotevilla and traveling internationally for his art exhibitions. Along with being a renowned artist, he was also leading her along with his teachings. She said:

> *Uncles* [are] *supposed to lead you along and tell you—that's the Hopi way, actually. Just staying with him* [while] *some other kids don't. They try something here, and then quit that and go to something else. But just being there, and just continuing to work with him…*
>
> …[He would be] *telling me to create a piece and just letting me do it. Then, I'm saying, "Oh, I don't know how. I can't. I don't think I can do it."*
>
> *But the thing he tells me is, "How can you say you can't do it if you haven't tried it?"*
>
> *That's really true…Just trying it and if it comes out what you wanted it to do, or if it was a casting and it comes out really nice, that really makes*

you feel good. [And you think,] *"Oh, then I'm going to try it again." And then again, and again.*

Charles used positive encouragement to motivate her development as a jeweler. He would say to her, "Oh, wow, this is so great. Let's do it this way. Maybe you can do it this way next time." She explained that his teaching method "makes you want to do even better or to design something different."

Verma is active with her responsibilities of her Badger and Butterfly clans, and fulfilling her duties to her clans is paramount to her. She carries out special tasks in regards to tribal ceremonies. One important responsibility for Verma's clan, and in the past for her uncle Charles, deals with home dance. She balances her ceremonial responsibilities with her jewelry-making. Verma's commitments to the Hopi community are a key part of her identity. Hopi comes first; jewelry comes second. In fact, when I was scheduling a studio visit, the artist and her husband noted that they were waiting to hear about the day of a summer dance in Hotevilla and would let me know her availability once they found out.

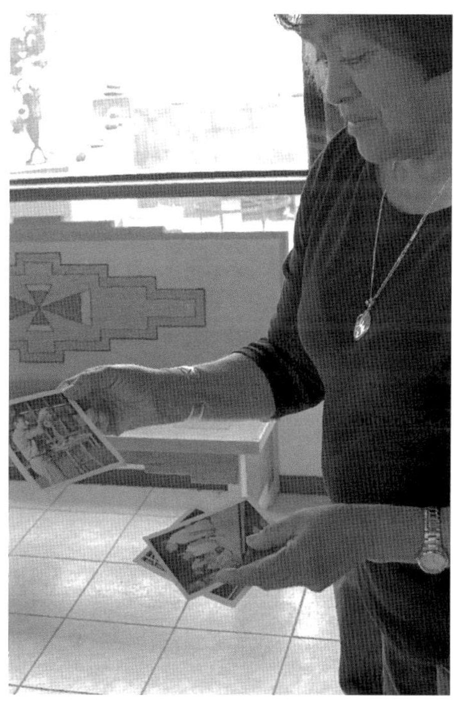

In her studio, Verma Nequatewa shows historical photographs of an Egyptian friend of Charles Loloma who created busts of Verma and Charles. *Photograph by Rory O'Neill Schmitt, all rights reserved.*

Verma also is grateful to be able to have a career and remain at home. Beauty surrounds her and inspires her artwork. She explains how she absorbs inspirations for her designs from nature: "Taking walks out at home and seeing what's on the outside, just the environment in itself. You point out certain things…look at the shapes of the mesas and the rocks, or even a plant that comes out with a nice little flower…There's all these little designs in a leaf or a tree or a plant, and pointing those things out, that's part of nature."

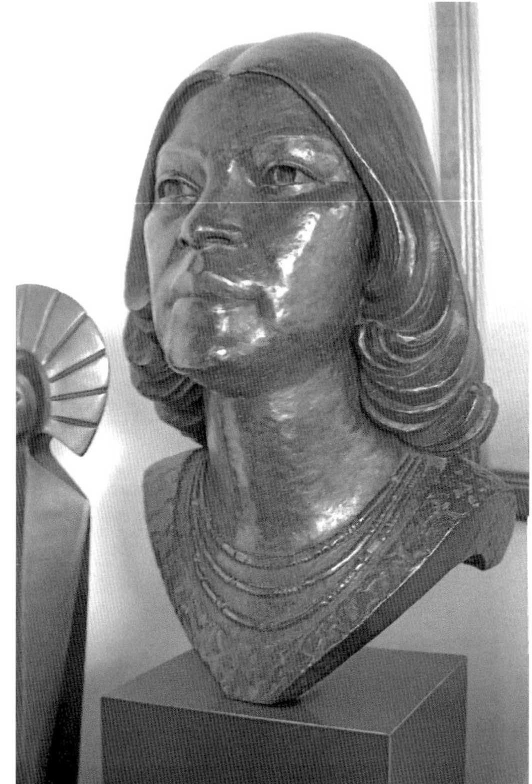

Right: Pictured here is a sculpture of Verma Nequatewa on display in her studio. Verma's art collection includes legendary and emerging artists. *Photograph by Rory O'Neill Schmitt, all rights reserved.*

Below: Famous Chiricahua Apache sculptor Alan Houser (1914–1994) gifted this sculpture to jeweler Charles Loloma (an uncle of artist Verma Nequatewa). *Photograph by Rory O'Neill Schmitt, all rights reserved.*

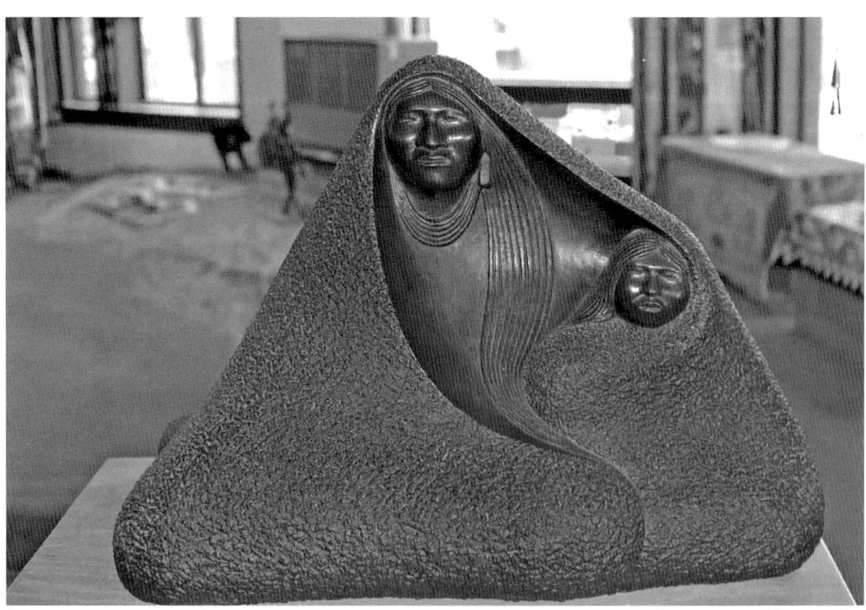

From her uncle, she learned the importance of the uniqueness of every piece of jewelry. Loloma set the highest standards and used the finest of materials. Examining rocks while on walks, he would point out that interesting material surrounds them.

Following a tragic car accident, Charles Loloma retired from jewelry-making. However, Verma remained at home and continued to make jewelry. She started her own company, Sonwai, which is a female form of *lol'ma* in the Hopi language. In the Badger and Butterfly clans, it is the female word for "beauty, pretty, exquisite." She described the transition of working with her uncle to working alone. She said, "It's not that bad. I'm missing him, yes, of course. But then knowing that his teachings and all, you work even harder and you have to aim more for the end zone. I know this is what he wants me to do, and I'm always working. It's a…real job. I don't do jewelry just when I feel like it. It's like an everyday kind of thing. I treat it like a real job."

Verma met her husband, Bob Rhodes, while he was a doctoral student in education at Arizona State University, and they married in 1977. Bob has worked with Hopi schools and has authored books on education and Hopi culture, including *Hopi Wicker Plaques and Baskets* (2007), *Nurturing Learning in Native American Students* (1994) and *Hopi Music and Dance* (1977). Verma has one son, Bryson Charles Nequatewa (born in 1967), who is a glass artist and traditional katsina doll carver. Bryson lives nearby and has two daughters, Alicia Jean and Lorene Rose.

Artistic Processes

Verma's technical process require patience and dedication to detail. She grinds, cuts and polishes stones. Materials include fossilized ivory, coral, opal, sugilite, Lone Mountain turquoise, lapis, ironwood, vermillion wood, ebony, jade, sugilite and other precious gems. She places stones in a line, called a corn row inlay, like Loloma did. She also utilizes tufa-casting methods that she learned from him. Tufa casting involves using molds of tufa, pumice-like hardened lava rock, which gives a unique texture. Her style, noted by its simplicity, elegance and vibrant colors, is a subtle progression from Loloma's. In silver and gold, she produces unique rings, belts, pendants, bolas, buckles, earrings, pins, necklaces and bracelets. She described her artistic processes:

> *This is constructed...from a sheet of gold...Then you solder your bezels on it and shape it, the metal section and the area where it's going to be inlaid, and solder the little piece on it here...We were working mostly with rough materials, like the turquoise that we buy in rough and lapis, and then cutting our own stones, shaping them. It's a lot of lapidary work, inlaying, and then he teaches you the colors, what color would work really* [well] *next to each other or bring out the colors. I guess it's kind of like painting, so all of this is all hand done...All of ours is all hand done and shaped, then the stonework. It takes a lot of time, but that's what it takes. You have to have patience—a lot of patience.*

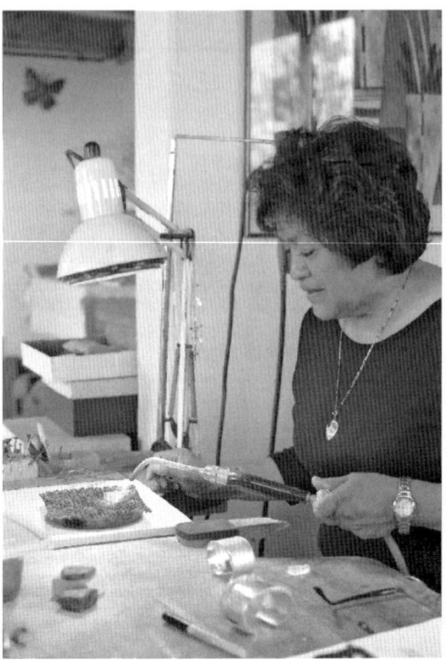

Verma Nequatewa adeptly demonstrates soldering jewelry in her studio. *Photograph by Rory O'Neill Schmitt, all rights reserved.*

Verma described the complex tools, solder torches and diamond-cutting machinery in an elegant way that made it seem they were easy to use. She selects a stone, grinds it to see what the true color is, shapes it, creates the tufa-stone casting for the frame (bracelet, necklace or whatever piece of jewelry she is making) and then glues the perfectly polished and sized stones. Her humility is considerable as so few people in the world today can produce such exquisite jewelry pieces.

Additional Information

Verma's artwork has been exhibited at several esteemed institutions, including the Heard Museum (1997, 1999, 2000, 2002, 2005, 2006 and 2011), the Arizona Historical Society Museum (2002), the Kentucky Art and Craft Gallery (1998) and the Institute of American Indian Arts Museum (1997). Verma has received numerous awards from the Southwestern Association for Indian Arts' Santa Fe Indian Market (1995, 1996 and 1998) and the

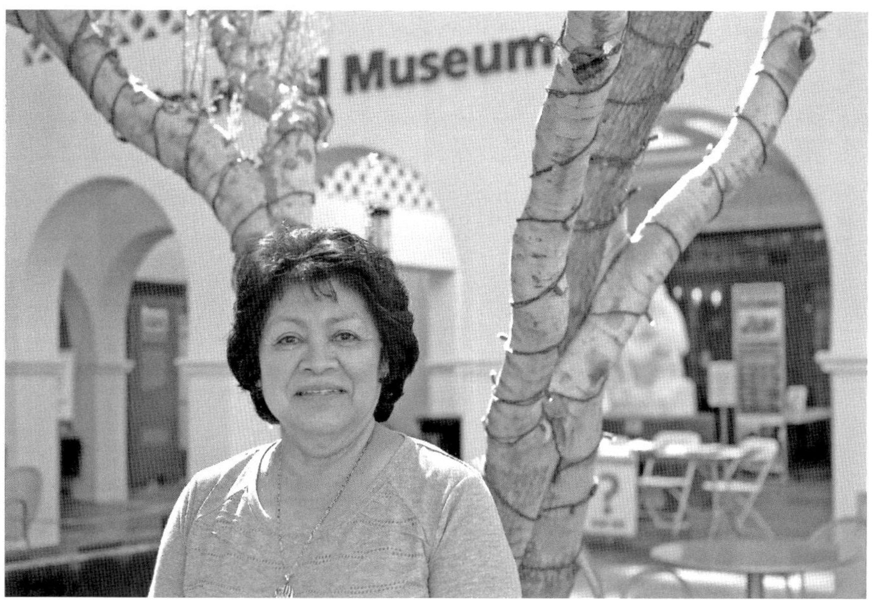

Verma Nequatewa is pictured here at the 2015 Heard Museum Guild Indian Fair and Market. An exhibit of a relative's legendary artwork (Charles Loloma) called "Loloma: Expressions in Metal, Ink and Clay" was on display at the museum. *Photograph by Rory O'Neill Schmitt, all rights reserved.*

Scottsdale National Indian Arts Exhibition (1972 and 1974). Collectors can purchase Verma's jewelry from the Sonwai website (www.sonwai.com), Faust Gallery in Scottsdale and Shiprock in Santa Fe.

12

PIKI WADSWORTH

GREEN VALLEYS

Emerging artist Piki Wadsworth was born at home on April 25, 1980, to jeweler parents, Cheryl Yestewa and Glenn Wadsworth. One of nine children (three boys and six girls), she was raised in Camp Verde, Arizona, a place where you feel enveloped by nature, grace and beauty. Piki described growing up as "busy. I was the third oldest so I helped out a lot. All of us older girls helped raise the younger kids." While the six eldest siblings were homeschooled, the three youngest children attended public school. This year, Piki's sister is graduating from high school and will be the first in the family to attend college by enrolling at Northern Arizona University. With her siblings, Piki is rooting for her success and accompanied her sister to fall college orientation.

Piki's mother is Hopi-Navajo and grew up in Phoenix. Cheryl introduced Piki to her native heritage through bringing her to visit her relatives on the First and Second Mesas of the Hopi reservation. Piki would enjoy going to ceremonial dances and spending time with her maternal grandfather, Carol "Cal" Yestewa. Cal was a katsina doll carver, known for his clown katsina dolls with watermelons. In fact, his artwork is a part of the Smithsonian Museum's collection. Until her grandfather's death in the mid-1990s, Piki visited the reservation quite frequently. With a name referring to the traditional Hopi piki bread, Piki takes pride in her heritage. She is extremely honored to belong to a tribe that is known for being a peaceful people.

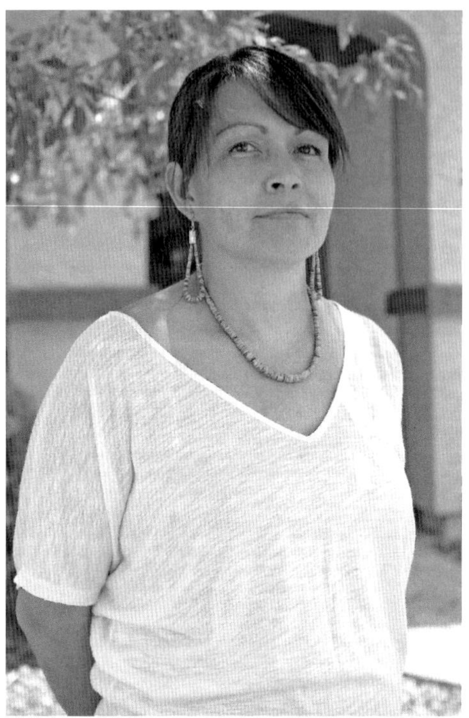

On a summer day, Piki Wadsworth stands outside a friend's home in Clarkdale, Arizona. *Photograph by Rory O'Neill Schmitt, all rights reserved.*

Piki described her Anglo father as "very hardworking" Glenn is from Rock Springs, Wyoming, but met Cheryl in Cave Creek, Arizona. Piki explained that her parents decided to become jewelers together and taught themselves the craft. She said, "He was a welder. And then he met my mom, and they kind of just brainstormed and said, 'Let's make jewelry.' My dad bought some turquoise and some jewelry equipment…and started making jewelry…They just picked it up and started doing it."

Piki's parents became world-renowned jewelers, silversmiths and bead makers, who hold the highest standards. Their artwork has been collected by the Smithsonian Museum and the Heard Museum and has been featured in *Arizona Highways* magazine and in Annie Osborn's 2012 book, *Turquoise: Jewel of the Southwest.*

Cheryl and Glenn taught their children the craft, and as a child, Piki would assist her parents with creating jewelry next to them on their workstation bench. She said, "I used to help my mom drill when I was really little, and then string beads and then graduate, which is like taking, say, a strand of beads, and graduating is taking it from one size and working it, bigger to smaller. I've grown up around turquoise my entire life." All of her training was gained from careful observation of her parents. When her parents asked how she learned, she told them: "I watched you."

Piki treasures childhood memories of accompanying her parents to Indian Market Days and shows in Santa Fe and Phoenix. When she was only eight years old, she sold her first pieces of jewelry: seed earrings made of small glass beads. She can still remember the name of the gentleman at the Heard Museum who purchased her seed earrings: Byron Hunter. Piki shared:

> *We've been going to the Heard, ever since I can remember. We would play outside while my mother went inside to do business. I first started making seed bead earrings when I was eight. My mom would help me sell them. It was so memorable to me because I would get my own check and felt so grown up. That was my first taste.*

PIKI, EMERGING JEWELER

As Piki was starting as a jeweler, Piki would prepare the turquoise beads and string the necklaces. As she was not familiar with how to do silverwork, her parents would initially finish her pieces for her and offer advice for improvement. She progressed in her skill set and decided to learn silverwork. She shared, "I watched my mom and dad. And then one day, I was like, 'Quit being afraid of the torch.' Because it is kind of intimidating, afraid you're going to burn something, melt something…One day, I picked it up and made a ring—that was my first, my first quest." Since then, Piki has excelled in her mastery of silverwork.

Piki's parents have supported her career as a jeweler. She said, "I'm really lucky because my mom and dad are really well known. And when I started making beads, my mom introduced me to all of her people. She took me in and said, 'Oh, my daughter is one of nine kids; she's just starting.'" Cheryl taught Piki about the business of jewelry. Piki described her mom as "an amazing people person." She stated, "She would just go into these places, not knowing anybody or anything, and take their stuff in there and try to sell it…It takes a lot of guts…just [to] go in there."

FOR THE LOVE OF TURQUOISE

Piki is one of a few female bead makers and is perhaps one of the only female Hopi bead makers. She creates jewelry in the traditional style and bases her designs on inspiration that she gets from the turquoise stones. She uses the highest-grade turquoise stones, in their perfect natural and rough form. All natural materials are never dyed, treated or stabilized, as her parents encouraged her to use materials that were not treated or processed with chemicals. Turquoise exists in incredibly diverse variations and colors. Piki pays careful attention to the different colors of the stone and can easily identify the mines from which they came. She pointed out the spider webbing coloration in the matrix of darker lines in turquoise from Indian Mountain. She said, "I've just always loved it, the color. It's amazing how it comes out of the ground, and just, so many different colors, and it's an amazing stone. My most favorite is probably Sleeping Beauty."

In addition to the Sleeping Beauty (Arizona) mine, the Castle Dome (Arizona), Morenci (Arizona) and Red Mountain (Nevada) mines also produce turquoise. When she goes to the post office to pick up a package of stones, the post officer often says, "It feels like you have a bunch of rocks in here." She replies, "Actually, it is."

Her Hopi culture influences her artworks. For example, one turquoise necklace holds three corn pieces at the center. The corn pieces are flattened turquoise stones or spiny oyster shells, which are shaped liked kernels. Central to Hopi life is corn, which is, indeed, sacred.

Viewing Piki's jewelry, one can note the family resemblance to her mother's artwork. Piki uses similar exquisite materials and reflects Yestewa designs. For example, both women have made dangling turquoise earrings on a U-shaped string, with spiny oyster shell details at the center. Cheryl is known for her high-quality beaded turquoise necklaces; she has sold over three hundred necklaces to Garland's Indian Jewelry.

Like her parents did when she was a child, Piki works from home while her children watch her. She said, "That's why I really like it. I have two children, so I get to stay at home: Savannah and Autumn...Girls are the best." Piki encourages her children to continue the family tradition. She is working on teaching her daughters how to make jewelry. She said, "I try to get them to do it, but they're not [interested]—even when I was little, we weren't interested in it.

Piki sits at a workstation that her father welded and uses equipment from her parents, who have retired. Her station is exactly like her parents' stations. They made extras, hoping that one day one of the children would make jewelry. Appearing similar to a drafting table, the station has orange metal legs, a tabletop with a lower shelf, and a metal border frame. A bright lamp is clamped onto the edge, providing extra light for her to examine stones and complete the silverwork. Often, when Piki works in her outdoor studio during Arizona summers, she has to take frequent breaks to cool off.

Dedicated to a highly labor-intensive process, Piki hand-shapes, drills and polishes the turquoise to form beads. Recently, a client ordered a triple-strand necklace, which will require six hundred beads. Piki's process for creating turquoise jewelry is a testimony to her commitment to having the highest-quality materials and the highest expectations for them. Her process includes the following steps:

Additional Information

Piki is proud to be an Arizonan and appreciates the beauty and creativity of the landscapes, the sunsets and, of course, the jewelry. Piki's love for jewelry-making has enabled her to pursue this art form despite any obstacle. In the past, she cleaned houses during the day and made her jewelry at night. Presently, she is pursuing jewelry-making as a full-time career. While some clients commission jewelry via contacting her on her Facebook page, Piki Wadsworth Jewelry, most of the jewelry she sells is through galleries across

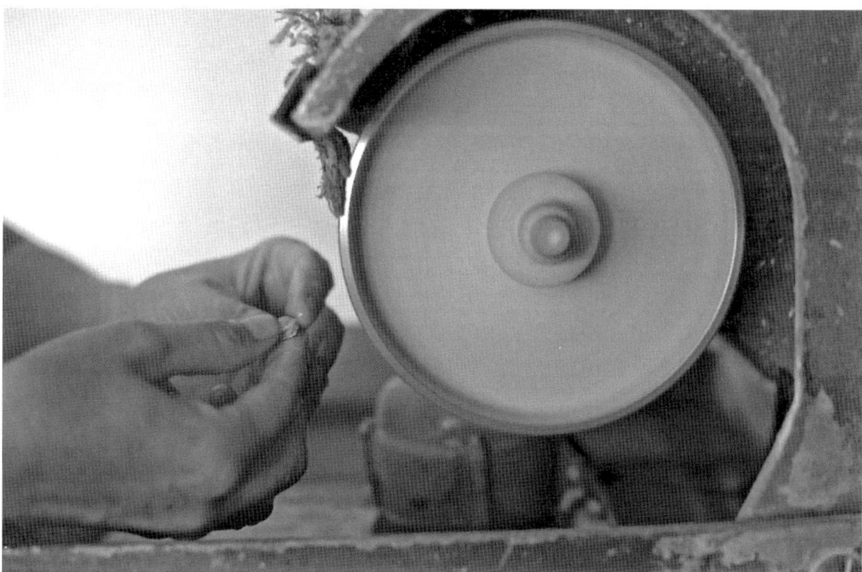

Piki Wadsworth carefully uses a grinder to polish, round and smooth the edges of turquoise stones. *Photograph by Rory O'Neill Schmitt, all rights reserved.*

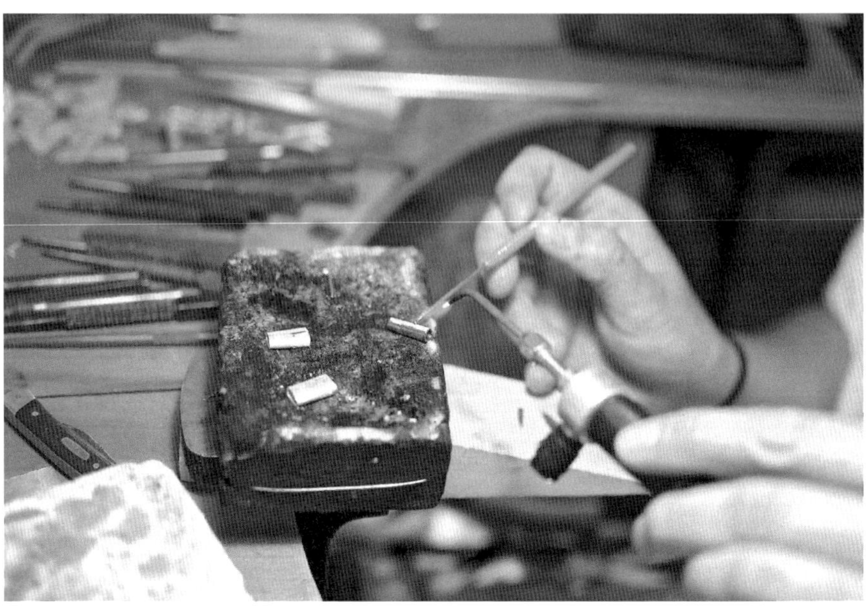

Piki Wadsworth skillfully solders silver cones that will be used to cover the ends of a strand of turquoise beads. *Photograph by Rory O'Neill Schmitt, all rights reserved.*

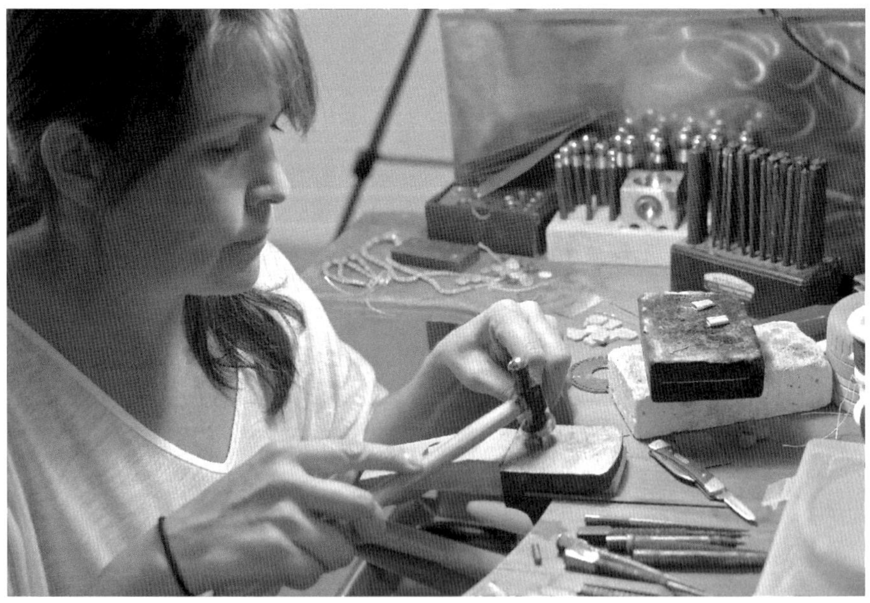

Piki Wadsworth uses a small hammer to shape sheet silver for her jewelry. *Photograph by Rory O'Neill Schmitt, all rights reserved.*

the country, including Faust Gallery and Territorial Indian Arts & Antiques (Scottsdale), the Heard Museum Gift Shop (Phoenix), Hoel's Indian Shop and Garland's Indian Jewelry (Sedona) and the Indian Craft Shop (Washington, D.C.). Piki is thrilled when her jewelry sells and recognized: "Somebody liked it enough to cherish it and buy and love it."

13

RAMSON LOMATEWAMA

Early Life

Ramson Lomatewama was born on October 20, 1953, in Victorville, California. When he was about seven years old, his family moved to Flagstaff, Arizona. Growing up, he lived in two different cultures. While he spent most of his childhood growing up in Flagstaff, he enjoyed weekends and summers on the Hopi reservation. As a teenager, he learned how to carve katsina dolls. Carving in the Old-school style, he uses traditional tools and materials, such as obsidian blades, hand-spun cotton and mineral paints.

After graduating from high school, Ramson studied premedicine at Northern Arizona University. When he realized he was not pursuing goals that were true to his heart, he stopped attending. He worked in various jobs, including as an exterminator, a salesman and a restaurant manager. Gaining a deep realization that his culture affected his own identity, Ramson turned to creative writing to express his culture and himself. In 1979, he attained his associate's degree from Northland Pioneer College in Holbrook, Arizona. In 1981, he earned his bachelor's degree at Goddard College, a small liberal arts school in Plainfield, Vermont. He worked as a junior high school teacher on the Hopi reservation instructing sixth through eighth grades.

With his wife, Jessica, a blue ribbon award–winning Hopi basketry artist, he lives on the Hopi reservation in Hotevilla, where he spends much time participating in ceremonial rituals. Jessica creates traditional wicker baskets

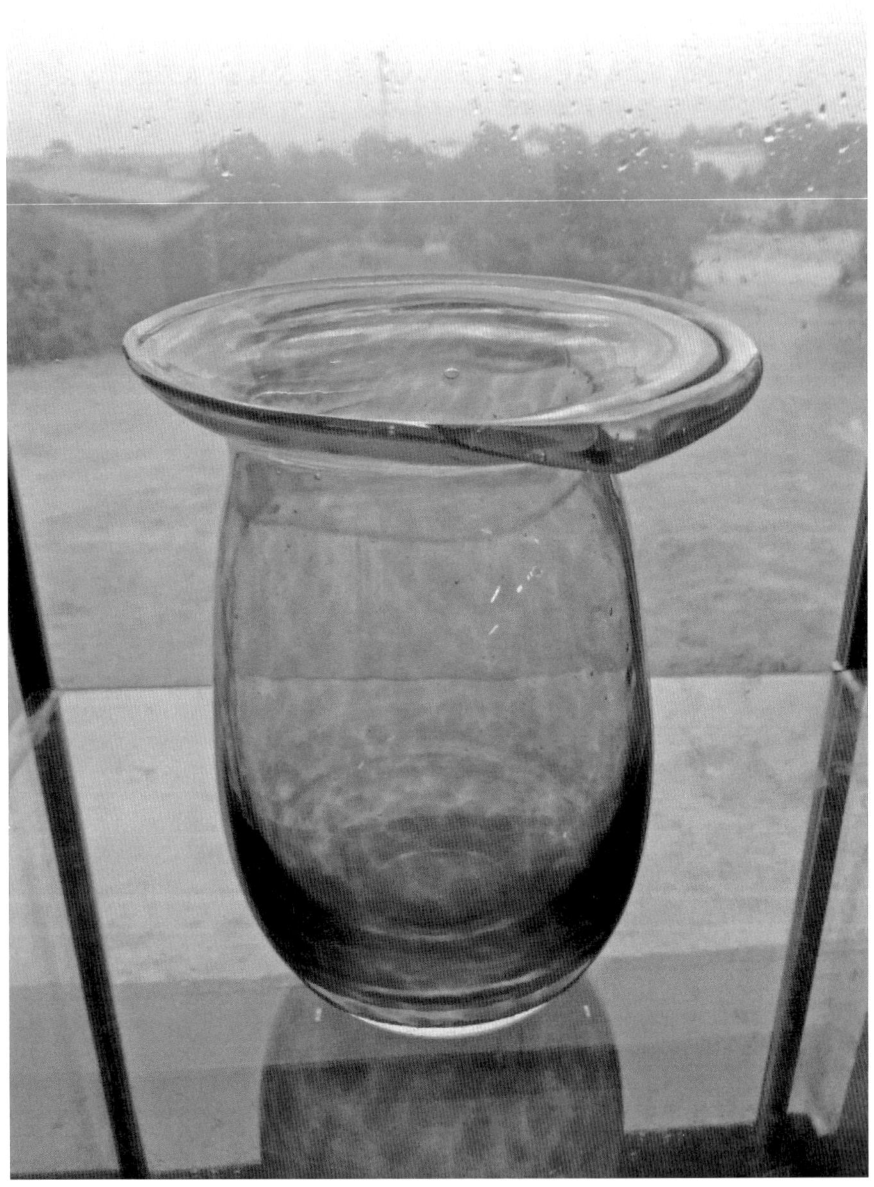

Pictured here is an example of Ramson Lomatewama's exceptional glasswork. *Courtesy of Ramson Lomatewama.*

of the Third Mesa. Knowledgeable about Hopi basketry, she has presented at various museums, including the Museum of Northern Arizona, the Southwest Museum and the Santa Fe Indian Market. A teacher, she has taught courses on the role of women in Hopi society and has instructed art courses at Idyllwild Summer Arts program for several years.

DISCOVERING HIS CALLING

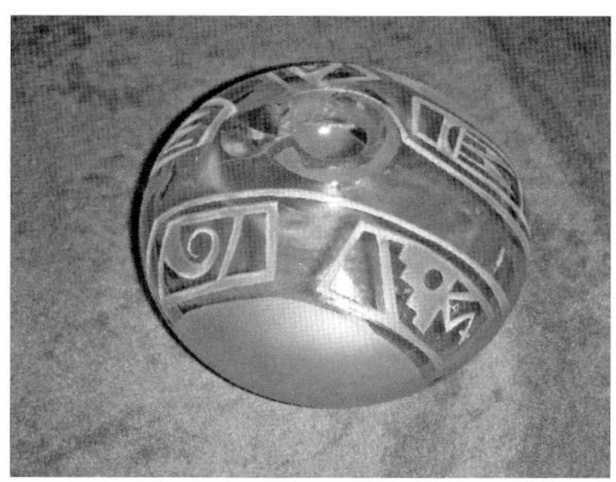

Ramsom Lomatewama creates geometric and organic designs on his sandblasted glass pottery. *Courtesy of Ramson Lomatewama.*

Ramson has been blowing glass for over twenty years. He was first introduced to this art form when visiting the Corning Museum of Glass in New York. The movement of the artists and the fluidity with which they worked inspired him. He stayed until closing and when the security guard was escorting him out, he asked, "So, did you enjoy what you saw today?" Ramson responded, "Yes, I think I found my calling." While clay work is seen as a female art form for Hopis, glass blowing is not a traditional art form that gender dictates. He chose to explore a new way.

DEVELOPING AND TEACHING HIS TECHNIQUES

When people ask if he is a self-taught artist, he replies that he can't teach himself something that he doesn't know. Rather, he is a "self-learned" artist. Ramson continues to develop his techniques through trying out different practices, as well as watching artist videos on YouTube. He noted that he has probably about forty hours of formal training, including a one-week workshop at a Tucson studio twelve years ago and an artist residency at a glass school in Washington State about twenty years ago. He has also learned from brief encounters with master glassblowers. He said, "I'm blessed by learning another art form. I've been doing glass blowing for over twenty years, but I'm still learning. I'm constantly reinventing…I'm learning new techniques. I watch YouTube all the time because you learn some techniques for working glass. I just kind of allow myself to be bombarded by all these new ideas. All the while I try [to] keep connections to the culture."

Ramson teaches glass blowing workshops, including a range of classes from a two-hour session to a two-week session. For the last twenty years, he has been part of a program called the Horn School of Arizona's Fine Arts Festival, where he teaches glass blowing to high school students. His latest project is with the Idyllwild Arts Academy in California. He is helping the school build its own glass blowing studio, where he will teach.

Ramson is deeply connected to the fears that students have when beginning to learn how to make glass works. He tells his students, "There's a lot of fear here with hot glass. You're going to have a fear of getting burned. You're going to have a fear of the heat. You're going to have a fear of being not understood. You're going to have a fear of miscommunication. You're going to have a fear of failure." Ramson's classes are about overcoming fear first and glass blowing second.

Ramson's Art

Ramson creates stunning glass artworks. His glass art is rich in color and movement. Examples of his artworks include hand-sculpture forms, such as spirit figures, inspired by his Hopi culture. He also makes glass artworks that are his interpretation of prehistoric rock found in the Southwest. He integrates aspects of his culture into his work. For example, there is cultural significance in the colors that are contained in a piece. Artwork expresses the cultural ideas that he was raised with and communicates important images of Hopi people.

His media includes leaded stained glass, acrylics and pastels and traditional Hopi weaving. Leaded stained glass has historically been a European medium. Through his art, he may be bringing together American Indian and European cultures. Found in his Artist Profile at the Heard Museum Library is Ramson's quote:

Ramson believes that, through viewing art, people gain a greater appreciation of the world around them; they respond to their environments and reflect on their spirituality. Art enables growth on the inside. Art is a catalyst for moving forward. Through art, people can learn about others and

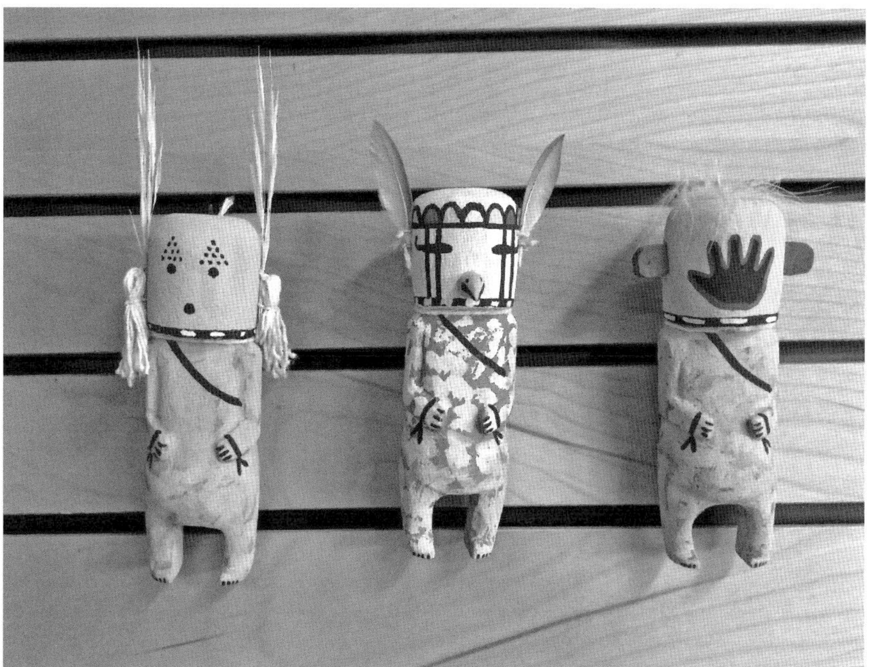

Ramson Lomatewama carves katsina dolls using traditional processes. *Courtesy of Ramson Lomatewama.*

open their minds to new expressions and new art forms, new ideas. Through his glass arts, he maintains a connection to his culture.

Ramson said the purpose of his art is to alleviate pain and find wisdom. He shared, "Basically if someone looks at one of my glass pieces and has a mini epiphany, and it just touches something in them, then I've done my job. They don't even have to like [it] because I look at glass art and all art as part of the human problem. As far as I would like to look at things, everybody has a certain degree of being. If I can have my artwork alleviate a small degree of that pain and help them a little bit closer to healing, then I've already done my job as an artist."

Viewers find meaning in artwork based on their relationship to the artwork. He finds that sometimes people project their feelings onto his glassworks. All art is a healing process. Ramson explained, "I think everybody is looking to have a greater appreciation of the world around them in terms of them relating to other people, them relating to their environment, them relating to their own concept of spirituality. My art form is there to practice a jumping off point. To me the artwork and what it does for a person's growth on the inside is more important than anything else."

A loyalist, Ramson is dedicated to respecting and practicing Hopi cultural beliefs and traditions. Ramson lives his Hopi cultural beliefs. An example is his long dark hair, which he has worn for many years. For Hopis, hair is symbolic of rain; they believed that long hair could lead to more rain. Aspects of his culture, such as the colors of the four cardinal directions and Hopis' friction with Navajos, are incorporated into his artworks, as well.

Ramson finds inspiration in life. He said, "I don't know if I could pinpoint to any one thing or even several things because I get my inspiration by waking up every day and looking at the world around me. Looking at landscapes here on the reservation. Looking at our history. All these things are, I guess, taken into my art and into my inner being. Through the glass arts I'm expressing all of those."

He wakes up and sees the landscape on the reservation. He appreciates life. Art reflects his inner being.

Ramson has been an exhibiting fine artist for over twenty-five years. His work has been shown in solo and group exhibitions, including at the following locations: Museum of Craft and Folk Art (2002), Eliteljorg Museum (1990), Lovena Ohl Gallery (1990), Coconino Center for the Arts (1989), Museum of Northern Arizona (1989, 1988), Tlaquepaque Plaza (1989), Yuma Art Center (1988) and National Handicrafts and Handloom Museum (1986). He has been given several prestigious awards, including the Arizona Senator's Arts Award from the American Indian Arts Foundation. He has also won best of division, first place and honorable mentions at the Hopi Show at the Museum of Northern Arizona.

A Poet and an Educator

All cultures share four common elements—values, laws, language and the arts. And although each facet has value in its own right, it is through the arts that we gain more understanding of those values, laws and languages; those ideas which make up the roots of all people. As an artist, my continual search for a greater appreciation and respect for others an only come through the practice of my own creativity. It is with this in mind that I have chosen both the visual and literary arts to broaden my quest for greater awareness.

Ramson has two written books of poetry, which were published by Badger Claw Press: *Ascending the Reed: Poems by Ramson Lomatewama* (1987) and *Silent Winds: Poetry of One Hopi* (1983). Later, he self-published *Drifting through Ancestor Dreams* (1993). In his poetry, Ramson describes nature and feelings. *Silent Winds* poems reflect Japanese haikus in their brevity and visual organization. Several of his poems, which are written in English and Hopi languages, have been published in newspapers, magazines and anthologies. He has led poetry readings and conducted writing workshops in New England, the Midwest and India. While Ramson spends about three-quarters of his life on making art, he spends the remaining time writing poems.

In the 1990s, Ramson worked as the Heard Museum's Artist on the Road, teaching poetry and creative writing to youth. This educational program promoted awareness and understanding through exposure to, and involvement with, native artist instructors. Ramson traveled to different schools throughout Arizona, in order to promote a better understanding of the native cultures to students in grades three through twelve. He supported the program in lessening misconceptions and prejudices about American Indians, stereotypes that were often based on movie depictions. He used his background for students to compare it to their own, and increase their awareness of self and other.

Who Are Hopis?

Ramson wants readers to learn that Hopis today are like anyone else and they also belong to a culture in transition. He said:

> *Number one, we're people just like anyone else. Our culture is in transition 24/7. We're not living in the 1800s anymore. It's 2015. One thing that I learned early on when I got into glass blowing was when I had my work set out in my booth, people would come and think, "Gee, this isn't an Indian art." It was a matter of people putting us in shoeboxes. If you're a Native American artist, you do porcupine quill work. You do basketry. You carve katsina dolls. You do this. You do that. I really believe that* [for] *a culture, art is the catalyst for moving forward.*

Additional Information

Ramson consults for international museums, including one in Japan, where he headed in 2015. He also leads university and museum lectures every so often. He frequently travels with his mobile glass blowing vehicle that is attached to his car as a trailer, participating in demonstrations at festivals and workshops around the country. His artwork can be found in galleries and stores, including at the University of Northern Arizona Museum, the Heard Museum gift shop, Bryce Canyon National Park and the Gilcrease Museum. He may be contacted via e-mail at lomatewama@yahoo.com or by visiting his Hotevilla Glassworks studio.

14

MANUEL CHAVARRIA JR.

Artist at an Early Age

A Hopi-Mexican, Manuel grew up in Phoenix but spent much time with his grandparents on the Hopi reservation. At an early age, Manuel knew that he wanted to become an artist. He admired his grandmother Savannah Denet, whom he described as: "A traditional Hopi potter, [who was] using traditional materials, traditional paints [and] firing traditional [processes]. She made painted pottery, I guess they call it polychrome pottery, when she was younger. And then as she got older, she started losing her eyesight, so she started making cookware…like bean pots, ladles, things like that."

As a boy, Manuel longed for his grandmother's lifestyle of participating in art exhibits in Phoenix. He shared, "I thought it was really so glamorous and just always traveling, seeing new places, meeting new people. I was like, 'Man, that's what I wanna do when I get older!'"

Additional artist family members influenced Manuel. His godmother, Ottile Jackson, taught him: "Never leave home without your tools." Ottile stressed that he could sell his artwork anywhere that he went.

Carrying on the Carving Tradition

After being initiated into Hopi society at age ten, Manuel was formally able to begin learning katsina doll carving. He carefully observed the carving techniques of his grandfather Fred Denet, as well as other male family members. They would offer him critique and give him support for whatever he needed. He said:

> *I learned the same way I taught Kevin* [my nephew], *and my brothers and my son, for one: I learned by observation, by watching and listening. Then there's simple instructions. But mainly it's just watch and learn the techniques, and then you try it yourself.*
>
> *Then, as you're going along, whoever—usually you'll carve with family members, male family members, or relatives or friends, family friends—as you go along, they'll still critique you...on whatever you need help with. Pretty much, you just learn like that. You observe, and then you get so far, and then you go on your own, and then you develop your own art style.*

Through experimenting with techniques, Manuel refined his own style. Around the age of fifteen, he came to the professional level of carvers and began to work directly with experienced traders.

Manuel spent part of his adult life in the military, but when he got out of the service in 1989, he decided to return to the Hopi reservation. He describes Arizona as his homeland: "This is our homeland. We've [Hopis] been here for thousands of years. This is where I belong and I love the landscape, the—I love everything about it...I hate people [who] come to Arizona, [and] they're like, "There's just sand and bushes!' But it's beautiful to me. I love living here. I love the—everywhere I go in Arizona. I love it. It's just a beautiful place to live. I wouldn't wanna live anywhere else."

On the Hopi reservation, Manuel married and started his own family. He resides with his wife, Marlinda Kooyaquaptewe, in Polacca. Marlinda is a traditional Hopi potter who also runs a small gallery at the Hopi Cultural Center. He has four children—Fred, Sonja, Lavonna and Angel—as well as nine grandchildren: Faylene, Eve, Alleea, Carmen, Chloe, Amaya, Kris, Marley and Andreas. During my visit, I was able to meet his kind granddaughters, who showed me their favorite katsina dolls. Outside during our photo shoot, with a beautiful sunset over a large field, the girls shared with me that the katsina dolls are indeed teaching tools. They teach them who each katsina is.

In order to support his family, Manuel sold his contemporary katsina dolls and sculptures. However, he struggled to make ends meet. He said, "You know there's not much work, so I had to start doing my art...Anyway, I had to do my art. I worked at it for a couple years, making the more contemporary

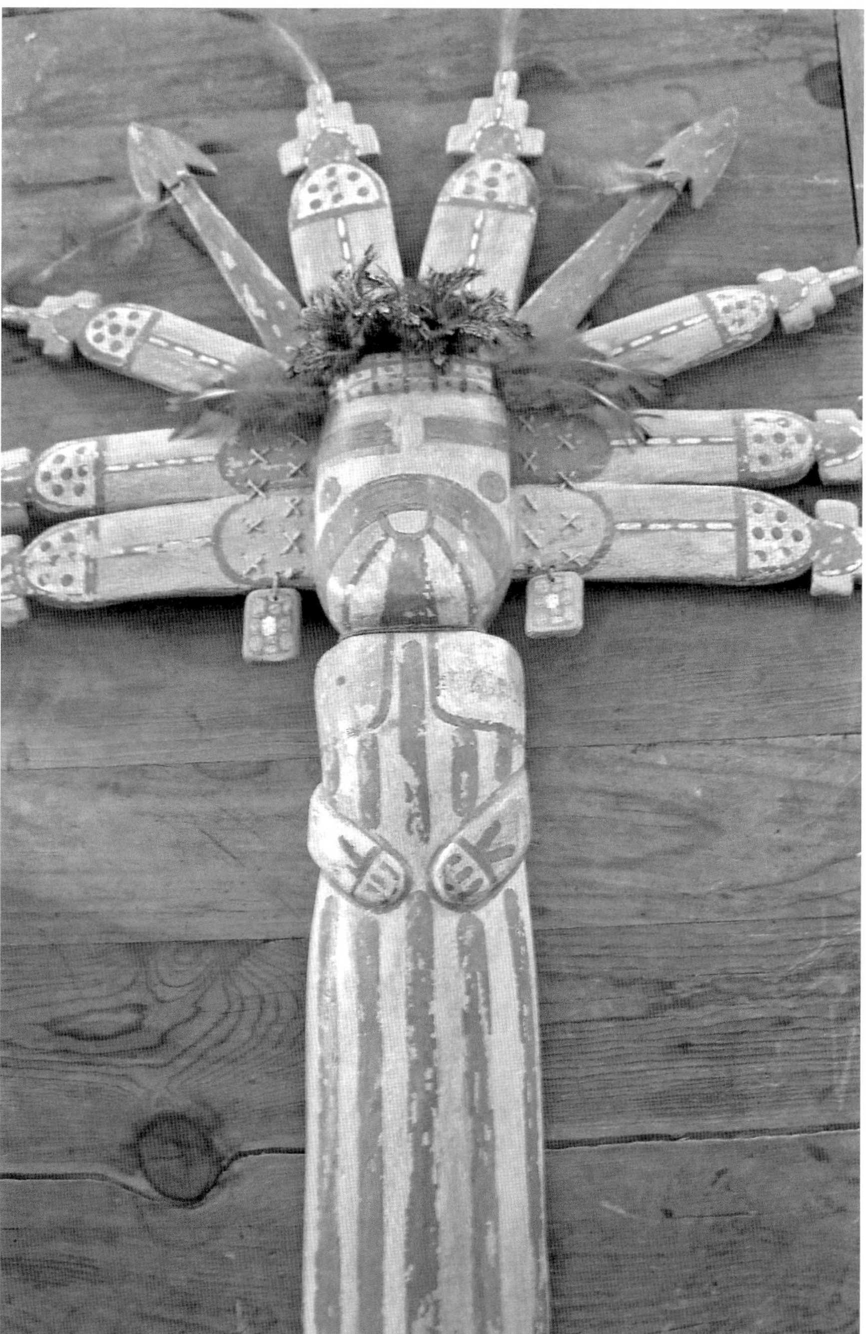

The distressed wood in this carving by Manuel Chavarria shows the artist's commitment to reviving historical techniques of katsina doll carving. *Photograph by Rory O'Neill Schmitt, all rights reserved.*

style of dolls, but they were really taking a long time—up to two weeks. I was making like $125, or something like that. And you can't raise a family on that."

In the 1990s, a trader at Second Mesa, Joseph Day, introduced Manuel to the older style of katsina doll carving. He explained, "He challenged me to make a doll. I made one in one night. I made a katsina. I remember I stayed up all night. I went and sold it to him. I sold it for $80, which was amazing to me because I made $80 in like six, eight hours. It never stopped from there. I just kept going and kept developing my style, and kept pursuing things, like being in books and—just things like that.

In 2000, Manuel was featured in a book by Jonathan Day, *Traditional Hopi Kachinas: A New Generation of Carvers*. Manuel began specializing in the Older-style katsina dolls after investigating historical katsina dolls and analyzing how to make carvings that look almost exactly like antiques. He shared, "I can just tell you like from people's reaction, they're just amazed that I made that and I just might have completed it yesterday. Because my technique, they [katsina dolls] really look old."

Though machines, such as power tools, are widely available in the twenty-first century, many katsina doll carvers prefer to use simple,

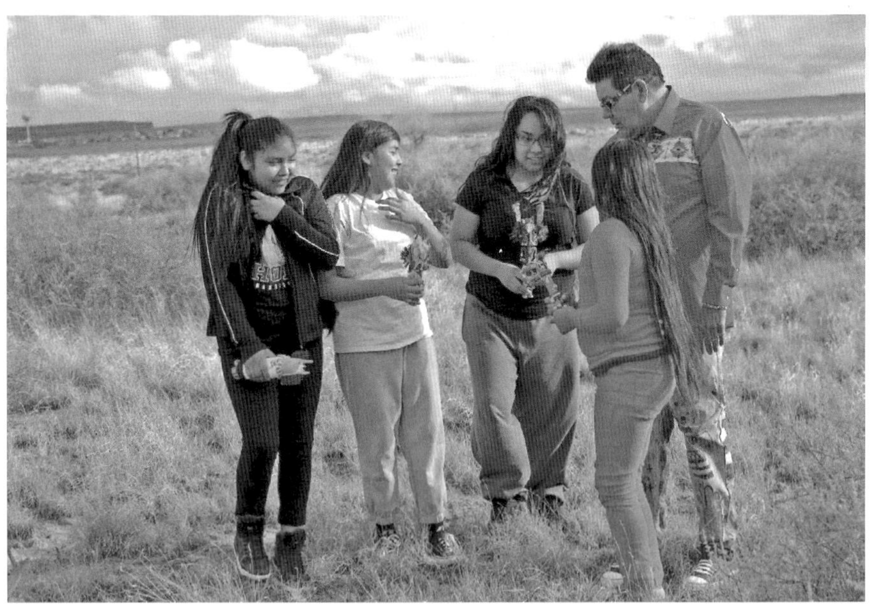

Manuel Chavarria interacts with his granddaughters outside their family home on the Hopi reservation. *Photograph by Rory O'Neill Schmitt, all rights reserved.*

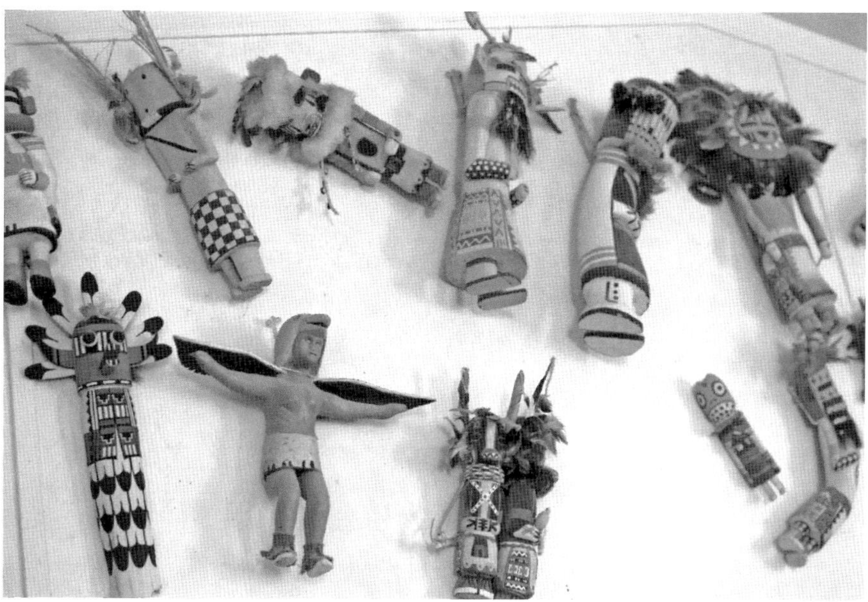

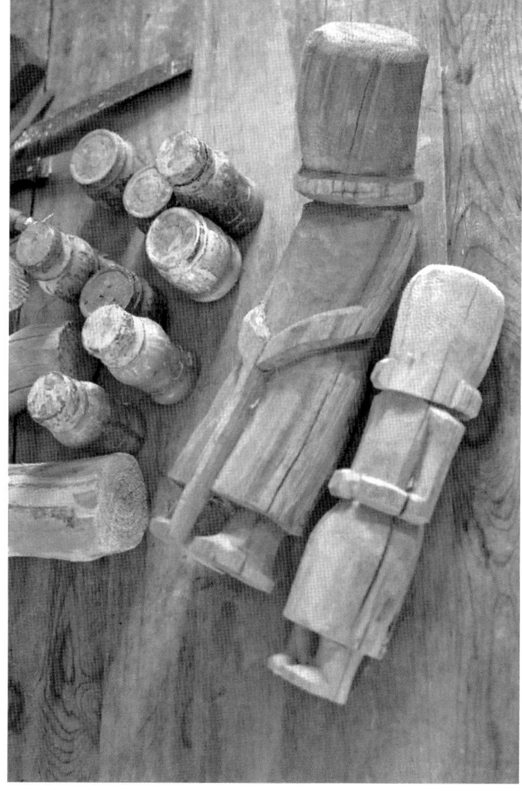

Above: Katsina dolls are displayed on the living room wall of Manuel Chavarria's home. *Photograph by Rory O'Neill Schmitt, all rights reserved.*

Right: These works-in-progress carvings show Manuel Chavarria's commitment to creating katsina dolls that resemble antiques. *Photograph by Rory O'Neill Schmitt, all rights reserved.*

This photograph depicts a sketch of the signature that Manuel Chavarria uses on his katsina doll carvings and stands for his Butterfly clan. Manuel Chavarria and Verma Nequatewa both belong to the Butterfly clan on the Hopi reservation and participate in shared ceremonies. *Photograph by Rory O'Neill Schmitt, all rights reserved.*

primitive tools. Manuel explained that he does not break any traditions in carving and is determined to continue as many traditional practices as he can. He is committed to reviving historical techniques. He said:

> *I really try to stay traditional as much as I can. I don't know why—it seems like it's so natural for me. I tried to use power tools, I tried to get modern, and I just can't. I have really primitive, simple tools. I don't know, I'm just comfortable with that.*
>
> *I don't really try to develop any new techniques. I try to revive old techniques and find old techniques, and then kind of start using those again, is what I like to do…*
>
> *I like investigating old katsinas and then reproducing them. I like looking at something and figuring it out, how that guy made—how whoever made that made it, and then reproduce it to almost exact. I don't know if you've seen any of my current work, but I do that, and they look like antiques. I've always been interested in antiques. When I first started doing traditional style, I started kinda playing around with that and trying to antique some pieces…Once I find something like that, that my customers and my friends like, I just kinda stick with and just keep going with it and keep—but I keep building on it, changing it, learning new things and then just keep building on it.*

FAMILY

Manuel is also committed to caring for his community, including those who suffer from drug and alcohol addiction. Currently, Manuel's full-time job is at a detoxification stabilization center, where he runs peer support groups.

He is also committed to expanding his worldview through studying other cultures. He said:

> *I think it's important for all people to learn about all cultures, not just to be in your own world with your own culture. Learn about people, and you can... When you learn about other cultures, you see how much we all have in common as humans...*
>
> *A lot of times, we can get caught up in our own culture and our own peoples, and we kind of think that's all there is out there and that's the only way or that's the right way. But once you start looking at other people and—you just get a broader view of things.*

ADDITIONAL INFORMATION

Currently, Manuel sells his katsina dolls in Albuquerque, New Mexico, at Corn Maiden Arts and Grey Dog Trading; in Phoenix, Arizona, at the Heard Museum Gift Shop; in Tucson, Arizona, at Bahti Arts; and online at Buffalo Barry's Indian Art. Each year, he also participates in SWAIA Santa Fe Indian Market.

FAMILY CONNECTIONS: KEVIN CHAVARRIA

Just as Manuel was inspired to pursue katsina doll carving by artists in his family, Kevin Chavarria also was inspired to pursue carving by his uncle Manuel. Born in Phoenix in 1987, Kevin spent much of his early adolescence and young adulthood in Sichomovi, a small village on the First Mesa of the Hopi reservation. As a child, Kevin attended book signings and exhibits with his uncle Manuel. He was inspired by how Manuel contributed to bringing back the traditional techniques of carving when this style was becoming obsolete.

In the evenings, Kevin would often spend time observing the carving practices of his uncles Manuel Chavarria and Larry Melendez. Larry also had extensive carving techniques, making items such as bows, rabbit sticks, dancing sticks and headdresses. He explained that his uncle would become upset with him because individuals are only supposed to learn katsina doll carving after they are initiated into adulthood. Kevin shared, "He used to work in the kitchen, and I used to go and watch him and stuff, and we're not really supposed to learn how to do it until we're initiated into higher society when you start to become a young adult. Sometimes, he would get mad by us still watching…[but] I was really interested."

After he was initiated at age fifteen, Kevin formally began carving. He said, "He [Manuel] showed me step by step. I used to sit with him, and I worked with him for a long time, and he showed me everything. He showed me how to start it out, how to mark it out and then how to carve it out, how to use my saw the right way. And how to sharpen my knife right because, if you don't sharpen your knife right, there's a whip on it, and it'll slip on the wood and you can hurt yourself."

Kevin remains committed to traditional katsina doll carving processes. He described his processes: "The traditional part is the way we make it as Old style, and it's been passed down for generations, and making it that way is a—that's traditional. The way I mix my paints is pretty traditional. The tool thing, I don't use no power tools. I just use a handsaw, a splitting knife…a saw, carving knife, wood file and sandpaper. I don't really break tradition when I make things."

Kevin remains conscientious when he carves, and he finds inspiration from pieces of cottonwood. He said, "Sometimes, it's just walking outside and just taking a look at my woodpile. And I'll see a certain piece of wood, and it has a certain shape in it. I'll pick it up, and I can already see the finished product."

Kevin would want someone new to understanding Hopi katsina dolls to learn:

> *A lot of thought goes into it. It's a lot of thoughtfulness, and prayers, and stuff going into them. You're not supposed to make them when you're mad or stuff because you can hurt yourself. It's just not good to put those kind of thoughts into it. It's like a prayer.*
>
> *They used to make them for the kids, and they're teaching tools, and the first one that a child would get when they're born is…a grandmother. And, when she comes, she is always smiling, and she is always talking. She'll never stop, so they'll give the baby that katsina doll, and you know how babies like to teeth on stuff? They'll chew on that katsina doll, and it's said to help them speak."*

Currently, Kevin resides in Phoenix and sells his katsina dolls at Kachina House in Sedona. Kevin is a youthful, optimistic, hopeful artist with burgeoning talent and humility. He possesses an authentic dedication to preserving the traditions of his craft, katsina doll carving. He explained that Arizona's natural environment, as well as Hopi cultural traditions, influence the artwork he makes. He said, "Because it's home…and I guess the influence is all around. There's all the rock arts and the petroglyphs and the old houses on the ruins…They were so interesting to me. They all have stories behind them, and they just influence me to keep the tradition going. Those are our ancestors' footprints they left for us."

Kevin treasures his ancestral homeland and yearns to one day return to the Hopi reservation to live. He said, "I can't wait. One day, I want to move back out there."

Part IV

Closing Remarks

15
CLOSING REMARKS

Critically Thinking About Art

Learning about art is a lifelong process. Recently, a student in my critical thinking class at Arizona State University asked, "How long does it take to become a critical thinker?" A discussion ensued: Do we really ever stop learning? We can always strive to learn more, expanding our minds, and perhaps our hearts, as well. The process of learning about Navajo and Hopi cultures in Arizona has been an incredible journey, but I realize there will always be more to learn. In this concluding chapter, I share some of the key themes that united these featured talented artists.

A Continuum of Native Art Forms

Contemporary native artists create art on a continuum. On the far side of the continuum, there is an adherence to traditional art-making practices of the tribe, such as types of art forms, symbols and the use of traditional tools, materials and processes. One artist in particular who might be considered on the traditional end of the continuum is Manuel Chavarria, katsina doll carver. He remains true to the tradition of his artistic processes and has taught others, including a nephew, to do the same. He makes painstaking efforts to create antique-like carvings, distressing the wood and paint. Manuel also deeply respects traditions associated with insider knowledge about katsina dolls and their carvers. For example, during our interview at his home on the reservation, he requested that his young granddaughter leave the room, as she had not yet been initiated and was not privy to the information.

On the polar opposite end of the continuum, there exists a use of artistic media and imagery that is quite different from native traditions. Artists might be using media that had not existed in their tribe hundreds of years ago or might transform traditional art forms. For example, Melanie Yazzie uses a variety of media that includes bronze sculpture, ceramics, lithography, painting, collage and installation art. She chose not to pursue the path of a Navajo weaver, which her mother, aunts and grandmother took. However, weaving, Navajo culture and family deeply influenced her identity and her use of new art forms. Like other artists in this book, she identified that her native traditions inspired her artwork and artistic development.

At this current period in history, contemporary art can never be as clear-cut as falling into either this or that category. To respect all artists and artworks, we must embrace complexity. Somewhere in the center of this continuum are native artists who practice traditional *and* contemporary art forms. Ramson Lomatewama uses a new form of art that was not traditionally used by his Hopi culture: glass. Concurrently, he carves katsina dolls and weaves, two processes traditionally associated with Hopi males. Other artists, such as Marlowe Katoney and Michael Teller Ornelas, follow an artistic tradition of their Navajo tribe: weaving. However, they break tradition by being male weavers. In addition, while female Navajo weavers Barbara Teller Ornelas and Lynda Teller Pete continue weaving in Two Grey Hills style and remaining true to the wool material and preparation traditions of their mothers, aunts and grandmothers, they also incorporate other regional styles.

Heritage Is Sacred

Navajo and Hopi artists in this book expressed that they cannot escape their heritage, nor do they want to. It affects the people they are, and the art forms they create. Participating artists are conscious of how tribal culture influences them. A message reverberates: "I have to continue this. If I don't, no one else will. I must continue this tradition so that it doesn't die, so that people don't forget the talents and contributions of their ancestors. We must hold close to us what is dear, what is sacred."

Jesse Monongya, Verma Nequatewa and Piki Wadsworth continue creating jewelry as their direct ancestors did. Barbara Teller Ornelas, Michael Teller Ornelas, Lynda Teller Pete and Marlowe Katoney continue their mothers' and grandmothers' practice of Navajo weaving. And thus, the story continues. Native art is a lifeline that connects the generations.

Combatting Expectations and Stereotypes of American Indian Art

Navajo and Hopi artists shared that they are often in the process of combatting stereotypes about American Indians through educating others about their cultures. They persist in fighting others' expectations that their artworks don't look "Indian enough." Native art, like art of other cultures, evolves. These artists are transforming what Native American art means today. Through their artwork, they are expressing some of what the native experience is. Marlowe Katoney and Lynda Teller Pete explained that they are reflecting their experiences through their weavings, as their relatives did. Navajo weavers have reflected what was happening in their lives and environments, whether it was through the type of wool used or through the pictorials represented. Each artwork is a snapshot of one time, revealing the individual and perhaps one piece of the cultural experience.

Art Training and Family Traditions

Many artists in this book learned through observation of, and instruction by, family members, as well as self-teaching. For many, individuals have always been artists. This identity is who, deep down, they are, whom they struggle to maintain. Barbara Teller Ornelas has always been an artist; weaving has been part of her family tradition for generations. She learned to weave the same way she learned to walk. Being an artist involves incorporating art-making into daily, habitual routines, creating innovative works within their homes—in their living rooms, backyards and garages. The artists merge their family values, ancestral histories and deepest beliefs into their identities and artworks. Often, they are in the process of educating others about who they are, who their tribe is, what their artworks mean and the special place from where it comes. Navajo and Hopi artists are breaking expectations, fighting society's drive to fit art into simple categories. Contemporary native art defies expectations and oversimplifications: It is encompassing, it is complicated, it holds amazing depth and it reflects a powerful beauty.

Thank you for reading this book, for participating in this journey with me and for embracing the new, innovative artists and art worlds of Arizona.

BIBLIOGRAPHY

"About Hubbell Trading Post." Hubbell Trading Post. http://www.nps.gov/hutr/index.htm.

"About the Heard Museum." Heard Museum. http://heard.org/about.

Adair, J. "Lanyade." *Southwest Crossroads*, 2012.

Anderson, Susan. "Letters from the Mesa Poet Writes of Corn Silk and the Eagle's Flight." *Citizen*, July 29, 1985.

Archuleta, Margaret. "The United States Federal Government's Role in the Development of the Native American Fine Art Movement, 1850–1936." *Heard Museum Journal*, July–December 1999: 11–14.

"Artist in Residence: Melanie Yazzie, July 25-29." Denver Art Museum. http://denverartmuseum.org/calendar/artist-residence-melanie-yazzie-0.

"Artist Profile (Ramson Lomatewama)." Native American Artists Resource Collection. Heard Museum.

"Barbara Ornelas Teller." Native American Artists Resource Collection. Heard Museum.

Benally, Michael. *Bitter Water: Diné Oral Histories of the Navajo-Hopi Land Dispute.* Tucson: University of Arizona Press, 2011.

Bix, C. *Art of the State: Arizona*. New York: Harry N. Abrams, 1998.

Chalmers, G. "Cultural Colonialism and Art Education: Eurocentric and Racist Roots of Art Education." In *Beyond Multicultural Art Education: International Perspectives*. New York: Munster, 1999.

Clark, Hattie. "Reflections on Hopi Life: Poet Ramson Lomatewama Shares His World Through Verse." *Christian Science Monitor*, December 1992.

Dwyer, Helen, and D.L. Birchfield. *Navajo: History and Culture*. New York: Gareth Stevens, 2012.

Ellis, Nancy. "Sonwai: The Sculptural Jewelry of Two Hopi Sisters." *Focus/Santa Fe*, August–September 1990.

"Exhibitions: Blessingway; Prints by Melanie Yazzie." Missoula Art Museum. January 2015.

"Fusing Traditions: Transformations in Glass by Native American Artists." Museum of Craft and Folk Art, 2002.

Gregg, James. "Weaving Is Part of Woman's Soul: Renowned Navajo Artist Has Strong Ties to Homeland." *Arizona Daily Star*, December 13, 2006.

Gude, Olivia. "Art Education for Democratic Life." In *Art Education* 62, no. 6 (2009).

Guthrie, Patricia. "Weaving the Big One: Sisters' Determination, Traditional Skills Produce History-Making Tapestry." *New Mexico Magazine*, August 1988: 67–69.

Hill, Liz. "Artistic Temperament." *Native Peoples Magazine*, July 1, 2013.

"Hopi Art and Culture." *Native American Arts*, 1992: 37.

"Introducing Yourself in Navajo." *Navajo WTOD*, January 2015.

Jacka, J., and L. Jacka. *Beyond Tradition: Contemporary Indian Art and Its Evolution*. Flagstaff, AZ: Northland Publishing, 1998.

Jacka, Lois. *Navajo Jewelry: A Legacy of Silver and Stone*. Flagstaff, AZ: Northland Publishing, 1995.

"Kachina Dolls: Ceremonial Carvings that Evoke the Rich World of Hopi Culture." *Antiques*, n.d.: 167, 194–95.

Kuwanwisiwma, Leigh. "Introduction: From the Sacred to the Cash Register; Problems Encountered in Protecting the Hopi Patrimony." In *Katsina* by Zena Pearlstone. Los Angles: UCLA Fowler Museum of Cultural History, 2001, 16–21.

Lavin, P. *Arizona: An Illustrated History*. New York: Hippocrene Books, 2001.

Mason, R. "Multicultural Art Education: Global Reform." In *Beyond Multicultural Art Education: International Perspectives*. New York: Munster, 1999.

McCoy, Ron. "Sonwai: Beautiful in Any Language." *Southwest Profile*, February, March, April 1994: 32–35.

"Melanie Yazzie." Artnet. http://www.artnet.com/artists/melanie-yazzie.

"Melanie Yazzie: Department of Art & Art History." University of Colorado Boulder. http://cuart.colorado.edu/people/faculty/melanie-yazzie.

"Melanie Yazzie: Geographies of Memory." University of New Mexico Art Museum. http://unmartmuseum.org/past-exhibitions/melanie-yazzie-geographies-of-memory.

"Melanie Yazzie." Glenn Green Galleries. http://glenngreengalleries.com/Artists/myazzie/index.html.

"Melanie Yazzie." Missoula Art Museum. http://www.missoulaartmuseum.org/index.php/ID/4c3f719c/fuseaction/exhibitions.artist.htm.

"Melanie Yazzie, 2014 & 2015." *Matrix Press.* http://www.matrixpress.org/melanie-yazzie.html.

"Native American Sand Painting." Indians. http://www.indians.org/articles/native-american-sand-painting.html.

"Navajo Clans." Navajo-Arts. http://navajo-arts.com/clans-navajo.html.

"News Release: Blessingway; Prints by Melanie Yazzie." Missoula Art Museum. http://www.missoulaartmuseum.org/files/documents/pressReleases/Yazzie.pdf.

Nickens, P., and K. Nickens. *Native Americans of Arizona*. Charleston, SC: Arcadia Publishing, 2007.

Nochlin, Linda. "Why Have There Been No Great Women Artists?" In *The Feminism and Visual Culture Reader*. Edited by A. Jones. New York: Routledge, 2003, 263–67.

Norris, T., P. Vines and M. Hoeffel. "American Indian and Alaska Native Population: 2010." United States Census Bureau. (2012). http://www.census.gov/prod/cen2010/briefs/c2010br-10.pdf.

Pearlstone, Z. *Katsina.* Los Angeles: UCLA Fowler Museum of Cultural History, 2001.

Phoenix Gazette. "Rug Brings in $60,000." October 6, 1989.

"Piki Wadsworth—Hopi Jewelry Maker." Hoel's Indian Shop. http://hoelsindianshop.com/artist-profiles/piki-wadsworth-hopi-jewelry-maker.

"Ramson Lomatewama: About the 'Artist on the Road' Press Release." Native American Artists Resource Collection. Heard Museum.

Regan, Margaret. "Intertwined Threads: An Exhibit at Arizona State Museum Depicts Navajo Weaving Throughout History." *Tucson Weekly*, December 23, 2004.

Reid, J., and S. Whittlesey. *The Archeology of Ancient Arizona*. Tucson: University of Arizona Press, 1997.

Rosenak, C. and J. Rosenak. *The People Speak: Navajo Folk Art*. Flagstaff, AZ: Northland Publishing, 1994.

Secakuku, Alph. "Authentic Hopi Katsina Dolls." In *Katsina* by Zena Pearlstone. Los Angles: UCLA Fowler Museum of Cultural History, 2001, 162–65.

"Selected Awards and Exhibits." Jesse Monongya Studios. http://www.jessemonongyastudios.com/about_awards.html.

Silas, A. *Journey to Hopi Land*. Tucson: Rio Nuevo Publishers, 2006.

Stephenson, Anne. "Cultural Exchange: Hopi Poet-Teacher Opens Kids' Eyes, Ears, Minds, Hearts." *Arizona Republic* 8 (January 1989): F1–F4.

Trevathan, L., and P. Nicosin. "Barbara Jean Teller Ornelas." *Cristof's News*, no. 10 (Third Quarter, 1995).

"What Is Lapidary?" Lizzadro Museum of Lapidary Art. http://www.lizzadromuseum.org/whatislap.html.

INDEX

G

H

I

K

L

M

N

U

W

Y

Z

ABOUT THE AUTHOR

I look at Arizona through the eyes of an adopted child. I'm not a native Arizonan. I was raised in New Orleans, Louisiana. Trips to my husband's family's home in Snowflake, Arizona, introduced me to a different way of life where people remain dedicated to the land and remain deeply connected to it. Vast, open spaces, dotted with junipers, prickly pears and yucca, stand in stark contrast to my previous urban living environments. (While pursuing my master's degree in art therapy, I lived in a fifth-floor walk-up apartment in the East Village of Manhattan. Looking out of my bedroom window, I could see a fire escape, a police department parking lot and a tiny community garden.) What I want my daughter to learn is where she is from: Arizona—the history of the land, the people and the native art.

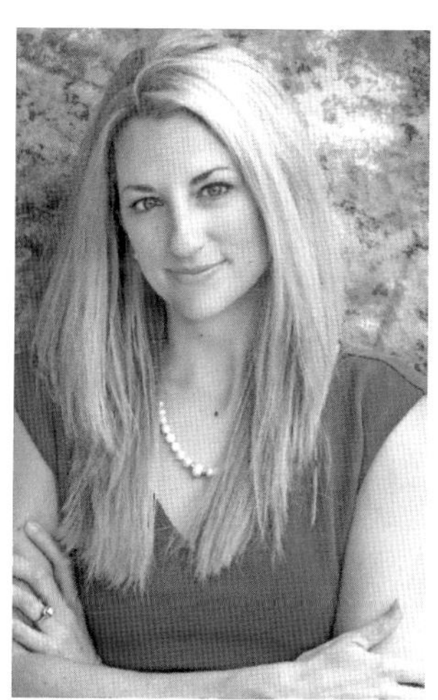

Photograph by Traci Bower, all rights reserved.

Rory O'Neill Schmitt, PhD, MPS, ATR-BC, is a writer, art therapist, professor and photographer. She earned her PhD in curriculum and instruction studies, with a concentration in art education, at Arizona State University. She has completed research work in museum, school and community settings. She serves on the faculty of the University College of Arizona State University. Rory has worked at museums and galleries in New York, California and Arizona, including at the International Center for Photography, Cristinerose Gallery, Visual Arts Gallery, the San Diego Chinese Historical Society and Museum and the ASU Art Museum. As a board-certified art therapist, she has worked with youth and adults in rehabilitation programs. She continues to advocate for art therapy through her volunteer work on the board of the Arizona Art Therapy Association. She is a fine art photographer who has exhibited her work in New York and Los Angeles and has published her photographs in print and online. Rory resides in Scottsdale, Arizona, with her husband, Dasan Schmitt; their daughter, Olivia Rose Schmitt; and their two French bulldogs, Ozzie and Bella.

Visit us at
www.historypress.net

This title is also available as an e-book